Early Childhood Leadership

Early Childhood Leadership

Motivation, Inspiration, Empowerment

LYNN MAROTZ

ROWMAN & LITTLEFIELD
Lanham • Boulder • New York • London

Published by Rowman & Littlefield
An imprint of The Rowman & Littlefield Publishing Group, Inc.
4501 Forbes Boulevard, Suite 200, Lanham, Maryland 20706
www.rowman.com

6 Tinworth Street, London, SE11 5AL, United Kingdom

British Library Cataloguing in Publication Information Available

Library of Congress Cataloging-in-Publication Data
Names: Marotz, Lynn R., author.
Title: Early childhood leadership : Motivation, inspiration, empowerment / Lynn Marotz.
Description: Lanham : Rowman & Littlefield, [2021] | Includes bibliographical references and index. | Summary: "Motivational and Inspirational Leadership is written in a reader-friendly style and offers a wealth of everyday strategies for creating a workplace environment that attracts and retains quality employees, motivates performance, boosts morale, and supports personnel development"—Provided by publisher.
Identifiers: LCCN 2020049973 (print) | LCCN 2020049974 (ebook) | ISBN 9781538137901 (cloth) | ISBN 9781538137918 (paperback) | ISBN 9781538137925 (ebook)
Subjects: LCSH: Early childhood educators—Professional relationships—United States. | Early childhood education—United States—Administration. | Educational leadership—United States. | School management and organization—United States. | Motivation in education—United States. | Employee motivation—United States. | Teacher turnover—United States.
Classification: LCC LB1775.6 .M3695 2021 (print) | LCC LB1775.6 (ebook) | DDC 372.210973—dc23
LC record available at https://lccn.loc.gov/2020049973
LC ebook record available at https://lccn.loc.gov/2020049974

♾️™ The paper used in this publication meets the minimum requirements of American National Standard for Information Sciences—Permanence of Paper for Printed Library Materials, ANSI/NISO Z39.48-1992.

Table of Contents

Table of Contents

Chapter 5   The Art of Effective Communication   99

Chapter 6   Problem-Solving and Conflict Management   129

Preface

Early Childhood Leadership: Motivation, Inspiration, and Empowerment addresses one of the most fundamental and challenging workplace issues facing employers today: the ability to recruit and retain highly qualified employees. Results from many studies consistently point to the negative effect that staff turnover in early childhood settings has on employee morale, recruiting and training costs, and children's development. Practices and policies that foster personnel motivation, inspiration, and empowerment are, thus, crucial to staff retention. Equally important are acknowledgment of their efforts, showing appreciation for their contributions, and supporting their professional development. In other words, every aspect of a program is dependent upon the effectiveness of its leadership and personnel.

Surprisingly, data show that strategies used by many leaders to administer their programs and guide employee behavior often contribute to personnel dissatisfaction and attrition—the opposite circumstances necessary for an organization's success. Many individuals who find themselves in leadership positions have not had an opportunity to acquire the knowledge, skills, and competencies that are necessary to be effective early childhood leaders. Efforts to address this need and build leadership capacity in the field have led to the development of director-credentialing programs and state mandates that require early childhood leaders to be credentialed.

Well-prepared leaders are needed to address current and emerging challenges, such as social and diversity issues, funding, public expectations, and a proposed restructuring of early childhood as a field of professional practice. Success will require leaders to possess effective communication, leadership, team-building, conflict resolution, and decision-making skills.

ORGANIZATION AND SPECIAL FEATURES

Early Childhood Leadership: Motivation, Inspiration, and Empowerment is written for administrators, directors, coordinators, team leaders, managers, lead teachers, office managers, and others who hold a leadership position, or aspire to one. The competencies, skills, and theoretical foundations that are fundamental to a leader's success are addressed in-depth in this book. Readers will gain an understanding of motivational theory, ways in which diversity influences motivation, and how motivational and inspirational leadership can be implemented to promote employee performance, personal and professional development, job satisfaction, and long-term commitment.

Examples specific to early childhood settings are provided throughout the book. Each chapter also includes highlighted tables with guidelines and suggestions for implementing critical leadership strategies. Additional features, such as Learning Objectives, Connecting Points, Director's Showcase, Review Points, and Application Activities, illustrate, reinforce, and encourage practice of the chapter content. Also included is an appendix with applicable federal laws that address work regulations, practices, and employee rights.

Leaders might not always have the answers or make the right decisions. They are, however, able to create positive, effective workplace environments through their use of a motivational, inspirational, and empowering leadership style.

Acknowledgments

First and foremost, I want to recognize the many exemplary early childhood leaders who strive to attract, motivate, inspire, and empower outstanding personnel. Your dedication deserves "thank you, well done" plaudits.

The production of any book involves the creative talents of many "behind-the-scenes" individuals. Their ability to turn a vision and pages and pages of manuscript into a worthy product is admirable. First and foremost, I wish to extend a special "thank-you" to Mark Kerr for his continued support and foresight in recognizing the importance of preparing effective leaders. Mark has long been an advocate for achieving quality and professionalism in the early childhood education field. I am also grateful to have worked with Courtney Packard and Andrew Yoder, who always offered excellent guidance and responded promptly and knowledgeably to my many queries. Also, thank you Amanda Wilson for a great cover design and Karen Cholak for your marketing support. My sincere appreciation is also extended to the many other unnamed individuals who were integrally involved in the culmination of this book. And, finally, a special thank-you to my husband for his never-ending patience, understanding, and inspiration.

1

Early Childhood Education: A Field of Practice

OBJECTIVES

After reading this chapter, you will be able to do the following:

- Briefly describe how social and economic factors have historically shaped the types of early childhood opportunities available at any given point in time.
- Explain why early childhood education continues to be perceived as having a weak identity.
- Discuss NAEYC's proposed initiative to establish a professional early childhood workforce, and the role effective motivational leadership will play in advancing the process.

KEY TERMS

- compensatory
- commensurate

■ ■ ■

Every child deserves a champion—an adult who will never give up on them, who understands the power of connection and insists that they become the best that they can possibly be.

—Rita Pierson, professional educator

INTRODUCTION

What young children should learn and how they are to be taught have been defined by the political, social, economic, and cultural conditions at any given moment in history. During the early nineteenth century, for example, concerns about the plight of disadvantaged children living in poverty led to the establishment of charitable infant schools in the United States. Those programs offered basic custodial care and supervision for children. Some religious and moral instruction was also provided because the children's parents were thought to be unqualified to instill proper socialization (Kamerman, 2006). Program organizers believed that their efforts would improve children's lives and help them to overcome poverty and "corruption." Infant schools also served another role: parents, particularly mothers, could participate in the workforce.

At the same time, nursery schools were being formed to provide enrichment education for the children of well-to-do families. Privately funded programs were operated primarily by women who were considered to have a better understanding about how children learned (Cahan, 1989). Their mission was to supplement what children were being taught in their home environment, which would prove to be advantageous when they entered kindergarten.

Middle-class families wanted the same benefits for their children, so they began sending them to public school at ages two and three (Vinovskis, 1993). Records suggest that approximately forty percent of the three-year-olds in Massachusetts were enrolled in public school in the early 1830s (Kaestle & Vinovskis, 1980; Vinovskis, 1993). Despite its popularity among families, the trend was short-lived because teachers considered very young children too unruly and difficult to manage!

Philosophers were opposed to this development and suggested that children should be taught at home because schools weakened the mother-child attachment (Cahan, 1989). Medical professionals warned parents that overstimulating children's minds "too early" would cause physical and mental health problems, including "epilepsy, insanity, and imbecility" (Brigham, 1833). Nursery schools were closed and upper-class families kept their children at home in response to medical advice. Infant schools remained open for a period of time until they, too, eventually closed due to a loss of public funding.

Renewed interest in early childhood education developed shortly after the Civil War. Kindergartens, modeled after those in Europe and supported by private philanthropy, were opened in cities throughout the East. The medical profession again criticized such programs as "penitentiaries" and accused them of harming young children because the process of learning caused "too much stimulation" (Winterer, 1992).

Educators acknowledged such arguments but countered that very young children did undoubtedly learn differently than older children. As a result, they began to implement a new kindergarten curriculum that was child-centered and reflected a "sensitive" balance of academic activities with play and relaxation (Bloch & Choi, 1990).

By 1914, publicly funded kindergartens for five-year-olds were integrated into many American school systems. The younger children of middle- and upper-class families continued to attend private nursery schools. However, such programs were again heavily criticized for their poor educational quality and for removing children from their mothers. This prompted a renewed interest among scientists to study issues related to child development, parenting, curriculum, and teacher training (Elkind, 1985; Stroud & Clark, 2000).

Results from many studies confirmed the positive outcomes that children gained as a result of attending kindergarten. These findings increased demands to improve nursery school programs and to make them more accessible to all children, but progress toward achieving these goals was slow. Personnel demands in two world wars forced programs to revert back to the provision of basic care in government-supported facilities for large numbers of children whose mothers and fathers were working in war-related industries or serving in the military.

Although research on children's learning and socialization moved steadily forward, early childhood education efforts and programs experienced few changes. Demands for child care continued to increase as a result of changes in the adult workforce and educational requirements (U.S. Bureau of Labor Statistics, 2020a). Some new intervention programs were developed to address the needs of children living in poverty and those at risk for abuse and developmental delays. Yet, the "traditional model" of early childhood education that seemed to have worked adequately for many years was still followed.

Interest in new approaches has occasionally been sparked by discoveries about how learning affects children's neurobiological development, the importance of positive parenting practices, and the implementation of developmentally appropriate pedagogy. Despite such efforts, early childhood education as a discipline continues to face significant obstacles and a disconnect, at times, between what we know and what we do.

--- *Connecting Points* ---

Many experts argue that government-funded pre-K programs should be made accessible to three- and four-year-olds in this country. Others suggest that the cost would be prohibitive and cite a lack of robust evidence supporting the benefits of pre-K education for all children. Some say schools are oppressive and overregulated.

- In what ways are these arguments similar to those made in the past?
- What are the advantages and drawbacks of making pre-K programs available to all children?
- Should there be a mandate that all four-year-olds enroll in a pre-K program if positive outcomes have been documented?

WHERE ARE WE NOW?

What does history have to do with the current state of early childhood education? The answer is, everything.

Ideas from the past provide a foundation for the evolution and development of new concepts. Some earlier practices have been modified to better serve contemporary audiences. Others, such as the provision of separate educational programs for children with disabilities, have been abandoned. In each case, research has informed decisions about the most effective pedagogy and practices and their implementation.

Public Perception

The field of early childhood education, which serves children from birth to age eight, has witnessed significant improvements over the years. Yet, it lacks a strong, unified identity. Many people understand the positive effects that early childhood education can have on children's development (Figure 1.1). Others simply regard these programs as settings where children will be kept safe and cared for while parents work.

FIGURE 1.1 Researchers continue to show long-term benefits for children who attend high-quality early childhood programs. *FatCamera, E+*

Why do these seemingly disparate perceptions exist? The reasons, in part, may be traced to a history of addressing children's needs through a two-tier system. For example, early custodial programs were established to care for the disadvantaged children of poor working parents. At the same time, enrichment programs were created to prepare the children of middle- and upper-class families for formal schooling.

An analogous division remains today. The diversity of programs available can be confusing and may make it difficult for the public to understand the role and purpose of early education. This situation also serves to weaken the field's identity. For example, **compensatory** programs (e.g., income-qualified, special needs, dual-language learners) serve a small percentage of the eligible children. Low-income families that do not qualify for special services often must settle for affordable and conveniently located child care over quality education (Herbst et al., 2020; NAEYC, 2019). Higher-income working families have the resources to place their children in quality programs that emphasize learning and social-emotional development. However, these programs can be costly and often consume fifteen to thirty percent of a family's annual disposable income (Child Care Aware, 2019; Gould et al., 2019; Malik, 2019).

The historical construct of women as innate nurturers and caretakers of children may also add to the public's mixed perceptions about the nature of early childhood education. Women provided most of the nonparental care for young children during the nineteenth and twentieth centuries. Today, ninety-seven percent of child care settings in the United States are operated by women in their homes (ChildStats.gov, 2019; Paschall & Tout, 2018). Ninety-three percent of the two million child caregivers in this country are female (DataUSA, 2018).

This similarity may create an illusion of equivalency between past and present. It may also perpetuate the belief that anyone can care for young children or that early childhood teachers are simply devoted babysitters (Build Initiative, 2020; Harwood & Tukonic, 2016). However, many of today's early childhood home-providers and center-based teachers are well-educated and offer rich learning environments that promote children's optimal development (Blasberg et al., 2019; Hooper, 2020). Another factor that raises questions about the field's identity and legitimacy may be related to the use of a play-based curriculum (Nilsson, Ferholt, & Lecusay, 2017; Taylor & Boyer, 2020; Zosh et al., 2017). Casual observers often view children's play as random behavior that fails to result in meaningful learning. Warash, Root, & Doris (2017) noted that there are even differences between mothers' and fathers' views on the worth of play as an educational tool. Mothers understand that play promotes learning. Fathers believe that formal instructional experiences are more important, especially as children approach school-age.

How might the early childhood education field address the public's misperceptions and gain improved identity and credibility? One approach would entail the standardization of training requirements and attainment of credentials for practitioners. So, too, would efforts to publicly communicate early education's important role and benefits for all children and society. Such efforts will require dedicated, effective motivational leaders and advocates who can work with policymakers to capitalize on the potential benefits and savings that investments in universal early childhood education can have for states and the nation.

Without progressive, continuous professional leadership, even well-founded and convincing evidence will make such changes difficult to implement. For example, results from several studies indicate that there is currently only moderate interest in implementing publicly funded early childhood programs (Fairbank et al., 2018; Greenberg, 2018).

Although people understand the benefits of early education, they are only willing to support universal access if it meets their needs, they see a personal benefit, and no additional taxes are necessary. People are not interested in funding universal early childhood programs if it reduces revenue earmarked for K–12 or increases their taxes (Greenberg, 2018).

Did You Know? ....

Every dollar of federal money spent on child care subsidies returns approximately $3.80 to state governments.

....

Career Opportunities

Career opportunities for early childhood educators are diverse and continue to expand as new programs and services are added (Textbox 1.1). Prospective educators find this characteristic attractive. However, career diversity can also present challenges, such as the formation of a clear and definitive explanation of the roles and responsibilities of early childhood educators. Furthermore, the lack of any consistent credential or required preparation further weakens the field's identity and acceptance as a legitimate professional endeavor.

EXAMPLES OF EMPLOYMENT OPPORTUNITIES
IN EARLY CHILDHOOD EDUCATION

A wide range of job opportunities are open to individuals who have an academic credential in early childhood education, including the following:

- home visitor or family support provider
- home-based early childhood educator (e.g., owner, teacher)
- consultant (e.g., airlines, hospitality and food industry, legislators, toy and clothing manufacturers, educational products)
- teacher or teacher coach (e.g., for profit/nonprofit community-based program, church-affiliated, charter school, kindergarten)
- administrator (e.g., center director, social service agency, civic organization)
- paraprofessional (e.g., preschool program, public or private school)
- curriculum development specialist
- child life specialist (e.g., hospital, clinic)
- private nanny
- sales representative (e.g., children's products)
- licensing regulator

The qualifications required for most early childhood positions range from a high school education to a graduate degree and they also vary significantly from state to state (Figure 1.2). An early childhood certificate may be accepted for some positions. Others may require a Child Development Associate (CDA) credential, an associate degree (AA), or an undergraduate degree in early childhood education or a closely allied field. Specialized coursework may be necessary to hold positions in administration, curriculum development, counseling, special education, or child life. An estimated 2.7 million individuals work in unlicensed, home-based child care and privately owned or church-affiliated programs where they are often exempt from meeting any minimal qualification standards (Whitebook et al., 2018; NSECE, 2016).

DIRECTOR'S SHOWCASE

Do you think NAEYC's proposal to restructure the early childhood workforce would help or hurt your programs?

I applaud NAEYC's efforts to improve the preparation and salaries of early childhood teachers. We try to pay our teachers more if they have a degree, but there isn't much extra room in the budget. NAEYC's plan will only work if subsidies are available so that we can provide better compensation. Families can't afford to pay fees any higher than they are right now.

—Tim H., multi-site director

FIGURE 1.2 The joy of working with children draws teachers to the field. *monkeybusinessimages*

WHY IS THE DEMAND INCREASING?

More than 12.5 million U.S. children younger than age six spend a portion of their day in a nonparental care arrangement (Haynie, 2019; Whitebook et al., 2018). Yet, the number of quality and affordable openings in early childhood programs is currently insufficient to meet existing and future demands (Committee for Economic Development, 2019). The reasons for this situation are several.

More mothers with young children continue to enter the workforce for personal and economic reasons (Figure 1.3). In 2019, approximately sixty-seven percent of mothers with children younger than six years old were employed in the United States; eighty percent of those individuals worked in full-time positions (U.S. Bureau of Labor Statistics, 2020b).

Locating affordable child care within a reasonable distance is reported to be a major obstacle, particularly for mothers in lower-paying jobs. It also prevents more women from seeking paid employment or working longer hours (Amaram, 2019; Schochet, 2019). Many also cite the lack of affordable and adequate child care as a reason for delaying or abandoning their careers.

Demand for early childhood programs, especially those of high quality, has also increased in response to research evidence that documents short- and long-term improvements in children's cognitive, language, social-emotional, and physical development. Some questions have been raised about the lasting effects of early learning experiences, but many robust study results support gains that are persistent well into adulthood (Garcia, Heckman, & Ziff, 2019; Kohl et al., 2020; Vandell et al., 2020; Yang et al., 2019).

FIGURE 1.3 Working parents rely on early childhood programs to nurture and care for their young children. *AzmanL, E+*

Bakken, Brown, and Downing (2017) found that children from disadvantaged homes who had attended high-quality early childhood programs continued to show significant improvements in their reading and math test scores into the third and fourth grades. These children also had better attendance records and fewer disciplinary referrals. Bai et al. (2020) followed approximately 900,000 students from the time they initially participated in an early childhood education program until the eighth grade. Students continued to achieve higher math and reading test scores, lower grade retention rates, and fewer special education placements than children who had not attended an early childhood program.

Positive health benefits have also been observed in children who participated in Head Start and other high-quality early childhood programs. These included reduced malnutrition, improved growth rates, early identification of health problems (e.g., dental, vision, hearing), increased immunization rates, less obesity, improved physical fitness, and reduced rates of child abuse, diabetes, and hypertension (high blood pressure) (Friedman-Krauss, Bernstein, & Barnett, 2019; Lee, 2020). Garcia, Heckman, and Ziff (2019) also found lower crime rates among adults, especially women, who had attended high-quality early childhood programs. Gender differences were attributed to women growing up in home conditions that were significantly worse than those of men in the study.

Despite extensive research supporting the benefits of early childhood education, families often struggle to find openings in high-quality, affordable programs. Licensed centers are reducing their capacity at the same time that many home-based programs are closing due to logistical and financial constraints (National Center on Early Childhood Quality Assurance,

2019). This is leaving many child care deserts in areas where programs are few in number and located far from where they are most needed (Malik et al., 2018).

These challenges have prompted the business sector to call for an expansion of publicly funded universal prekindergarten programs in the United States (CED, 2019; U.S. Chamber of Commerce Foundation, 2020). Their reasoning is twofold. More parents who want to work could do so if they were able to find affordable, quality early education programs for their children. This would potentially increase the size of the nation's workforce and its productivity (Belfield, 2018; Delalibera & Ferreira, 2019; Grunewald, 2019). It would also reduce the revenue losses that businesses experience when workers must take time off to care for their children.

The business community also supports universal early education for its role in preparing the next generation of skilled leaders and employees. Economists have estimated that states could expect a substantial return on their investment in early education (Jessen-Howard & Workman, 2019). They would also see cost savings associated with reductions in remedial and special education placements (Bai et al., 2020; Karoly, 2016; Meloy, Gardner, & Darling-Hammond, 2019). Although there are significant economic gains to be realized, such benefits must not overshadow the most important outcome: the opportunity for young children to develop to their fullest potential.

Did You Know? ·

Employed parents report losing approximately two hours of worktime per week due to child care–related issues.

· ·

WHAT DOES THIS ALL MEAN FOR EARLY CHILDHOOD LEADERS?

At present, the field of early childhood education finds itself at a crossroad. It is caught between a tradition of simply providing basic child care and a current emphasis on the promotion of high-quality early learning opportunities for young children. As a result, it is becoming increasingly apparent that the current disjointed array of early childhood programs and lack of well-trained leaders and educators no longer reflects what is known to be best for children and their families.

Demands that all young children have equitable access to high-quality early childhood education programs are increasing. More families are relying on these programs so they can work or attend school. Researchers continue to validate positive neurobiological outcomes for young children who participate in these programs, particularly those who are growing up in disadvantaged families (Kulic et al., 2019; Shonkoff & Phillips, 2000; Sinclaire-Harding, Vuillier, & Whitebread, 2018). Business leaders are beginning to recognize the significant contribution that early childhood education makes to the nation's economy in terms of wages paid, monetary savings, and future workforce preparation and productivity (CED, 2019).

The National Institute of Medicine (IOM) and the National Research Council (NRC) (now called the National Academies of Science, Engineering, and Medicine) completed a comprehensive study of the early childhood education system in 2015. Their findings were published in a document entitled *Transforming the Workforce for Children Birth through*

Age 8: A Unifying Foundation (Institute of Medicine and National Research Council, 2015). Among the stakeholders' primary recommendations was a call for the establishment of a uniform system of competency-based qualifications, evaluation measures, and appropriate compensation for early childhood educators. These measures would strengthen the preparation, retention, and identity of a quality workforce. It was also suggested that higher education improve its academic programs to provide training that was relevant, interdisciplinary, rigorous, and exemplary. Subsequently, practitioners would also have access to a continuous system of high-quality professional development opportunities.

Several years after this report was released, the National Association for the Education of Young Children (NAEYC), which represents over 60,000 members, embarked on an ambitious campaign to redefine the field. Their vision for developing a coherent system worthy of professional status is outlined in the document entitled *Unifying Framework for the Early Childhood Education Profession*. The plan presents a strategic career development framework of "competencies, qualifications, standards of practice, and compensation for all early childhood educators who work with children birth through age eight across a variety of early learning settings" (NAEYC, 2020).

NAEYC's proposed restructuring of early childhood education as a field of professional practice has the potential to achieve several objectives. First, it establishes a clearly defined purpose and identity. All educators would be required to be licensed in one of three designated categories: Early Childhood Educator I, II, or III. Practitioners at each level would be expected to master a set of standardized competencies and demonstrate proficiency. This change would produce a highly trained workforce and achieve the field's objective of improving the quality and consistency of children's educational experiences. It also has the potential to develop new early childhood leaders and leadership capacity. And, perhaps most importantly, the restructuring would strengthen the organization's quest to achieve professional recognition and **commensurate** compensation for early childhood educators.

NAEYC's proposed systemic restructuring of early childhood education as a professional field of practice conveys a strong, long-awaited sense of optimism. Although many obstacles remain to be addressed, the proposed changes will afford educators the identity, respect, and compensation that is long overdue. Early childhood education will become a more desirable and sustainable career choice. Efforts to recruit and retain a highly qualified, diverse early childhood workforce will improve. Children will benefit from programs that are consistently of a higher quality and developmentally appropriate. And newly trained motivational leaders who can keep the professional momentum moving forward will gradually emerge.

These bold changes will require strong leadership and advocacy. Early childhood leaders will need to use effective communication skills to help teachers understand why these changes are necessary and how they and the field will ultimately benefit. Motivational leaders must know how to engage teachers in meaningful decision-making so they can navigate the change process successfully. In addition, it will be incumbent upon leaders to support, motivate, and inspire early childhood educators throughout a challenging transitional period. Clearly, there may be no time more important than the present for individuals to develop and exercise effective motivational leadership skills if these momentous changes are to be realized.

SUMMARY

- Throughout history, young children's care and educational needs have been met through an uncoordinated system of publicly funded programs and private pay services.
- Numerous factors, including a lack of regulated training and credentialing, teachers who are primarily women, and misunderstood pedagogy, continue to raise questions about early childhood education's purpose and legitimacy. Yet, many individuals are drawn to the field by the variety of opportunities, settings, and populations to be served.
- NAEYC has proposed a major restructuring of the early childhood education workforce. Its primary objectives are to achieve recognition as a professional field of practice by establishing consistent training requirements and assuring that practitioners receive commensurate compensation.

APPLICATION ACTIVITIES

1. Locate and read several seminal studies that describe the long-term benefits of early education: Abecedarian Project (North Carolina); Perry Preschool Project (High Scope); Early Childhood Longitudinal Study (National Center for Education Statistics); Head Start Impact Study; and, *From Neurons to Neighborhoods: The Science of Early Childhood Development*. Prepare a one-page argument, based on evidence from these studies and neurobiological research, that would counter critics who suggest that early education does not have long-lasting benefits. Provide your response on Application Sheet 1-1.
2. Add a minimum of five job opportunities/titles to those included in Textbox 1.1. Record your responses on Application Sheet 1-2.
3. Survey fifteen to twenty early childhood teachers in your area to determine their highest education attainment. Record your findings on Application Sheet 1-3, and comment on what you learned. How do your findings compare with the perception that early childhood teachers are not educated?

REVIEW POINTS

1. What purpose did early infant schools serve in the United States?
2. Historically, what gender were most teachers and caretakers of young children?
3. What factors have limited the field of early childhood education from establishing a strong professional identity?
4. What is the minimal degree required to work as an early childhood teacher in most states?
5. Why has the demand for early childhood education programs continued to increase?
6. What recommendations did the National Institute of Medicine and National Research Council offer to improve the quality of early childhood education in this country and the field's potential for achieving professional recognition?

KEY TERMS DEFINED

compensatory—to make up for a loss or deficiency

commensurate—appropriate or suitable according to specific criteria

REFERENCES

Amaram, D. I. (2019). Attracting and retaining women talent in the global labor market: A review. *Journal of Human Resources Management and Labor Studies, 7*(1), 1–10.

Bai, Y., Ladd, H. F., Muschkin, C. G., & Dodge, K. A. (2020). Long-term effects of early childhood programs through eighth grade: Do the effects fade out or grow? *Children and Youth Services Review, 112* (104890), 1–10.

Bakken, L., Brown, N., & Downing, B. (2017). Early childhood education: The long-term benefits. *Journal of Research in Childhood Education, 31*(2), 255–269.

Belfield, C. R. (2018). *The economic impacts of insufficient child care on working families.* Ready Nation: Council for a Strong America. Retrieved from https://strongnation.s3.amazonaws .com/documents/522/3c5cdb46-eda2-4723-9e8e-f20511cc9f0f.pdf?1542205790&inline;%20 filename=%22The%20Economic%20Impacts%20of%20Insufficient%20Child%20Care%20on%20 Working%20Families.pdf%22.

Blasberg, A., Bromer, J., Nugent, C., Porter, T., Shivers, E. M., Tonyan, H., Tout, K., & Weber, B. (2019). *A conceptual model for quality in home-based child care.* OPRE Report #2019-37. Washington, DC: Office of Planning, Research and Evaluation, Administration for Children and Families, U.S. Department of Health and Human Services.

Bloch, M. N., & Choi, S. (1990). Conceptions of play in the history of early childhood education. *Child Youth Care Forum 19*, 31–48.

Brigham, A. (1833). *Remarks on the influence of mental cultivation and mental excitement upon health.* (2nd ed.). Boston, MA: Marsh, Capen, & Lyon.

Build Initiative. (2020). *Aligning early learning with K-12.* Retrieved from https://www.buildinitiative .org/The-Issues/Early-Learning/Birth-to-Eight/Early-Childhood-K-12-Alignment.

Cahan, E. D. (1989). *Past caring: A history of U.S. preschool care and education for the poor, 1820–1965.* National Center for Children in Poverty. Retrieved from https://www.researchconnections.org/ childcare/resources/2088/pdf.

Child Care Aware. (2019). *The U.S. and the high price of child care.* Retrieved from https://www .childcareaware.org/our-issues/research/the-us-and-the-high-price-of-child-care-2019.

ChildStats.gov. (2019). *America's children: Key national indicators of well-being, 2019.* Retrieved from https://www.childstats.gov/americaschildren/family3.asp.

Committee for Economic Development (CED). (2019). *Child care in state economies (2019).* Retrieved from https://www.ced.org/assets/reports/childcareimpact/181104%20CCSE%20Report%20Jan30 .pdf.

DataUSA. (2018). *Child caregivers.* Retrieved from https://datausa.io/profile/soc/childcare-workers #demographics.

Delalibera, B. R., & Ferreira, P. C. (2019). Early childhood education and economic growth. *Journal of Economic Dynamics and Control, 98*, 82–104.

Elkind, D. (1985). Child development research. In S. Koch & D. E. Leary (Eds.), *A century of psychology as science* (pp. 472–488). New York: McGraw-Hill.

Fairbank, Maslin, Maullin, Metz, & Associates. (2018). *Meta-analysis of public opinion data on support for early childhood services.* Retrieved from https://s3-us-west-2.amazonaws.com/mcf-redesign -assets/pdfs/ECF-EC-Research-Meta-Analysis-Final-1-29-2018.pdf?mtime=20180206140737.

Friedman-Krauss, A., Bernstein, S., & Barnett, W. S. (2019). *Early childhood education: Three pathways to better health.* National Institute for Early Education Research (NIEER). Retrieved from http:// nieer.org/policy-issue/early-childhood-education-three-pathways-to-better-health.

Garcia, J. L., Heckman, J. J., & Ziff, A. L. (2019). Early childhood education and crime. *Infant Mental Health Journal, 40*(1), 141–151.

Gould, E., Whitebook, M., Mokhiber, Z., & Austin, L. (2019). *Breaking the silence on early child care and education costs. A values-based budget for children, parents, and teachers in California.* Economic Policy Institute. Retrieved from https://www.epi.org/publication/breaking-the-silence-on-early-child-care-and-education-costs-a-values-based-budget-for-children-parents-and-teachers-in-california.

Greenberg, E. H. (2018). Public preferences for targeted and universal preschool. *AERA Open, 4*(1), 1–20.

Grunewald, R. (2019). Early childhood development as economic development. *Economic Development Journal, 18*(1), 10–15.

Harwood, D., & Tukonic, S. (2016). Babysitter or professional? Perceptions of professionalism narrated by Ontario early childhood educators. *International Electronic Journal of Elementary Education, 8*(4), 589–600.

Haynie, K. (2019). *Checking in on the child care landscape: 2019 state fact sheets.* Retrieved from https://cdn2.hubspot.net/hubfs/3957809/State%20Fact%20Sheets%202019/2019StateFactSheets-Overview.pdf.

Herbst, C. M., Desouza, K. C., Al-Ashri, S., Kandala, S. S., Khullar, M., & Bajaj, V. (2020). What do parents value in a child care provider? Evidence from Yelp consumer reviews. *Early Childhood Research Quarterly, 51*(2), 288–306.

Hooper, A. (2020). "I'm a teacher, unofficially": How home-based providers perceive and navigate their roles. *Journal of Research in Childhood Education, 34*(2), 223–237.

Institute of Medicine and National Research Council. (2015). *Transforming the workforce for children birth through age 8: A unifying foundation.* Washington, DC: The National Academies Press. https://doi.org/10.17226/19401.

Jessen-Howard, S., & Workman, S. (2019). *Early learning in the United States: 2019.* Center for American Progress. Retrieved from https://www.americanprogress.org/issues/early-childhood/reports/2019/09/16/474487/early-learning-united-states-2019/.

Kaestle, C. F., & Vinovskis, M. A. (1980). *Education and social change in nineteenth-century Massachusetts.* New York: Cambridge University Press.

Kamerman, S. B. (2006). *A global history of early childhood education and care. Education for all global monitoring report 2007.* United Nations. Retrieved from https://unesdoc.unesco.org/ark:/48223/pf0000147470.

Karoly, L. A. (2016). The economic returns to early childhood education. *The Future of Children, 26*(2), 37–55.

Kohl, K., Bihler, L. M., Willard, J. A., Agache, A., & Leyendecker, B. (2020). Linking quantity and quality of early childhood education and care to children's socio-emotional adjustment: A German cross-sectional study. *Early Education and Development, 31*(2), 177–199.

Kulic, N., Skopek, J., Triventi, M., & Blossfeld, H. (2019). Social background and children's cognitive skills: The role of early childhood education and care in a cross-national perspective. *Annual Review of Sociology, 45*, 557–579.

Lascarides, V. C., & Hinitz, B. F. (2000). *History of early childhood education.* New York: Routledge.

Lee, K. (2020). Long-term Head Start impact on developmental outcomes for children in foster care. *Child Abuse & Neglect,* 101:104329.

Malik, R. (2019). *Working families are spending big money on child care*. Center for American Progress. Retrieved from https://www.americanprogress.org/issues/early-childhood/reports/2019/06/20/471141/working-families-spending-big-money-child-care.

Malik, R., Hamm, K., Schochet, L., Novoa, C., Workman, S., & Jessen-Howard, S. (2018). *America's child care deserts in 2018*. Center for American Progress. Retrieved from https://www.americanprogress.org/issues/early-childhood/reports/2018/12/06/461643/americas-child-care-deserts-20.

McLean, C., Whitebook, M., & Roh, E. (2019). *From unlivable wages to just pay for early educators*. Berkeley, CA: Center for the Study of Child Care Employment, University of California, Berkeley. Retrieved from https://cscce.berkeley.edu/from-unlivable-wages-to-just-pay-for-early-educators/.

Meloy, B., Gardner, M., & Darling-Hammond, L. (2019). *Untangling the evidence on preschool effectiveness: Insights for policymakers*. Learning Policy Institute. Retrieved from https://learningpolicyinstitute.org/sites/default/files/product-files/Untangling_Evidence_Preschool_Effectiveness_REPORT.pdf.

National Association for the Education of Young Children (NAEYC). (2020). *Unifying framework for the early childhood education profession*. Retrieved from http://powertotheprofession.org/.

National Association for the Education of Young Children (NAEYC). (2019). *Growing the demand for quality: Parents and early childhood educators talk about the financing of early learning*. Retrieved from https://www.naeyc.org/sites/default/files/globally-shared/downloads/PDFs/our-work/public-policy-advocacy/Growing%20the%20Demand%20for%20Quality.Executive%20Summary.FINAL__0.pdf.

National Center on Early Childhood Quality Assurance. (2019). *Addressing the decreasing number of family child care providers in the United States*. Retrieved from https://www.researchconnections.org/childcare/resources/37075/pdf.

National Survey of Early Care and Education Project Team (NSECE). (2016). *Early care and education usage and households' out-of-pocket costs: Tabulations from the National Survey of Early Care and Education (NSECE)*. OPRE Report #2016-09, Washington DC: Office of Planning, Research and Evaluation, Administration for Children and Families, U.S. Department of Health and Human Services.

Nilsson, M., Ferholt, B., & Lecusay, R. (2017). The playing-exploring child: Reconceptualizing the relationship between play and learning in early childhood education. *Contemporary Issues in Early Childhood Education, 19*(3), 231–245.

Paschall, K., & Tout, K. (2018). *Most child care settings in the United States are homes, not centers*. Retrieved from https://www.childtrends.org/most-child-care-providers-in-the-united-states-are-based-in-homes-not-centers.

Schochet, L. (2019). *The child care crisis is keeping women out of the workforce*. Center for American Progress. Retrieved from https://cdn.americanprogress.org/content/uploads/2019/03/19103744/ECPP-ChildCare-Crisis-report-2.pdf.

Shah, R. K. (2019). Child-centered education: Criticisms. *Shanlax International Journal of Education, 8*(1), 22–27.

Shonkoff, J. P., & Phillips, D. A. (Eds.). (2000). *From neurons to neighborhoods: The science of early childhood development*. National Research Council (US) and Institute of Medicine (US). Committee on Integrating the Science of Early Childhood Development. Washington, DC: National Academies Press.

Sinclaire-Harding L., Vuillier L., & Whitebread, D. (2018). Neuroscience and early childhood education. In M. Fleer & B. van Oers (Eds.), *International Handbook of Early Childhood Education* (pp. 335–361). Springer International Handbooks of Education.

Stroud, J. C., & Clark, P. (2000). Obstacles and opportunities: Creating early childhood professional development schools. *Journal of Early Childhood Teacher Education, 21*(1), 39–46.

Taylor, M. E., & Boyer, W. (2020). Play-based learning: Evidence-based research to improve children's learning experiences in the kindergarten classroom. *Early Childhood Education Journal, 48*, 127–133.

U.S. Bureau of Labor Statistics. (2020a). *Families with own children: Employment status of parents by age of youngest child and family type, 2018–2019 annual averages (Table 4)*. Retrieved from https://www.bls.gov/news.release/famee.t04.htm.

U.S. Bureau of Labor Statistics. (2020b). *Preschool teachers*. Retrieved from https://www.bls.gov/ooh/education-training-and-library/preschool-teachers.htm.

U.S. Chamber of Commerce Foundation. (2020). *A world-class workforce begins with a world-class education system*. Retrieved from https://www.uschamberfoundation.org/early-childhood-education/the-business-case.

U.S. Department of Education. (2016). *Fact sheet: Troubling pay gap for early childhood teachers*. Retrieved from https://www.ed.gov/news/press-releases/fact-sheet-troubling-pay-gap-early-childhood-teacher.

Vandell, D. L., Lee, K. T., Whitaker, A. A., & Pierce, K. M. (2020). Cumulative and differential effects of early child care and middle childhood out-of-school time on adolescent functioning. *Child Development, 91*(1), 129–144.

Vinovskis, M. A. (1993). Early childhood education: Then and now. *Daedalus, 122*(1), 151–176.

Warash, B. G., Root, A. E., & Doris, M. D. (2017). Parents' perceptions of play: A comparative study of spousal perspectives. *Early Child Development and Care, 187*(5–6), 958–966.

Whitebook, M., McLean, C., Austin, L. J., & Edwards, B. (2018). *Early childhood workforce index—2018*. Berkeley, CA: Center for the Study of Child Care Employment, University of California, Berkeley. Retrieved from http://cscce.berkeley.edu/topic/early-childhood-work-force-index/2018/.

Winterer, C. (1992). Avoiding a "hothouse system of education": Nineteenth-century early childhood education from the infant schools to the kindergartens. *History of Education Quarterly, 32*(3), 289–314.

Yang, W., Datu, A. D., Lin, X., Lau, M. M., & Li, H. (2019). Can early childhood curriculum enhance social-emotional competence in low-income children? A meta-analysis of the educational effects. *Early Education and Development, 30*(1), 36–59.

Zosh, J. M., Hopkins, E. J., Jensen, H., Liu, C., Neale, D., Hirsh-Pasek, K., Solis, S. L., & Whitebread, D. (2017). *Learning through play: A review of the evidence* (White paper). The LEGO Foundation, DK. Retrieved from https://www.legofoundation.com/media/1063/learning-through-play_web.pdf.

ONLINE RESOURCES

Center for the Study of Child Care Employment: https://cscce.berkeley.edu

Institute of Education Sciences: https://ies.ed.gov/topics/earlyChildhood.asp

National Association for the Education of Young Children (NAEYC): https://www.naeyc.org

National Institute for Early Education Research: http://nieer.org

Office of Head Start: https://www.acf.hhs.gov/ohs

APPLICATION SHEET 1-1

Do young children benefit from participation in early childhood education? What are some of the benefits cited in the literature?

APPLICATION SHEET 1-2

Additional early childhood job opportunities/titles:

a) _____

b) _____

c) _____

d) _____

e) _____

APPLICATION SHEET 1-3

Number of teachers whose highest education degree is a

a) high school diploma =

b) completion of classes beyond high school =

c) associate's degree in early childhood education =

d) associate's degree in another field =

e) bachelor's degree in early childhood education =

f) bachelor's degree in another field =

g) master's degree in early childhood education =

h) master's degree in another field =

i) PhD in early childhood education =

j) PhD in another field =

Comments about my findings:

2

The Early Childhood Education Workforce

OBJECTIVES

After reading this chapter, you will be able to do the following:

- Discuss three features that often draw preservice teachers to the early childhood field.
- Identify the fundamental expectations that employees have when they accept a job.
- Explain why the early childhood field continues to experience a shortage of highly qualified teachers.
- Discuss how working conditions in early childhood education programs may contribute to a high teacher turnover rate.
- Describe four motivational strategies that leaders can use to attract and retain quality employees.

KEY TERMS

- demographic
- stress
- subjective
- burnout
- attrition

■ ■ ■

The vision is really about empowering workers, giving them all the information about what's going on so they can do a lot more than they've done in the past.

—Bill Gates, philanthropist, Microsoft co-founder

INTRODUCTION

Science-based evidence has validated immediate and long-term beneficial outcomes for children who participate in high-quality early childhood education programs (Cornelissen & Dustmann, 2019; Garcia, Heckman, & Ziff, 2019; Thompson, 2018). These results are typically attributed to well-trained early childhood teachers who are knowledgeable about children's development, positive behavior guidance, cultural diversity, assessment, developmentally appropriate learning experiences, and family engagement (Boyd-Swan & Herbst, 2020; Nocita et al., 2020; Ramírez, López, & Ferron, 2019).

Although early childhood education continues to gain favorable attention and support, it suffers from a critical shortage of trained teachers. Currently, too few such teachers are available for hire, or they chose to remain in their positions for only a short time. As a result, programs are often unable to maintain a stable, qualified workforce. Understanding why this situation is occurring requires an examination of several factors: the fundamental reasons why people choose to work and pursue careers in early childhood education; what they want and expect from their employer; and why some teachers leave the field. Although this information is unlikely to eliminate the teacher shortage problem, it will help program leaders to be more effective in recruiting, motivating, inspiring, and retaining dedicated personnel.

WHAT ATTRACTS TEACHERS TO EARLY CHILDHOOD EDUCATION?

Why are some individuals drawn to the field of early childhood education? What do they find satisfying and motivating about working with young children? These are important questions to ask when a person enters the field and as they move through their career. An understanding of the answers to these questions enables leadership to provide inspiration and adapt motivational strategies so they are meaningful to individual employees.

The most commonly cited reason for choosing this career path is to earn a reliable income. Jobs in the early childhood field are relatively available and easy to secure. Positions are offered in diverse settings, such as private and public centers, public schools, home-based programs, travel and hospitality venues, and community agencies. Early childhood teachers often find this variety of choices appealing.

Many individuals also note that they are attracted to the field by children's laughter, enthusiasm for learning, endless curiosity, and an opportunity to interact with children's families (Bergmark et al., 2018). They describe their work as intrinsically rewarding and fulfilling, and find pleasure in introducing children to new ideas, encouraging their efforts, fostering their understanding, and nurturing their success (Figure 2.1). Other individuals become early childhood teachers for altruistic reasons, such as helping to improve children's lives, giving back to their communities, or contributing to society (Fray & Gore, 2018). In other words, people choose to become early childhood educators for many of the same fundamental reasons that individuals seek employment in other fields, namely,

- financial considerations;
- personal fulfillment; and
- the opportunity to make professional contributions to an endeavor or program.

Each of these factors is subject to a host of influences, such as an individual's career stage, personal interests, training and experience, cultural background, and the prestige and reinforcement associated with a professional position (Moon, Hur, & Hyun, 2019; Van Wingerden & Van der Stoep, 2018).

FIGURE 2.1 Early childhood teachers work in diverse settings. *Kritchanut, iStock / Getty Images Plus*

Currently, the child care industry employs approximately two million paid caregivers and early childhood educators to care for and teach more than 12.5 million children under the age of six (Haynie, 2019; Whitebook et al., 2018). Of this number,

- less than three percent of preschool and kindergarten teachers are male (U.S. Bureau of Labor Statistics, 2019);
- nearly 50 percent of early childhood teachers are individuals of color or foreign-born (Whitebook et al., 2018);
- one-third of all positions involve part-time employment with no benefits;
- 98 percent of all early childhood teachers are younger than age 50; and
- early childhood teachers are among the lowest paid educators (Table 2.1) (U.S. Bureau of Labor Statistics, 2019).

The early childhood workforce includes individuals who represent four different generations for the first time in history (Table 2.2). Each group is often described as having different values, work ethics, and career goals. However, research does not support these distinctions (The National Academies of Science, Engineering, and Medicine, 2020). In fact, age cohorts have many characteristics in common with regard to their job and personal requirements (Cucina et al., 2018; Standifer & Lester, 2020). For example, all employees expect to work in a safe environment, earn a livable wage, be treated respectfully, and be recognized for their effort and contributions.

Table 2.1: Early Childhood Educators: Entry Requirements and Salary

Occupation	Entry Requirement	Median Salary
Child Care Worker	High school diploma or equivalent	$24,230
Teacher Assistant	Some college preferred; no degree required	$27,920
Preschool Teacher	Associate Degree (AA)	$30,520
Kindergarten & Elementary School Teachers	Bachelor's Degree	$59,420
Special Education Teachers	Bachelor's or Master's Degree	$61,030
Preschool & Childcare Center Directors	Bachelor's Degree	$48,210

Source: U.S. Bureau of Labor Statistics, Department of Labor (2019). 2019 *Occupational Outlook Handbook*. Retrieved from https://www.bls.gov/ooh/education-training-and-library/home.htm.

Table 2.2: Generational Differences in Work-Related Values

Work-related values and preferences associated with current generational cohorts:

✓ Baby Boomers—born 1944 to 1964 (currently 56–76 years old*)	Hardworking; dedicated; goal-oriented; prefers a defined work structure and clear expectations.
✓ Generation X—born 1965 to 1980 (currently 40–55 years old)	Seeks autonomy and flexible work schedule; ambitious; values collaboration; loyal; strong work ethic.
✓ Millennials (Gen Y)—born 1981 to 1996 (currently 24–39 years old)	Strives for work/life balance vs. advancement; questions authority; values challenge and meaningful work; completes task efficiently and moves on; team-oriented.
✓ Generation Z (Gen Z)—born after 1997 (currently 23 years old and under)	Desires mentoring and skill acquisition; goal-oriented; tolerant; considers civic engagement important; is creative; seeks flexible work schedule.

*Ages calculated as of the year 2020.

Kalleberg & Marsden (2019) suggest that factors other than an employee's age may explain the differences often attributed to individual cohort groups. For example, they found that gender plays an important role. Women, especially those who have children, were more likely than men to value a flexible work schedule, meaningful work, and job security. In contrast, men believed that job promotion and greater income were primary goals that could be achieved through ambition and hard work. Career stage also had an influential effect on a person's work values. Younger employees sought interesting work and opportunities to acquire new skills that would help them to advance in their field. In contrast, employees in their prime working years tended to focus more on income, job security, and a balance between their work commitment and personal life.

Leaders should be cautious not to make age-based, stereotyped assumptions about an employee's personal and work-related characteristics. Each individual is a unique product of their social, economic, cultural, religious, and experiential backgrounds. These differences exert a strong influence on individuals' reasons for seeking employment, what they want and expect from a position, and how much time and effort they are willing to invest in performing the job (Kalleberg & Marsden, 2019). Successful motivational leaders take time to meet with individual employees and learn about their personal needs, values, and preferences. They may be surprised to discover that employees seek to work in their programs for many similar reasons and are not as different as might have been assumed.

The demand for early childhood educators, especially those from diverse backgrounds and with advanced training, is expected to increase between four and seven percent in the next few years (U.S. Bureau of Labor Statistics, 2019). This growth rate is significantly higher than predicted for many other occupations. It reflects anticipated social and **demographic** changes, including an increase in the number of mothers with children under age six who are likely to seek employment outside of their home. It also addresses the growing number of families who are enrolling their child(ren) in early childhood programs for the learning and social opportunities (Ansari, 2018; Conger et al., 2019; Garcia, Heckman, & Ziff, 2019). More special education educators will also be needed to serve the increasing number of children with health and developmental challenges who attend early childhood programs.

Did You Know? ·

Seventy-eight percent of early childhood teachers are employed in community-based early childhood services and programs; 19 percent work in elementary and secondary schools.

· ·

WHAT DO EMPLOYEES WANT FROM THEIR JOB?

Although personal reasons for becoming an early childhood teacher may differ, employees often have similar expectations in terms of what they want and expect from an employer, including:

- job security
- safe working conditions
- recognition/acknowledgment of job performance
- respect

Job Security

Employees want assurance that their jobs will continue well into the future. This point may seem somewhat curious given the high teacher turnover rate and frequent program closures in the early childhood education field. However, employees who are looking for job stability want the decision about whether to stay or leave a position to be their personal choice. Leaders' acknowledgment of employees' concerns about job security should result in measures taken to make them feel genuinely valued. Engaging teachers in program decisions, recognizing their efforts, and maintaining good communication are some of the motivating strategies that leaders can practice to make employees feel needed and appreciated. Supporting teachers' continued education through informal (e.g., in-service, workshop, conference attendance) and/or formal certification or degree completion classes also conveys a powerful message regarding their importance to the program.

Safe and Healthy Working Conditions

Employees value their personal health and safety and expect employers to provide workplace environments that protect them from unnecessary harm (Otten et al., 2019). Caring for young children can have potential risks, such as exposure to communicable illnesses, injuries incurred from improper lifting of children, and occasional scratches, bites, and bruises. However, steps can be taken to create clean, safe environments. For example, reducing noise levels and maintaining proper room temperatures will contribute to teachers' comfort. Providing adult-sized chairs for teachers' use and making sure that countertops and changing tables are adult-height can reduce the risk of muscle strain and joint injuries. Implementing sick leave and immunization requirement policies help to protect teachers' health. Arranging a fitness or yoga class can promote staff wellness, improve energy and stamina, and reduce the potential for injury.

Measures should also be taken to address teachers' mental health. Providing a quiet room where teachers can relax, stretch, socialize with one another, and take a break from classroom noise and responsibilities can be effective for reducing **stress**. The addition of a small refrigerator, coffeemaker, and/or water dispenser also sends a supportive message to teachers that their well-being is important. Windows that let in sunshine and fresh air provide added benefits that are also known to have positive psychological effects (Young, McGrath, & Adams, 2018).

Recognition

Employees want meaningful work and to feel that their efforts and contributions are sincerely appreciated (Grant, Jeon, & Buettner, 2019). However, many leaders fail to recognize this essential need, find it difficult to put into practice, or do not devote sufficient time and effort to addressing it in the workplace.

Understanding when and how to motivate and encourage employees plays a critical role in performance improvement, reduction of stress and job dissatisfaction, and burnout prevention (Ford et al., 2019). For example, a director may bring in a health consultant to mentor a teacher who has a new child enrolled in her classroom who is in a wheelchair or requires tube feedings. The director recognizes that this step may reduce the teacher's anxiety and enable her to work more effectively with this child. A simple thank-you also goes a long way in letting an individual know that their efforts are valued. For example, "I appreciate the extra time you spent yesterday straightening up the resource room."

Respect

Maslow (1968) described respect as a fundamental human need for belonging and essential to the formation of one's self-esteem. Respect provides an individual with critical feedback about what others value in terms of a person's behavior, performance, and/or contributions. Employees who are treated with respect experience less stress, show improved performance, are more engaged in their work, and are more likely to remain with the organization (Ng, Hsu, & Parker, 2019; Rogers & Ashforth, 2017).

Motivational leaders understand the importance of treating employees with respect, encouraging their input, listening to their ideas in a nonjudgmental manner, and implementing their suggestions whenever appropriate. They meet regularly with individual employees to stay informed about their interests and concerns and to let them know they are an important team member. Effective motivational leaders provide employees with opportunities to develop and showcase their individual talents, such as managing a special project or assuming new job responsibilities. They place a high value on strengthening communication and building effective working relationships among employees.

Early childhood leaders also have a moral and ethical responsibility to establish a culture of respect, dignity, sensitivity, understanding, and acceptance in their programs. This role is an especially important one given the increasingly diverse workforce and child and family populations being served.

Motivational leaders also have an obligation to model the same exemplary behaviors that they expect of their employees. Harassment, stereotyping, discrimination, or insensitive comments and practices are unacceptable in the workplace, and violate the NAEYC Code of Ethical Conduct and Statement of Commitment (NAEYC, 2011). Such behaviors also lead children to believe that intolerance is acceptable.

WHY IS THERE A TEACHER SHORTAGE?

Despite a favorable job market, the field suffers from a significant shortage of qualified teachers. Fewer students are enrolling in teacher-training degree programs. They are choosing instead to pursue other academic disciplines in higher-paying professions (AACTC, 2018; Sutcher, Darling-Hammond, & Carver-Thomas, 2019). Challenging working conditions, lack of adequate resources and opportunities for advancement, and improved access to other fields of study are also frequently cited reasons for the declining interest in a teaching career.

The pool of qualified early childhood teachers is further compromised by the relatively high number who leave the field each year (Grant, Jeon, & Buettner, 2019; Hughes & Mc-Cartney, 2019). The annual turnover rate among early childhood educators is reported to be approximately thirty percent (Whitebook et al., 2018). This figure is nearly twice the average attrition rate experienced by other businesses in the United States.

These facts are particularly noteworthy and draw attention to the critical issue of how to retain highly qualified employees. When employees leave, programs face substantial direct and indirect costs, including those associated with recruiting, rehiring, and retraining new personnel. In addition, the loss of a teacher or other staff member can temporarily disrupt the quality of services a program provides and contribute to poor morale among the remaining employees.

However, economic factors are secondary to the negative effects that high staff turnover rates can have on children's development, such as a sense of loss, insecurity, or delayed language and/or social skills (Choi et al., 2018). Researchers have identified stable, consistent teacher-child relationships as critical to young children's learning ability, emotional health, and self-regulation (Kwon et al., 2020; Magnuson & Schindler, 2019).

Connecting Points

Two months ago, you were hired on as an assistant teacher in the toddler room at the See Saw Center. When the head teacher left for another position, the director asked you to take over her classroom responsibilities. This is your first job, and you have only taken a few early childhood classes at the local community college.

- How would you feel about being asked to assume the head teacher position?
- Would you feel adequately prepared to take on this level of responsibility? Why? Why not?
- If you decided not to accept the position, do you think your decision might jeopardize future promotion opportunities ? Explain.

DIRECTOR'S SHOWCASE

Is there anything teachers can do to address the low wages they are typically paid?

That is a really tough question. There is no doubt that early childhood teachers deserve better compensation. However, most centers and home-based programs are not able to pay higher salaries without some additional source of financial support. Families are already paying high child care fees, so charging them more is not an option.

We encourage our teachers and administrators to advocate for better compensation by joining their local, state, and national NAEYC organizations. It is also important for them to share their concerns with city leaders, Chamber of Commerce personnel, state legislators, and local business owners to build support for improved pay. This isn't a problem that will be resolved quickly, but it must be addressed soon to prevent more good teachers from leaving the field.

—Mica, cooperative director

WHY DO TEACHERS LEAVE?

Qualities that make the field of early childhood education attractive to teachers were discussed at the beginning of this chapter. Among them were a dependable income and the desire to make a difference in children's lives. Despite its challenges, many early childhood teachers remain in their job because they consider it important work and continue to find it personally fulfilling and energizing (Arnup & Bowles, 2016; McDonald, Thorpe, & Irvine, 2018).

So, what causes some teachers to leave the early childhood field with such frequency? The answer, in part, may be related to the population with which they work. Unlike other forms of teaching, the care and education of young children present a number of unique challenges, including:

- working with highly dependent children who often require considerable assistance to meet their physical needs (e.g., feeding, toileting, dressing, handwashing, sleeping);
- serving a population with limited language, motor, and social-emotional skills;
- teaching and caring for children of multiple ages within a single group;

- maintaining safe and healthful environments for young children who are at greater risk of injury and illness;
- identifying children who may have developmental challenges, and arranging for appropriate intervention services; and
- working with families who are juggling multiple responsibilities and, perhaps, leaving their child in another person's care for the first time.

Early childhood educators may also find themselves working in conditions that are often less than ideal (Grant, Jeon, & Buettner, 2019; Lambert et al., 2019). Some of the concerns frequently cited include the following:

- long shifts that may involve eight to ten hours daily
- low wages
- lack of employee benefits, such as health insurance, retirement plans, paid vacation, and sick days
- lack of affordable professional development opportunities
- limited opportunities for advancement
- stress caused by exposure to continuous noise and responsibilities that are emotionally and physically demanding
- frequent personnel turnover and resulting staff shortages
- lack of professional recognition
- insufficient resources for purchasing supplies and equipment

Salaries

Concerns, such as long working hours and lack of advancement opportunities, arise from the very nature of the early childhood profession (Figure 2.2). Others, such as salaries, present a different and significant challenge. Progress in addressing salary inequities has been difficult and slow due to a number of unrelated factors. One relates to gender and racial bias: historically, women's salaries in almost all professions have lagged, and continue to lag, behind those of their male counterparts. Given that the majority of early childhood teacher positions are held by women, nearly half of whom are women of color, salaries have traditionally remained low (Allvin, 2019; Whitebook et al., 2018).

A second factor involved in the struggle to improve salaries relates to the lack of consistent educational qualifications necessary to be hired as an early childhood educator. Currently, individual states establish their own eligibility requirements, which has led to much variability across the nation (Institute of Medicine and National Research Council, 2015). In many states, a desire to work with children and the equivalent of a high school diploma are the only credentials required for employment as an early childhood teacher.

The absence of any defined advanced qualifications has made it difficult to argue for, and justify, higher wages. However, the current state of inadequate salaries also presents a significant barrier for many individuals who may be interested in obtaining an advanced degree but cannot afford to do so. Clearly, improved salary compensation is needed to attract, educate, and retain early childhood educators (The National Academies of Sciences, Engineering, and Medicine, 2018; Totenhagen et al., 2016; Whitebook et al., 2018).

FIGURE 2.2 Fair and equitable compensation is essential for retaining high-quality teachers.
iStock / Getty Images Plus

Did You Know? ···

Approximately 30 percent of early childhood teachers who work in in-home programs and 50 percent who work in center-based programs have attained an associate or higher degree.

···

A third factor that has impeded public policy and support for salary improvements is a general misperception regarding the critical role that early childhood educators play in fostering young children's development, and an inaccurate assumption that "anyone can take care of children" (Cassidy et al., 2019; LiBetti, 2018). However, attitudes are slowly changing as politicians, business leaders, administrators, and the public at-large are becoming better informed about the difference that high-quality early childhood education can make in children's lives (Bishop-Josef et al., 2019; Kulic et al., 2019; Sparling & Meunier, 2019). Continued efforts to reduce high teacher turnover rates will, in turn, help to build a stronger, unified base of organizational commitment necessary to advocate for and achieve improved compensation.

Stress

Everyone experiences **stress** from time to time. Early childhood teachers, in particular, experience considerable stress related to the physical and emotional demands associated with their work (Figure 2.3). Stress is often a topic of negative workplace conversation. A little reflection, though, suggests that stress is not always a bad or undesirable quality (Brulé & Morgan, 2018). It is known to spark a person's interest and energy levels; improve learning, productivity, and performance; and serve as a personal and professional motivator (Dhabhar, 2019; McEwen, 2016).

An absence of stress is likely to leave us feeling bored and disinterested. Most people enjoy a certain amount of stress in their daily lives, and often actively seek it out despite knowing that they may encounter frustration, anxiety, or obstacles along the way. For example, athletes train and compete, students return to enroll in challenging courses each semester, people choose to move and begin new jobs, and novices attempt to learn a new skill or language, or to play a musical instrument.

Periods of intermittent and short-term stress can be invigorating (Strack et al., 2017). However, excessive or prolonged stress may lead to a range of physiological and/or psychological problems (Felix et al., 2019; Jeon, Buettner, & Grant, 2018) (Textbox 2.1). The key is to find a healthy balance between too little and too much stress in order to avoid its negative effects.

Stress is a highly individualized physical and emotional response to any number of stressors. It is the result of a person's **subjective** interpretation of external events that can

FIGURE 2.3 Working with young children can be stressful at times. *globalmoments, iStock / Getty Images Plus*

cause feelings of anger, anxiousness, or distress. For example, one teacher may lash out at her team members because an activity was not set up the way she expected, while another teacher may simply overlook the incident and view it as a creative alternative. Why do these teachers react differently to the same situation? Differences in their personalities, temperament, life experiences, self-efficacy, health, culture, and coping mechanisms influence their perception of the event as being either a threatening or stressful but manageable challenge (Khedhaouria & Cucchi, 2019).

TEXTBOX 2.1

BEHAVIORAL INDICATORS OF ACUTE OR PROLONGED STRESS

An employee who is experiencing excessive stress may exhibit one or more of the following symptoms:

- loss of interest, creativity, or ability to remain focused
- resentment; not feeling appreciated
- irritability; defensive behavior
- lack of energy
- difficulty sleeping
- loss of appetite
- inability to have fun
- decreased interaction/communication with colleagues
- depression or sadness
- frequent tardiness and absenteeism

A person's response to stress is also influenced by the nature and/or number of additional stressors they may be experiencing at any given time (Arvidsson et al., 2019). For example, a lead teacher, who has been without his assistant for several days due to an illness, may become visibly upset when informed by the director that she has enrolled two additional children who have special needs in his classroom. Under ordinary circumstances, the teacher may not have responded in this fashion. However, his combined feelings of frustration, an added workload, and lack of control over the decision may cause him to react in an uncharacteristic fashion. Illness, pain, lack of sleep, personal problems, or an overextension of one's time and energies can also intensify a person's stressful feelings. An effective motivational leader notices when there are changes in an employee's behavior and should meet privately to determine what may be troubling the individual and if they can be of any assistance.

Results from numerous studies suggest that the more control an individual has in a given situation, the less stressful they perceive it to be (Brough, Drummond, & Biggs, 2018; García et al., 2019). For example, an announcement informing teachers that the center will stay open an hour longer each day with no additional pay, or that one of the classrooms is being eliminated, is likely to be met with an angry and aggressive response. However, involving teachers in decisions that directly affect their work or personal lives can be an effective strategy for reducing the initial elements of surprise and stress they may otherwise experience. Learning and practicing stress-reducing strategies can also help teachers to maintain their own good health and continued work-related interests (Textbox 2.2).

TEXTBOX 2.2

STRESS-REDUCING STRATEGIES

Strategies that can reduce stress include

- taking advantage of opportunities to learn new information and skills that will improve your effectiveness on the job;
- learning and practicing time-management techniques;
- maintaining a healthy lifestyle: getting plenty of sleep, exercise, and consuming a nutritious diet;
- developing new interests, hobbies, and other outlets for releasing tension;
- joining professional organizations, networking and expanding your interactions with other early childhood educators, becoming involved in advocacy issues;
- being spontaneous on occasion: taking an unplanned shopping trip, going for a walk, attending a sporting event, going out to eat, visiting an art museum or local park;
- practicing progressive relaxation techniques and mindfulness: setting aside a few minutes each day to relax, meditate, and/or daydream; and
- planning some "me time" each day: reading a favorite book, listening to music, watching a movie or favorite TV program, taking a long walk, scheduling a massage.

Job Dissatisfaction

Some teachers become disillusioned and dissatisfied with their jobs by the often stressful working conditions and demands involved in caring for young children. They may feel that their contributions are not appreciated. Others simply do not have adequate training or experience in early childhood education. As a result, they may become frustrated and find themselves unprepared to develop meaningful learning environments or to manage children's difficult behavior in a positive way.

Chronic job dissatisfaction can take a toll on teachers' physical and emotional stamina and gradually lead to a condition known as **burnout** (Jeon, Buettner, & Grant, 2018). In an investigative study to determine why many special education teachers leave the field, Robinson et al. (2019) noted a strong correlation between job dissatisfaction, burnout, and

attrition. In the early stages, teachers are tardy or absent more often than usual or they may be unwilling to volunteer for extra projects. They may also become defensive and make statements such as, "I am working as hard as I can" more frequently, even in casual conversations. Eventually, a teacher may exhibit a lack of motivation, increased irritability, and resentment, and begin to complain frequently about working conditions, other staff, the director, the children, or almost anything else.

Perceived and prolonged dissatisfaction with one's job can cause talented early childhood educators to leave their position and pursue other interests. Their departure may contribute to a sense of loss, frustration, and low morale among their colleagues who remain. It may also necessitate a reassignment of job responsibilities, which can increase the burden and stress placed on other personnel.

There appear to be critical times in a teacher's career when job dissatisfaction and early departure seem to peak. The highest attrition rates occur during the first and fifth years, when teachers seem to make decisions about whether to remain with the same program or organization. However, the reasons for the first- and fifth-year decisions are also quite different.

Connecting Points

Think about your least favorite position as a salaried employee.

- What motivated you to look for the job?
- Why did you accept the position?
- What factors caused you to become frustrated or dissatisfied with the job?
- What motivators might your supervisor/administrator have offered to improve your job satisfaction?

First-year teachers are more inclined to become frustrated with working conditions and administrative support and, thus, quickly leave the field (Kelly et al., 2019; Perrone, Player, & Youngs, 2019). Teachers who remain with a program for four or five years are more likely to become disillusioned by a perceived lack of advancement opportunities or feeling that their original expectations have not been met (Glazer, 2018; Hester, Bridges, & Rollins, 2020). Consequently, they decide to either find another job in early childhood education or abandon teaching altogether and begin a new career.

Motivational leaders can anticipate and address many of these potential problems if they understand stress and its effect on employees' career decisions. Early recognition of behavioral changes often provides leaders with an opportunity to intervene before a situation reaches a potential crisis stage. Leaders who devote time each day to acknowledging employees' contributions and implementing various motivational strategies create a more enjoyable workplace. Their efforts are also likely to yield significant rewards in terms of reducing stress, improving self-efficacy, and retaining quality employees (Hagaman & Casey, 2018; Holmes, Parker, & Gibson, 2019).

DIRECTOR'S SHOWCASE

What is one thing you do to motivate and support your teachers?

We are a relatively small center (50 three- and four-year-olds), so our budget doesn't have room to give teachers big pay increases. But I do try to come up with simple ways to let our teachers know they are appreciated and important to the program. One thing they really look forward to is the drawing we hold during our weekly staff meetings. I have a small budget that I use to purchase inexpensive items like a coupon for a free car wash or a five-dollar gift card to a local store for groceries, a coffee shop treat, or something special for their classroom. Local businesses and restaurants will make small donations from time to time, such as logo T-shirts or coffee mugs, gift certificates for fast food meals, or even a flower bouquet. One lucky teacher is the winner each week. If the same teacher wins twice during the month, there is a redrawing. Although the "treats" are relatively small tokens of appreciation, our teachers always look forward to the event. It also boosts morale and brings us closer together as a team.

—Darnell T., administrative director

Connecting Points

Your teachers have been complaining about having trouble locating certain pieces of outdoor play equipment because the storage shed is in complete disarray. After listening to their complaints, you decide to come in on a Saturday morning and reorganize the shed.

- What were your motives for coming in on your own time to clean out and reorganize the storage shed? (Be honest.)
- If no one notices or thanks you, how will that make you feel?
- When others acknowledge your efforts, how does this affect your willingness to help them in the future?
- Identify three or four situations in the past two months when you have acknowledged something special that another person has done or complimented someone on their work.

Did You Know? . . . .

An increasing number of states are requiring program directors to be credentialed.

. . . .

LEADERSHIP THAT MAKES A DIFFERENCE

It is important that motivational leaders understand an individual's purpose for seeking employment and the reasons why he or she has chosen to work in the early childhood field.

This information can be used to meet the person's real and perceived needs, inspire their development, motivate performance, and encourage a desire to remain with the program. For example, financial concerns may be a priority for newly graduated teachers in their first job. They may depend upon a reliable income to pay basic living expenses or to make special purchases and are more likely to be motivated by a salary increase, small bonus, tuition assistance, or gift certificate to a local business. A teacher who has been with a program for several years may find a job redesign or promotion rejuvenating and, thus, more rewarding than a small salary increase.

Some people work because they find it meaningful, personally fulfilling, and a way to validate their own feelings of self-worth (Van Wingerden & Van der Stoep, 2018). On-the-job performance provides them with an opportunity to display their abilities and develop new skills. Their self-worth is validated through feedback and acknowledgment of their efforts in the form of a promotion, title change, or change of assignments.

The workplace also provides some employees with an important forum for socializing and the establishment of friendships with colleagues who share similar interests (Ratner et al., 2018; Willis, Reynolds, & Lee, 2019). Motivational leaders can use this understanding to create a motivating workplace by scheduling occasional social events, such as picnics, team sports, recognition dinners, birthday celebrations, or group movie nights. They can also provide mentoring opportunities and support employees' participation in professional development events.

Still other employees have a strong desire to work in jobs where they can make a significant contribution. They prefer jobs that take advantage of their demonstrated and potential skills, and provide relative workplace freedom and flexibility. Many such individuals find the teaching profession, especially the field of early childhood education, an ideal career choice because they believe they can make a difference in children's lives (Fray & Gore, 2018; Magaldi, Conway, & Trub, 2018). They tend to be people-oriented, nurturing, and patient, and often have good organizational, leadership, and creative talents. Leaders can foster and support these qualities by assigning special projects that acknowledge teacher's autonomy, skills, and creativity.

These efforts represent only a few of the small steps that motivational leaders can take to create workplace environments that are meaningful and likely to reduce teacher turnover rates. Additional strategies for inspiring and motivating personnel will be discussed in chapter 8. Leaders should also look beyond their individual programs and assume an active role in advocating for significant improvements in teacher compensation and professional recognition.

SUMMARY

- Many early childhood programs struggle to attract and retain highly qualified teachers.
- Teachers are often drawn to the early childhood field for a variety of reasons, including a source of income, a desire to contribute to the lives of children and families, and personal fulfillment.

- Employees expect employers to provide job security, safe working conditions, recognition for their efforts, and respect.
- Employee turnover rates are exceptionally high in the field of early childhood education compared to other professions.
- Inadequate compensation, stressful working conditions, inadequate job preparation, and lack of recognition often lead to job dissatisfaction and early departure.
- Innovative motivational leadership is essential to the retention of quality employees.
- Adapting a motivational style can yield positive outcomes, including improved employee morale, engagement, performance, and reduced staff turnover.

APPLICATION ACTIVITIES

1. Conduct an Internet search to learn about the T.E.A.C.H. and WAGE$ programs. Use Application Sheet 2-1 to develop an informational flyer that describes one of the programs.
2. Locate the NAEYC Code of Ethical Conduct on the organization's website, (https://www.naeyc.org/resources/position-statements/ethical-conduct). Read section III, "Ethical responsibilities to colleagues." Identify several key issues addressed in this section that could be used for a staff in-service training session. For each issue, develop a brief outline highlighting the major points to be discussed and record the information on Application Sheet 2-2.
3. Compile a list of stress-relieving activities that you would personally find helpful, and record them on Application Sheet 2-3. Select two or three activities, and develop a realistic goal for each (e.g., I will walk at least 30 minutes three days per week; I will include two more servings of fruits and vegetables each day; I will enroll in the aerobics or painting class that I have always wanted to take).
4. Interview eight early childhood education teachers regarding their current level of job satisfaction. Determine what workplace conditions they find most frustrating or stressful. Prepare a graph that illustrates your findings.
5. Select four problems or conditions that the teachers in question 4 identified. Develop a workable solution for each one. Record your suggestions on Application Sheet 2-4. Present your ideas to the class or your team and have them critique your solutions.

REVIEW POINTS

1. What expectations do employees have with regard to a job they are considering?
2. What role do respect and recognition play in employee retention?
3. What factors may be contributing to the current shortage of early childhood teachers?
4. What is stress? Why may some stress actually be beneficial? Explain why two teachers in the same classroom might experience the same stressful event differently.
5. A colleague confides in you that he no longer enjoys his first teaching job in a small early childhood center. What may he be experiencing? What could you encourage him to do, knowing that he is a good teacher and has always wanted to work with young children?
6. Why is it particularly important for early childhood leaders to adopt a motivational leadership style?

KEY TERMS DEFINED

demographic—a statistical description of various human population characteristics, such as the number of employed fathers or the number of children per family

stress—a sense of frustration, tension, or anxiety that may develop when an event or response differs from what a person expected

subjective—relating to a personal belief, bias, or interpretation that is not based on fact

burnout—a physical or emotional response to prolonged stress; a lack of interest and commitment

attrition—the loss of employees due to intentional choice, death, or retirement

REFERENCES

Allvin, R. E. (2019). Radical transformation in higher education is required to achieve real equity. *Young Children, 74*(5), 60–66.

American Association of Colleges for Teacher Education (AACTC). (2018). *Colleges of education: A national portrait.* Retrieved from https://aacte.org/resources/colleges-of-education-a-national-portrait.

Ansari, A. (2018). The persistence of preschool effects from early childhood through adolescence. *Journal of Educational Psychology, 110*(7), 952–973.

Arnup, J., & Bowles, T. (2016). Should I stay or should I go? Resilience as a protective factor for teachers' intention to leave the teaching profession. *Australian Journal of Education, 60*(3), 229–244.

Arvidsson, I., Leo, U., Larsson, A., Håkansson, C., Persson, R., & Björk, J. (2019). Burnout among school teachers: Quantitative and qualitative results from a follow-up study in southern Sweden. *BMC Public Health, 19,* 655.

Bergmark, U., Lundström, S., Manderstedt, L., & Palo, A. (2018). Why become a teacher? Student teachers' perceptions of the teaching profession and motives for career choice. *European Journal of Teacher Education, 41*(3), 266–281.

Bishop-Josef, S., Beakey, C., Watson, S., & Garrett, T. (2019). Want to grow the economy? Fix the child care crisis. Retrieved from https://strongnation.s3.amazonaws.com/documents/602/83bb2275-ce07-4d74-bcee-ff6178daf6bd.pdf?1547054862&inline;%20filename=%22Want%20to%20Grow%20the%20Economy?%20Fix%20the%20Child%20Care%20Crisis.pdf%22.

Boyd-Swan, C., & Herbst, C. M. (2020). Influence of quality credentialing programs on teacher characteristics in center-based early care and education settings. *Early Childhood Research Quarterly, 51*(2nd Quarter), 352–365.

Brough, P., Drummond, S., & Biggs, A. (2018). Job support, coping, and control: Assessment of simultaneous impacts within the occupational stress process. *Journal of Occupational Health Psychology, 23*(2), 188–197.

Brulé, G., & Morgan, R. (2018). Working with stress: Can we turn distress into eustress? *Journal of Neuropsychology & Stress Management, 3,* 1–3.

Cassidy, D. J., Lippard, C., King, E. K., & Lower, J. K. (2019). Improving the lives of teachers in the early care and education field to better support children and families. *Family Relations, 68*(3), 288–297.

Choi, J. Y., Horm, D., Jeon, S., & Ryu, D. (2018). Do stability of care and teacher-child interaction quality predict child outcomes in Early Head Start? *Early Education and Development, 30*(3), 337–356.

Conger, D., Gibbs, C. R., Uchikoshi, Y., & Winsler, A. (2019). New benefits of public school pre-kindergarten programs: Early school stability, grade promotion, and exit from ELL services. *Early Childhood Research Quarterly, 48*, 26–35.

Cornelissen, T., & Dustmann, C. (2019). Early school exposure, test scores, and noncognitive outcomes. *American Economic Journal: Economic Policy, 11*(2), 35–63.

Cucina, J. M., Byle, K. A., Martin, N. R., Peyton, S. T., & Gast, I. F. (2018). Generational differences in workplace attitudes and job satisfaction: Lack of sizable differences across cohorts. *Journal of Managerial Psychology, 33*(3), 246–264.

Dhabhar, F. S. (2019). The power of positive stress. *Stress, 22*(5), 526–529.

Felix, A. S., Lehman, A., Nolan, T. S., Sealy-Jefferson, S., Breathett, K., Hood, D. B., Addison, D., Anderson, C. M., Cené, C. W., Warren, B. J., Jackson, R. D., & Williams, K. P. (2019). Stress, resilience, and cardiovascular disease risk among black women. *Circulation: Cardiovascular Quality and Outcomes, 12*(4), e005284. Retrieved from https://www.ahajournals.org/doi/full/10.1161/CIRCOUTCOMES.118.005284.

Ford, T., Olsen, J., Khojasteh, J., Ware, J., & Urick, A. (2019). The effects of leader support for teacher psychological needs on teacher burnout, commitment, and intent to leave. *Journal of Educational Administration, 57*(6), 615–634.

Fray, L., & Gore, J. (2018). Why people choose teaching: A scoping review of empirical studies, 2007–2016. *Teaching and Teacher Education, 75*, 153–163.

García, G., Gonzales-Miranda, D., Gallo, O., & Roman-Calderon, J. (2019). Employee involvement and job satisfaction: A tale of the millennial generation. *Employee Relations, 41*(3), 374–388.

Garcia, J. L., Heckman, J. J., & Ziff, A. L. (2019). Early childhood education and crime. *Infant Mental Health Journal, 40*(1), 141–151.

Glazer, J. (2018). Learning from those who no longer teach: Viewing teacher attrition through a resistance lens. *Teaching and Teacher Education, 74*, 62–71.

Grant, A. A., Jeon, L., & Buettner, C. K. (2019). Relating early childhood teachers' working conditions and well-being to their turnover intentions. *Educational Psychology, 39*(3), 294–312.

Hagaman, J. L., & Casey, K. J. (2018). Teacher attrition in special education: Perspectives from the field. *Teacher Education and Special Education, 41*(4), 277– 291.

Haynie, K. (2019). *Checking in on the child care landscape: 2019 state fact sheets.* Retrieved from https://cdn2.hubspot.net/hubfs/3957809/State%20Fact%20Sheets%202019/2019StateFactSheets-Overview.pdf.

Hester, O. R., Bridges, S. A., & Rollins, L. H. (2020). "Overworked and underappreciated": Special education teachers describe stress and attrition. *Teacher Development, 24*(3), 348–365.

Holmes, B., Parker, D., & Gibson, J. (2019). Rethinking teacher retention in hard-to-staff schools. *Contemporary Issues in Education Research (CIER), 12*(1), 27–32.

Hughes, M., & McCartney, H. (2019). Investigating the experiences of first year early childhood and elementary teachers: A pilot study. *Teacher Educators' Journal, 12*, 93–128.

Institute of Medicine and National Research Council. (2015). *Transforming the workforce for children birth through age 8: A unifying foundation.* Washington, DC: The National Academies Press. Retrieved from https://doi.org/10.17226/19401.

Jeon, L., Buettner, C. K., & Grant, A. A. (2018). Early childhood teachers' psychological well-being: Exploring potential predictors of depression, stress, and emotional exhaustion. *Early Education and Development, 29*(1), 53–69.

Kalleberg, A. L., & Marsden, P. V. (2019). Work values in the United States: Age, period, and generational differences. *The ANNALS of the American Academy of Political and Social Science, 682*(1), 43–59.

Kelly, N., Cespedes, M., Clara, M., & Danaher, P. A. (2019). Early career teachers' intentions to leave the profession: The complex relationships among preservice education, early career support, and job satisfaction. *Australian Journal of Teacher Education, 44*(3), 93–113.

Khedhaouria, A., & Cucchi, A. (2019). Technostress creators, personality traits, and job burnout: A fuzzy-set configurational analysis. *Journal of Business Research, 101,* 349–361.

Kulic, N., Skopek, J., Triventi, M., & Blossfeld, H. P. (2019). Social background and children's cognitive skills: The role of early childhood education and care in a cross-national perspective. *Annual Review of Sociology, 45*(1), 557–579.

Kwon, K., Malek, A., Horm, D., & Castle, S. (2020). Turnover and retention of infant-toddler teachers: Reasons, consequences, and implications for practice and policy. *Children and Youth Services Review, 115,* 105061. https://doi.org/10.1016/j.childyouth.2020.105061.

Lambert, R., Boyle, L., Fitchett, P., & McCarthy, C. (2019). Risk for occupational stress among U.S. kindergarten teachers. *Journal of Applied Developmental Psychology, 61,* 13–20.

LiBetti, A. (2018). *Let the research show. Developing the research to improve early childhood teacher preparation.* Retrieved from https://files.eric.ed.gov/fulltext/ED592467.pdf.

Magaldi, D., Conway, T., & Trub, L. (2018). "I am here for a reason": Minority teachers bridging many divides in urban education. *Race, Ethnicity and Education, 21*(3), 306–318.

Magnuson, K., & Schindler, H. (2019). Supporting children's early development by building caregivers' capacities and skills: A theoretical approach informed by new neuroscience research. *Journal of Family Theory & Review, 11*(1), 59–78.

Maslow, A. (1968). *Toward a psychology of being.* (2nd ed.). New York: Van Nostrand Reinhold Company.

McDonald, P., Thorpe, K., & Irvine, S. (2018). Low pay but still we stay: Retention in early childhood education and care. *Journal of Industrial Relations, 60*(5), 647–668.

McEwen, B. S. (2016). In pursuit of resilience: Stress, epigenetics, and brain plasticity. *Annals of the New York Academy of Sciences, 1373,* 56–64.

Moon, T. W., Hur, W. M., & Hyun, S. S. (2019). How service employees' work motivations lead to job performance: The role of service employees' job creativity and customer orientation. *Current Psychology, 38*(2), 517–532.

National Association for the Education of Young Children (NAEYC). (2011). *Code of ethical conduct and statement of commitment.* Retrieved from https://www.naeyc.org/sites/default/files/globally-shared/downloads/PDFs/resources/position-statements/Ethics%20Position%20Statement2011_09202013update.pdf.

Ng, T. W., Hsu, D. Y., & Parker, S. K. (2019). Received respect and constructive voice: The roles of proactive motivation and perspective taking. *Journal of Management.* doi.org/10.1177/0149206319834660.

Nocita, G., Perlman, M., McMullen, E., Falenchuk, O., Brunsek, A., Fletcher, B., Kamkar, N., & Shah, P. S. (2020). Early childhood specialization among ECEC educators and preschool children's outcomes: A systematic review and meta-analysis. *Early Childhood Research Quarterly, 53*(4th Quarter), 185–207.

Otten, J. J., Bradford, V. A., Stover, B., Hill, H. D., Osborne, C., Getts, K., & Seixas, N. (2019). The culture of health in early care and education: Workers' wages, health, and job characteristics. *Health Affairs, 38*(5), 709–720. Retrieved from https://www.healthaffairs.org/doi/full/10.1377/hlthaff.2018.05493.

Perrone, F., Player, D., & Youngs, P. (2019). Administrative climate, early career teacher burnout, and turnover. *Journal of School Leadership, 29*(3), 191–209.

Ramírez, R., López, L. M., & Ferron, J. (2019). Teacher characteristics that play a role in the language, literacy, and math development of dual language learners. *Early Childhood Education Journal, 47*(1), 85–96.

Rasheed, D. S., Brown, J. L., Doyle, S. L., & Jennings, P. A. (2020). The effect of teacher-child race/ ethnicity matching and classroom diversity on children's socioemotional and academic skills. *Child Development, 91*(3), e597–e618.

Ratner, H. H., Bocknek, E. L., Miller, A. G., Elliott, S. L., & Weathington, B. (2018). Creating communities: A consortium model for early childhood leaders. *Teacher Development, 22*(3), 427–446.

Robinson, O. P., Bridges, S. A., Rollins, L. H., & Schumacker, R. E. (2019). A study of the relation between special education burnout and job satisfaction. *Journal of Research in Special Educational Needs, 19*(4), 295–303.

Rogers, K. M., & Ashforth, B. E. (2017). Respect in organizations: Feeling valued as "We" and "Me." *Journal of Management, 43*(5), 1578–1608.

Sparling, J., & Meunier, K. (2019). Abecedarian: An early childhood education approach that has a rich history and a vibrant present. *International Journal of Early Childhood, 51*(2), 207–216.

Standifer, R. L., & Lester, S. W. (2020). Actual versus perceived generational differences in the preferred working context: An empirical study. *Journal of Intergenerational Relationships, 18*(1), 48–70.

Strack, J., Lopes, P. N., Esteves, F., & Fernández-Berrocal, P. (2017). Must we suffer to succeed? When anxiety boosts motivation and performance. *Journal of Individual Differences, 38*(2), 113–124.

Sutcher, L., Darling-Hammond, L., & Carver-Thomas, D. (2019). Understanding teacher shortages: An analysis of teacher supply and demand in the United States. *Education Policy Analysis Archives, 27*(35). Retrieved from http://dx.doi.org/10.14507/epaa.27.3696.

The National Academies of Sciences, Engineering, and Medicine. (2020). *Are generational categories meaningful distinctions for workforce management?* Retrieved from https://www.nap.edu/read/25796/chapter/1.

The National Academies of Sciences, Engineering, and Medicine. (2018). *Transforming the financing of early care and education.* Backes, E. P. & Allen, L. R. (Eds.). Washington, DC: National Academies Press (US).

Thompson, O. (2018). Head Start's long-run impact: Evidence from the program's introduction. *Journal of Human Resources, 53*(4), 1100–1139.

Totenhagen, C. J., Hawkins, S. A., Casper, D. M., Bosch, L. A., Hawkey, K. R., & Borden, L. M. (2016). Retaining early childhood education workers: A review of the empirical literature. *Journal of Research in Childhood Education, 30*(4), 585–599.

U.S. Bureau of Labor Statistics (BLS). (2019). *Occupational outlook handbook.* Retrieved from https://www.bls.gov/ooh/education-training-and-library/home.htm.

U.S. Bureau of Labor Statistics (BLS). (2018). *Labor force statistics from the current population survey.* Retrieved from https://www.bls.gov/cps/cpsaat11.htm.

Van Wingerden, J., & Van der Stoep, J. (2018). The motivational potential of meaningful work: Relationships with strengths use, work engagement, and performance. *PLOS.* Retrieved from https://journals.plos.org/plosone/article?id=10.1371/journal.pone.0197599.

Whitebook, M., McLean, C., Austin, L. J., & Edwards, B. (2018). *Early childhood workforce index—2018.* Berkeley, CA: Center for the Study of Child Care Employment, University of California, Berkeley. Retrieved from http://cscce.berkeley.edu/topic/early-childhood-work-force-index/2018/.

Willis, L., Reynolds, K. J., & Lee, E. (2019). Being well at work: The impact of organizational climate and social identity on employee stress and self-esteem over time. *European Journal of Work and Organizational Psychology, 28*(3), 399–413.

Wymer, S. C., Williford, A. P., & Lhospital, A. S. (2020). Exclusionary discipline practices in early childhood. *Young Children, 75*(3), 36–44.

Young, J., McGrath, R., & Adams, C. (2018). Fresh air, sunshine and happiness: Millennials building health (salutogenesis) in leisure and nature. *Annals of Leisure Research, 21*(3), 324–346.

ONLINE RESOURCES

Child Care Aware of America: https://usa.childcareaware.org

National Association for the Education of Young Children: https://www.naeyc.org

National Association of Early Childhood Teacher Educators: https://naecte.org/

National Education Association: http://www.nea.org/home/18163.htm

National Resource Center for Health and Safety in Child Care and Early Education: https://nrckids.org/

APPLICATION SHEET 2-1

Program overview:

APPLICATION SHEET 2-2

NAEYC Code of Ethical Conduct: Section III. Ethical responsibilities to colleagues.

Key discussion points:

APPLICATION SHEET 2-3

My stress-relieving activities and goals:

1.

2.

3.

APPLICATION SHEET 2-4

Challenging conditions cited by interviewed teachers and strategies to address them:

1.

2.

3.

4.

3

The Role of Motivation in Organizations

OBJECTIVES

After reading this chapter, you will be able to do the following:

- Define the term *motivation.*
- Discuss several factors that shape what an individual may find motivating.
- Contrast the motivational theories of Maslow, Herzberg, McClelland, and Bandura.
- Discuss how intrinsic and extrinsic motivators differ.
- Identify the positive outcomes that leaders can anticipate when they create a motivational workplace environment.

KEY TERMS

- motivation
- environment
- physiological needs
- self-actualization
- regression
- hygienes
- self-efficacy
- extrinsic motivators
- intrinsic motivators

■ ■ ■

Outstanding leaders go out of their way to boost the self-esteem of their personnel. If people believe in themselves, it's amazing what they can accomplish.

—Sam Walton, founder, Walmart

INTRODUCTION

How often have you made decisions and later questioned why you made the choices you did? For example, why did you agree to work on your afternoon off when you already had other plans? What made you purchase a shirt just because it was on sale, although you really dislike the color blue? Why did you decide to return to school? What made you accept your current job?

Our motivations influence our decisions and actions, give us direction and purpose, maintain our interest, and energize us to begin a new project or continue in the face of adversity. In some instances, we can identify the things that motivate our behaviors, but not always. We may know that completing a degree is likely to help us land a better paying job but may not understand why we became short tempered with a parent or colleague this afternoon.

WHAT IS MOTIVATION?

Behavior is an intriguing phenomenon that is driven primarily by **motivation**. Our decisions, choices, and actions are continually influenced by a complex system of human needs. Efforts to satisfy these needs cause us to behave in specific ways. And, once a need is satisfied, it loses its motivating power. Some needs, such as thirst and hunger, are common to everyone while others, such as the need for affection, recognition, or self-esteem, are of a higher order and, therefore, unique to an individual. Differences in biological makeup, culture, ethnicity, **environment**, and lifelong experiences collectively influence and shape the things we each find personally motivating. Consequently, things that motivate one employee may not prove to be motivating to another. Also, things that an employee finds motivating today may not be as fulfilling a year from now. In some instances, we are able to recognize these powerful emotions for what they are and understand how they affect our behavior—but this is not always the case.

Connecting Points

It is a beautiful Saturday morning. You have a final budget report to prepare for the board meeting on Monday evening. So, you decide to go into your office where you can work quietly but forget to turn off your cell phone. An hour later, your friends call and invite you to spend the weekend at the lake. You anticipate that the report will take several hours to complete.

- Identify all of the motivating factors in this situation.
- What consequence is each factor likely to produce?
- How is the outcome likely to differ depending upon your decision?
- Which motivating factor would you be most likely to choose? Why?

WHY IS MOTIVATION IMPORTANT?

Motivation explains why we find certain opportunities attractive and are willing to dedicate time and energy to pursue them. How valuable or invaluable an individual perceives an experience to be, or not to be, ultimately influences the direction of his or her behavior. For example, what makes some employees volunteer to assist with a weekend fundraising event when they won't be paid for the time that they donate? Why are parents willing to make cookies for the school's annual bake sale or costumes for the school play? Or, why is an experienced teacher not interested in applying for the assistant director position? In each case, these individuals were motivated by something they found personally rewarding.

The concept of motivation is also useful for understanding the amount of effort a person is willing to invest to accomplish a goal (Figure 3.1). For example, what makes one teacher perform above and beyond the requirements of their position description, while another simply does what he or she must to get by? Why does the same teacher volunteer whenever the director needs help with a special project while other teachers must be asked? What we do know is that when employees experience pleasure and satisfaction from their work, the quantity and quality of their effort typically increases until their needs are meet. The opposite is also true. A decline in a teacher's performance and productivity may indicate a lack of interest and personal fulfillment.

An individual's willingness to persist at a given task is also influenced by their degree of motivation. For example, sharing a few words of gratitude with a teacher who has done something special can prove to be energizing: "I appreciate the many hours it took you to plan and set up our new science center. It is very innovative, and I know the children are really going to enjoy it." When employees believe that no one cares about their contributions, they may gradually lose interest and leave. The leader who builds challenge, opportunity, and recognition into work activities increases the likelihood that employees will be motivated to stay.

FIGURE 3.1 Personally fulfilling work serves as a powerful motivator. *Rawpixel, iStock / Getty Images Plus*

Retention of dedicated employees is the number one concern of leaders in any business or organization. This is an especially critical issue in the field of early childhood education, which typically experiences an annual turnover rate of greater than thirty percent (Sarver et al., 2018; Whitebook et al., 2018). Although motivational leadership plays a key role in retaining employees, it will not fully eliminate the problem until other issues, such as wages, are also addressed.

It is important that leaders understand the basic principles of motivation and how to put them into practice. Motivation exerts a direct influence on employees' interests, efforts, and persistence in accomplishing a program's goals and objectives. However, determining what motivates individual employees and how to create workplace environments that encourage optimum performance can present a major leadership challenge.

DIRECTOR'S SHOWCASE

What strategies have you used and found to be effective in motivating staff performance?

I believe that one of the most important things I practice as the director of a large early childhood program is to spend one-on-one time with each of my staff members. Getting to know each person as an individual helps me to identify their strengths and limitations. I can then use this information to provide motivational strategies that promote the staff member's self-esteem and professional growth.

—Cindy M., center administrator

THEORETICAL MODELS OF MOTIVATION

Several classical theories have been proposed to improve our understanding of human motivational needs, and how they can be satisfied in the workplace. It is unlikely that any particular theory provides a completely satisfactory explanation. However, elements from each of these theories can be useful for understanding the concept of motivation. Persons in leadership positions can use elements from theoretical frameworks to better understand their employees' needs, and to design reward systems that are individualized, efficient, and effective motivators.

Maslow's Hierarchy of Needs

Abraham Maslow, a noted psychologist, was intrigued by what motivated people to act on a real or perceived need or task. Why, for example, do some individuals seek employment while others do not? What causes some early childhood educators to leave a program, while others remain for years? Why do people seek out friends and desire companionship? Why are some teachers seemingly more productive than others?

Maslow described five categories of basic human needs based on his observations (Maslow, 1968). These categories are typically represented in a triangular model, commonly referred to as Maslow's Hierarchy of Needs, and arranged in ascending order, from needs he considered to be the most fundamental and life-sustaining to those of the highest intellectual order :

- *physiological needs*—requirements necessary to sustain life, including food, water, shelter, and air
- *physical and psychological safety*—feelings of safety, security, and freedom from harm in one's environment
- *belongingness*—the drive for social connection, friendships, acceptance, love, and group membership
- *self-esteem*—an internal need to achieve respect, establish a positive reputation, and feel appreciated by others
- *self-actualization*—the feeling of personal satisfaction derived from utilizing one's talents and potential to achieve independent thinking, creative expression, and problem-solving.

Maslow's theory provided a valuable starting point for understanding the forces that motivate individual behavior. He assumed that humans have multiple layers of need, that everyone is motivated by the same basic needs, and that an unmet need causes a person to act in certain ways until the deficit is satisfied. For example, a hungry child will usually stop crying and begging his mother for food once he has been given something to eat. Maslow also believed that a person's needs had to be completely satisfied at each level before they were able to progress to the next higher one, and that upward movement could only be achieved in a step-wise manner. His ideas also acknowledged a person's ultimate desire for personal and professional growth. Only when all lower-level needs had been met would a person be ready and able to realize their creative interests and talents (self-actualization). This concept has valuable implications for early childhood education programs and reinforces the motivational importance of providing teachers and staff with professional development opportunities.

Maslow's ideas have been criticized for overgeneralizing the motivational process. Some critics have suggested that the hierarchical theory fails to acknowledge individual differences in terms of cultural values, gender, personal experiences, and motivational preferences. Others reject Maslow's theory due to his emphasis on the satisfaction of individual needs as opposed to a team or collaborative philosophy that is often practiced in contemporary organizations today (Acevedo, 2018; Gambrel & Cianci, 2003). Some psychologists have suggested that Maslow's ideas are not supported with sound research, and that his interpretations of human behavior may not be entirely correct (Heylighen, 1992; Wahba & Bridwell, 1976). However, others support his ideas and the notion that humans share many basic physical and psychological needs in common (Compton, 2018; Taormina & Gao, 2013). Despite these differences, Maslow's theory remains an important contribution to our fundamental understanding of human motivational needs.

ERG Theory

Clayton Alderfer saw merit in Maslow's ideas, and attempted to address criticism of the Hierarchy of Needs Theory by simplifying his concepts. Alderfer proposed the ERG Theory, which recognizes three basic motivational needs that he believed all humans share (Alderfer, 1972):

- *Existence*—includes physiological and physical safety needs; combines Maslow's physiological and safety categories. For example, earning a salary enables an individual to survive by securing shelter, food, clothing, etc.
- *Relatedness*—an individual's need or desire to form social relationships and to communicate with other people; this need is similar to Maslow's belongingness.
- *Growth*—an internal drive for personal achievement, peer recognition, and lifelong interest in learning; combines Maslow's self-esteem and self-actualization categories.

The ERG theory differs on several fundamental points from Maslow's ideas about motivation. Alderfer believed that

- individuals have different needs: not everyone is motivated by the same things;
- needs can be satisfied on multiple levels simultaneously;
- needs do not have to be entirely satisfied on one level before an individual can begin to address motivational needs on a higher level;
- satisfying a lower-level need may be more motivating if an individual becomes frustrated in attempts to fulfill a higher-order need;
- it isn't necessary to satisfy motivational needs in any particular order; and
- frustration and **regression** play an important role in need satisfaction.

Alderfer suggested that if individuals experience frustration when attempting to satisfy higher-level motivational needs, they often regress to a comfort level where their needs are currently being met or are easier to meet. For example, an employee who is in line for a promotion (Growth), but does not receive the promotion, may begin to devote more time and energy to socializing with colleagues (Relatedness). Or a teacher who is assigned to a challenging classroom that she did not request (Relatedness) may find a salary increase (Existence) more personally motivating. Temporary regression, apparent in the previous examples, should not be viewed as failure. In many cases, it can have positive outcomes for an individual by providing additional time to acquire new skills, build confidence, or rethink his or her strategies.

Herzberg's Two-Factor Theory

Fredrick Herzberg's ideas also helped to shed light on the role of motivation in the workplace (Herzberg, 1987; Herzberg, Mausner, & Snyderman, 1959). He was intrigued with Maslow's theory but believed that it was overly complicated and set out to propose a more simplified model. After surveying hundreds of employees, Herzberg concluded that employee satisfaction or dissatisfaction with their job is determined by two primary factors:

- Motivators—opportunities that foster an employee's personal sense of job satisfaction, such as formal recognition, assignment of new responsibilities, and promotions.
- **Hygienes**—workplace conditions or job characteristics, such as the physical environment, relationships with colleagues and/or supervisors, company policies, or lack of job security that can contribute to an employee's sense of job dissatisfaction.

Herzberg believed that motivators and hygienes functioned relatively independent of each other. Eliminating a source of job dissatisfaction does not necessarily produce job satisfaction. For example, painting the teachers' break room (hygienes) is not likely to have much effect on improving their motivation or performance if they are unhappy about poor salaries or a director's demanding oversight. In contrast, an assistant teacher who is promoted to a lead position (motivator) in the same classroom that she has worked for several years may feel a sense of renewed commitment.

Herzberg's ideas have been criticized for overlooking the effect that working conditions can have on employee attitude and performance. However, his theories have drawn positive attention to the idea that a person's job responsibilities and workplace support may reduce turnover intention by serving as significant motivators in and by themselves (Bassett-Jones & Lloyd, 2005; Chiat & Panatik, 2019; Jeon & Wells, 2018). When employees believe their work or role is personally fulfilling and appreciated by others, the job itself becomes an important motivator. This insight suggests that motivational leaders should look for ways to add interest, pizzaz, responsibility, and challenge to an employee's position, and to adapt a leadership style that supports and acknowledges employees' contributions on a regular basis.

―――――――――――――――― *Connecting Points* ――――――――――――――――

As the director of Sunny Days Early Education Center, you would like to give every staff member a small raise this coming year. However, after reviewing the annual budget you realize this is not financially feasible. Should you just forget about trying to reward your employees for now?

- What no-cost "hygiene" alternatives could you provide in place of a raise?
- Do you think your employees will find these motivators as rewarding as a small salary increase?
- What advantages do "hygienes" offer over a twenty-five-cent-an-hour pay raise?

McClelland's Theory of Learned Needs

David McClelland was also interested in Maslow's categorization of motivational needs. He conducted experimental studies to better understand the origin of such needs, and how they might ultimately influence an individual's behavior. Based on this work, McClelland proposed three major categories, which he believed serve as human motivators: the need for achievement, affiliation, and power (McClelland, 1961; McClelland & Burnham, 1976).

The Need for Achievement

McClelland observed that some individuals appear to seek out and thrive on challenge (Figure 3.2). He described this group as having a strong motivational need for achievement, and that they typically exhibit a high level of personal energy, initiative, and persistence in their work. McClelland also noted their preference for assuming responsibility, taking on leadership positions, engaging in problem-solving activities, and requesting feedback to improve their performance and success. Although these individuals possess many positive characteristics, McClelland also observed that high achievers are often reluctant to delegate

FIGURE 3.2 Employees differ in what they find personally motivating. *julief514, iStock / Getty Images Plus*

tasks to other workers, preferring instead to maintain control of decisions and outcomes. When work or work environments no longer provide adequate challenge, these individuals are likely to leave.

The Need for Affiliation

McClelland recognized that some individuals have an intense need for social interaction and establishing close social relationships with others. He noted that these individuals prefer to work cooperatively in teams or groups, engage in social activities, conform, seek out approval, and be liked by others. They typically avoid positions that require assertiveness, initiative, independent decision-making, or assuming major supervisory responsibility. McClelland suggested that individuals with a high need for affiliation do not make effective leaders or supervisors, because they find it difficult to give critical feedback, often show favoritism, and are reluctant to enforce rules or policy (McClelland & Burnham, 1976).

The Need for Power

McClelland believed that the quest for power serves as a primary motivating factor for individuals who assume leadership positions. He suggested that status, social recognition, and influence over others satisfy a fundamental human need for self-fulfillment. Although some individuals utilize their position for personal gain and career advancement, others are committed to advancing their organization's mission or goals. McClelland also argued that these same qualities are necessary for one to be an effective leader, and that leaders are morally obligated to perform their duties in an ethical manner.

McClelland suggested that these need behaviors are learned as the result of socialization and reinforcement through parental influence, cultural values, and individual personality traits. Rybnicek, Bergner, and Gutschelhofer (2019) confirmed McClelland's ideas in a recent study that demonstrated enhanced neural activity in the brain's reward centers when participants' motivational needs for power, achievement, or affiliation were addressed. They noted that other reward types (e.g., monetary, office space, flowers) did not elicit a similar response. These findings also reinforced McClelland's beliefs that employees have motivational needs that may differ from person to person. Thus, leaders who appreciate and are sensitive to these individual differences can tailor their inspirational and motivational efforts to meet employees' specific personal and professional needs.

DIRECTOR'S SHOWCASE

What do you do as a leader to create a motivating workplace for your staff?

I work hard to establish trust and transparency with my employees by communicating frequently and openly, giving them autonomy to do their jobs, showing appreciation for their efforts, and encouraging their input. We also make time to laugh and have fun together.

—Deisha H., director, Early Childhood Education Consultants

Bandura's Theory of Self-Efficacy

Albert Bandura introduced his Theory of Self-Efficacy as a contribution to the positive psychology movement and an attempt to explain the concept of human motivation (Bandura, 1977). He believed that people have the power to succeed in overcoming difficulties or a challenging task, whether it be personal, academic, athletic, or job-related, when they are confident in their ability to do so (**self-efficacy**). In other words, he proposed that individuals are able to make decisions and alter their behavior in ways that will allow them to achieve a desired goal or outcome. For example, a track athlete who decides to improve her 200-meter time by .5 of a second may spend more time conditioning, running sprints, and changing her diet. Words of encouragement and small improvements in her timing, in turn, will reinforce her continued commitment to work toward achieving her goal (Wright, O'Halloran, & Stukas, 2019).

Bandura suggested that several factors are involved in achieving self-efficacy. He believed that people form their self-efficacy beliefs based on information gathered from four sources:

- verbal persuasion or words of encouragement (or discouragement) from others;
- vicariously, by observing the outcome that other individuals experience in similar situations;
- past experiences that have led to success or failure; and
- physiological and emotional reactions (e.g., interest, excitement, anxiety, dread).

He explained that people who have a strong sense of self-esteem are more likely to accept challenge, establish a course of action, and persist in accomplishing a desired goal (Bandura, 1997). Additionally, these individuals tend to gravitate toward activities that are like those in which they have previously experienced success. Past learning experiences that led to mastery or a positive outcome often prove to be motivating because they boost a person's confidence in his or her capabilities, increase the individual's resilience to failure, and enable the person to recover more quickly if failure does occur. In other words, the environment plays a significant role in shaping a person's self-efficacy by eliciting some type of response or feedback, or remaining unresponsive.

Bandura thought that self-efficacy is also an important consideration in the event of failure. He believed that any lack of motivation or serious doubts that a person might have about her or his ability to achieve a desired goal will likely contribute to an unsuccessful outcome. For example, the track athlete who wants to improve her 200-meter time by .5 of a second may avoid making any serious changes because she is not convinced that the goal is achievable. Or she may give up after a week because there is no immediate time improvement, which reinforces her belief that the goal was unattainable in the first place.

Bandura's Theory of Self-Efficacy has important implications for early childhood leaders. It provides a framework for understanding the significant effect that inspiration and encouragement have on employee attitudes, performance, persistence, and motivation to tackle new challenges. This is an important point to remember when providing evaluative feedback during performance reviews or asking an employee to assume a new role. Bandura's ideas also help to explain why some employees, especially those who have experienced prior frustration or defeat, may require more support, encouragement, and mentoring than others.

The Expectancy Theory

Vroom's Expectancy Theory suggests that people make certain choices and are motivated to perform because they expect to be rewarded appropriately for their efforts (Vroom, 1964). Three conditions are implied in his theory (Figure 3.3):

Effort—whether an individual believes the effort invested will pay off or enable them to accomplish a given task. For example, "If I devote more time to preparing lesson plans, my day will probably run more smoothly."

Performance—whether an individual believes that good performance will be acknowledged and rewarded. For example, "My supervisor will notice how efficiently I am running my classroom and consider me for the lead teacher position."

Reward—how personally satisfying (or not satisfying) an individual finds a reward that acknowledges their effort: "My director brought in brownies today to celebrate my one-year anniversary as a teacher with this program. However, she knows that I am allergic to eggs and chocolate."

Early childhood leaders will find Vroom's theory particularly helpful in understanding the connection between employee performance, motivation, and retention. When employees are confident in their abilities and believe their efforts will be sincerely appreciated, they tend to

FIGURE 3.3 Expectancy Theory

work even harder in achieving a goal. Teachers are a prime example. Most would agree that it is the acknowledgment of their efforts and the children and families, not paychecks, that motivate them to devote as much time and energy to their jobs as they do (Ansley, Houchins, & Varjas, 2019). On the other hand, when employees perceive that their efforts are no longer appreciated or acknowledged, or that opportunity is lacking, they may begin to lose interest, perform poorly, and eventually leave their job (Iwu et al., 2018).

Vroom's theory implies that individuals can determine and express what they find motivating. However, people are not always able to identify what really inspires their behavior. Vroom's theory is also limited by the fact that programs may offer incentives for qualities other than employee performance. For example, higher salaries may be paid to teachers who have advanced education, skills, or experience. It is also important to recognize that a leader's personal values and biases may influence the nature of incentives provided and the decision-making processes used to recognize employee performance. However, effective leaders can address some of these challenges by utilizing strategies, such as holding individual or group discussions, providing self-evaluation tools, or inviting motivational speakers to assist employees in identifying rewards that may be personally and professionally satisfying.

The Equity Theory

Employees expect to be treated fairly and equitably for their contributions. No employee wants to feel that an organization or leader is taking advantage of their time, skills, or efforts. However, how just or fair an employee considers the amount and distribution of rewards to be can have either a positive or negative effect on their behavior. For example, a teacher who believes that she deserves the "teacher of the month" award, but is passed over, may feel resentment toward her colleagues. On the other hand, a first-grade teacher who is promoted to a curriculum coordinator position is likely to experience an immediate boost in self-esteem and confidence.

The Equity Theory recognizes the fundamental human precepts of fairness and equitable treatment by program leaders (Adams, 1963; Kollmann et al., 2020). It acknowledges that employees not only expect to be rewarded fairly, but also that the reward is comparable to what their colleagues are receiving for similar work. If employees believe, or discover, that they are being treated unfairly and not receiving equivalent compensation or acknowledgment for the same or similar work, they may convey their resentment in a variety of ways.

For example, if I find out that my raise is half of what my co-teacher received, I may consider quitting, calling in sick more often, or not volunteering to assist with any special center events. In other words, I am not inclined to exert any more effort than required. On the other hand, if I received a larger pay raise than other teachers, it may motivate me to work even harder or offer to take on extra projects.

An employee's interpretation of fairness and equity is generally subjective and influenced by one's personal values, belief systems, culture, and access to information. Inequities, whether real or perceived, have a direct effect on employee motivation, performance, retention, and trust in leadership. Consequently, leaders must make a concerted effort to reward employees in a way that is impartial, consistent, and fair to everyone. It is also important that motivational leaders maintain open communication with employees, listen carefully to an employee who has concerns about unfair workplace treatment, and involve employees in policy development. Getting to know your employees, documenting their contributions and efforts, understanding how various incentives are likely to affect their behavior, and eliminating favoritism can avoid many unhappy experiences.

EXTRINSIC AND INTRINSIC REWARDS

DeCharms (1968) offers yet another explanation for how motivation influences employee performance. He described motivators as being either extrinsic or intrinsic based upon their primary source of origination. Examples of **extrinsic motivators** (external factors) could include a pay raise, assignment to a better office space, a new job title, a prize, an extra day off, or a flexible work schedule. They are tangible rewards offered by another individual in acknowledgment of an employee's performance. **Intrinsic motivators** (internal factors) are derived from an internal or personal sense of accomplishment, and include feelings such as excitement, increased interest or energy, enjoyment, and pleasure. Consider, for example, how thrilling it is to watch a toddler take his first steps or a child write her name for the first time or the feeling of pride experienced when a co-worker offers a compliment!

Extrinsic and intrinsic motivators each have their own distinct advantages and disadvantages. Researchers have determined that employees who have only limited control over their jobs or few opportunities for creative input are more likely to respond to extrinsic rewards (Eisenberger, Rhoades, & Cameron, 1999; Malik, Choi, & Butt, 2019; Thibault Landry et al., 2017). They simply perform their work, and then expect to be compensated in some manner. Although extrinsic motivators can have a positive initial effect on employee behavior, the effect is often short-lived and tends to decrease intrinsic motivation. Once the reward exhilaration passes, employees often resume their typical efforts. Consider, for example, how rewarding you would still find the twenty-five-cent-an-hour raise that you received six months ago on a day when three of your teachers and the cook just called in sick!

Intrinsic rewards, on the other hand, generally have a more lasting effect on employee performance and commitment. Teachers, for example, who enjoy greater autonomy and control in their job are more likely to be motivated by things that contribute to their personal feelings of satisfaction and accomplishment. However, as we have previously seen, individuals are seldom motivated by a single factor. Zhang, Zhang, and Li (2018) noted that new employees may initially be motivated more by extrinsic rewards (e.g., money, work schedules). However, they also suggested that leaders should gradually shift to providing more intrinsic motivators (e.g., mentoring, professional development, training) to increase employee performance and retention. Thus, effective leaders must be sensitive to employees' individual needs, recognize that needs change over time, and utilize a variety of motivating strategies to insure optimal performance and long-term commitment.

MOTIVATIONAL THEORIES: IMPLICATIONS FOR EARLY CHILDHOOD PROGRAMS

Multiple theories have contributed to our understanding of motivation and what motivates people to behave in a certain way (Table 3.1). Although they provide somewhat different perspectives, each theory offers elements that can be applied in the workplace to encourage and support employee performance.

The motivation, inspiration, and empowerment of employees is clearly important to a program's success. They can improve recruitment and retention rates, help to assure high staff productivity, and boost employee morale (Figure 3.4). The opposite is also true. Programs that fail to create a positive work environment or to address their employees' intrinsic motivational needs are unlikely to experience lasting success.

Working conditions in early childhood programs make it especially important to adapt a motivational and inspirational leadership style (Grant, Jeon, & Buettner, 2019; Thomas et al., 2020). Limited resources, low wages, challenging diversity issues, long hours, and demanding work have led to consistently high turnover rates (Whitebook et al., 2018). Numerous

Table 3.1: Theoretical Models of Motivation

Maslow's Needs Hierarchy	Humans have an internal drive to fulfill basic physiological, physical/psychological, belonginess, self-esteem, and self-actualization needs.
Alderfer's ERG Theory	Humans have three common needs that must be satisfied: existence, relatedness, and, growth.
Herzberg's Two-Factor Theory	Some job characteristics (motivators) foster employees' job satisfaction; others (hygienes) produce job dissatisfaction. They are not opposites; each factor operates independently.
McClelland's Theory of Learned Needs	All humans have three learned motivational needs: achievement, affiliation, and power. One tends to become dominant as a result of a person's culture and life experiences.
Bandura's Theory of Self-Efficacy	Humans have the ability to control their own destiny through the decisions they make. Success builds confidence (self-efficacy), which motivates desire and ambition.
Vroom's Expectancy Theory	People expect their efforts to be rewarded and equivalent to performance quality and/or output. Rewards motivate and reinforce a person's work behavior.
Equity Theory	A person's degree of motivation is directly related to his/her perception of fair, impartial, and equitable treatment.

FIGURE 3.4 Successful leaders make an effort to identify and meet employees' intrinsic motivational needs. *FatCamera*

studies have documented a strong relationship between employee satisfaction, motivation, and retention (Jeon & Wells, 2018; Lambert et al., 2019). The degree of motivation and inspiration an employee perceives in his or her job can have a positive or negative effect on attendance, performance, morale, self-esteem, personal interest, and professional growth (Jeon & Wells, 2018; Shahid, 2018). When teachers feel valued and respected, they are also more likely to remain in their positions, whereas employees who feel unappreciated tend to leave sooner (McDonald, Thorpe, & Irvine, 2018; McMullen et al., 2020). Supportive workplace environments can also have a positive effect on a program's recruiting efforts, outcome for children, and other substantial returns for the organization.

Productivity is also directly influenced by the motivational climate established in the workplace. Teachers may possess all the required skills and experience, but it is up to program leaders to create an atmosphere that encourages individuals to utilize their full potentials. Leaders must be willing to invest time and effort in building a positive motivational environment, and to respect their staff as individuals—to know their personal interests, preferences, needs, and values—in order to provide reinforcers that are meaningful. This process must also be ongoing because circumstances and teachers' needs are continuously changing. Motivational leaders who are sensitive to these changes are able to create challenging, rewarding, and enjoyable workplace environments. They can also inspire and empower employees to assume responsibility, develop new skills, make decisions, become independent thinkers, and assume leadership roles.

SUMMARY

- Several classical theories have proven helpful for understanding human motivational needs, and how they can be satisfied in the workplace.
- Maslow's Hierarchy of Needs Theory identifies five levels of fundamental human needs: physiological, safety, belongingness, esteem, and self-actualization.
- The ERG Theory groups human motivational needs into three categories:
  o Existence—meeting essential physiological needs
  o Relatedness—the need for social interaction and relationships
  o Growth—the internal drive to achieve positive self-esteem and recognition
- Herzberg describes two basic categories of motivators—those associated with one's job responsibilities and those related to working conditions (e.g., policies, facilities).
- McClelland attributes motivation to the satisfaction of human desires for achievement, affiliation, and power or control. He also believed that these needs are learned through experience, modeling, and socialization.
- Bandura's Theory of Self-Efficacy contributes to an understanding of how leadership can use motivation to build employees' confidence in their ability to master challenges, perform, and achieve.
- The Expectancy Theory acknowledges that people expect their efforts to be recognized and rewarded; when this is lacking, employees develop apathy toward their work.
- The Equity Theory recognizes that employees expect to be treated fairly.
- Motivators can be either intrinsic or extrinsic.
  o Extrinsic motivators consist of external rewards.
  o Intrinsic rewards create an internal sense of satisfaction or pleasure.
  o Employees must have both their intrinsic and extrinsic needs met to remain inspired and motivated.

APPLICATION ACTIVITIES

1. Develop seven questions, one for each theory presented in this chapter, to assess employee motivation. Your questions should reflect the central idea proposed by each theorist. Record your questions on Application Sheet 3-1.
2. Conduct an online search for sites that address the concept of motivational leadership. Select five of the most useful sites. Summarize the information found on each site and record your findings on Application Sheet 3-2.
3. Interview the administrator of two different early childhood programs. Ask them to describe what they do to motivate staff members. Evaluate the effectiveness of their motivational incentives and practices based on what you have learned in this chapter. Record your interview and assessment summary on Application Sheets 3-3a and 3-3b.
4. List five incentives that would motivate you to change your current eating or exercise habits. Record your responses on Application Sheet 3-4.

REVIEW POINTS

1. What short- and long-term effects is a ten-cent-an-hour raise likely to have on employee motivation?

2. Should all employees who perform similar jobs be rewarded equally? Explain your answer.

3. Have you ever participated in a group project and felt that you were not treated fairly for your contributions? Use the Equity Theory to explain why you might feel this way.

4. How can a motivational leader use the need for affiliation to build effective team relationships?

5. Examine several of the personal and professional decisions you've made recently. What fundamental needs do you think your choices satisfied?

6. Person X is running for the mayor of your home town. His campaign ads air nightly on the local TV station, he is invited to frequent speaking engagements, and he appears at numerous public events. After losing the election, he removes himself from all political activities and resumes his office job. How would Alderfer explain this transition?

KEY TERMS DEFINED

motivation—a perceived need that shapes the purpose and direction of a person's behavior

environment—the sum of an individual's surroundings; includes physical and psychological factors

physiological needs—basic functions (e.g., food, water, shelter) that are required for survival

self-actualization—the personal need for satisfaction that an individual derives from using their skills and talents to accomplish a task

regression—to retreat or move backward

hygienes—a term Herzberg used to describe workplace conditions that contribute to employee satisfaction or displeasure

self-efficacy—a person's belief in her or his ability to succeed in accomplishing a desired task or goal

extrinsic motivators—tangible rewards (e.g., salary increase, designated parking space, birthday gift, movie tickets) that an individual finds personally gratifying

intrinsic motivators—rewards or recognition (e.g., job promotion, title change, praise, being named employee of the month) that provide a feeling of personal satisfaction, pride, or pleasure

REFERENCES

Acevedo, A. (2018). A personalistic appraisal of Maslow's Needs Theory of Motivation: From "humanistic" psychology to integral humanism. *Journal of Business Ethics, 148*(4), 741–763.

Adams, J. (1963). Towards an understanding of inequity. *Journal of Abnormal and Social Psychology, 67*(5), 422–436.

Alderfer, C. P. (1972). *Existence, relatedness, and growth: Human needs in organizational settings.* New York: Free Press.

Ansley, B. M., Houchins, D., & Varjas, K. (2019). Cultivating positive work contexts that promote teacher job satisfaction and retention in high-need schools. *Journal of Special Education Leadership, 32*(1), 3–16.

Bandura, A. (1977). Self-efficacy: Toward a unifying theory of behavioral change. *Psychological Review, 84*(2), 191–215.

Bandura, A. (1997). *Self-efficacy: The exercise of control.* New York: W. H. Freeman.

Bassett-Jones, N., & Lloyd, G. (2005). Does Herzberg's motivation theory have staying power? *Journal of Management Development, 24*(10), 929–943.

Chiat, L. C., & Panatik, S. A. (2019). Perceptions of employee turnover intention by Herzberg's motivation-hygiene theory: A systematic literature review. *Journal of Research in Psychology, 1*(2), 10–15.

Compton, W. C. (2018). Self-actualization myths: What did Maslow really say? *Journal of Humanistic Psychology.* https://doi.org/10.1177/0022167818761929.

DeCharms, R. (1968). *Personal causation: The internal affective determinants of behavior.* New York: Academic Press.

Eisenberger, R., Rhoades, L., & Cameron, J. (1999). Does pay for performance increase or decrease perceived self-determination and intrinsic motivation? *Journal of Personality and Social Psychology, 77*(5), 1026–1040.

Gambrel, P., & Cianci, R. (2003). Maslow's Hierarchy of Needs: Does it apply in a collectivist culture? *Journal of Applied Management and Entrepreneurship, 8*(2), 143–161.

Grant, A., Jeon, L., & Buettner, C. (2019). Relating early childhood teachers' working conditions and well-being to their turnover intentions. *Educational Psychology, 39*(3), 294–312.

Herzberg, F. (1987). One more time: How do you motivate employees? *Harvard Business Review, 65*(5), 1–16.

Herzberg, F., Mausner, B., & Snyderman, B. (1959). *The motivation to work.* New York: John Wiley.

Heylighen, F. (1992). A cognitive-systemic reconstruction of Maslow's theory of self-actualization. *Behavioral Science, 37*(1), 39–58.

Iwu, C., Ezeuduji, I., Iwu, C., Ikebuaku, K., & Tengeh, R. (2018). Achieving quality education by understanding teacher job satisfaction determinants. *Social Sciences, 7*(2), 25. https://doi.org/10.3390/socsci7020025.

Jeon, L., & Wells, M. (2018). An organizational-level analysis of early childhood teachers' job attitudes: Workplace satisfaction affects Early Head Start and Head Start teacher turnover. *Child & Youth Care Forum, 47*(4), 563–581.

Kollmann, T., Stöckmann, C., Kensbock, J. M., & Peschl, A. (2020). What satisfies younger versus older employees, and why? An aging perspective on equity theory to explain interactive effects of employee age, monetary rewards, and task contributions on job satisfaction. *Human Resource Management, 59*(1), 101–115.

Lambert, R., Boyle, L., Fitchett, P., & McCarthy, C. (2019). Risk for occupational stress among U.S. kindergarten teachers. *Journal of Applied Developmental Psychology, 61*, 13–20.

Landry, A. T., Forest, J., Zigarmi, D., Houson, D., & Boucher, É. (2017). The carrot or the stick? Investigating the functional meaning of cash rewards and their motivational power according to Self-Determination Theory. *Compensation & Benefits Review, 49*(1), 9–25.

Malik, M. A., Choi, J. N., & Butt, A. N. (2019). Distinct effects of intrinsic motivation and extrinsic rewards on radical and incremental creativity: The moderating role of goal orientations. *Journal of Organizational Behavior, 40*(9–10), 1013–1026.

Maslow, A. (1968). *Toward a psychology of being.* (2nd Ed.). New York: Van Nostrand Reinhold Company.

McClelland, D. C. (1961). *The achieving society.* Princeton, NJ: Van Nostrand.

McClelland, D. C., & Burnham, D. H. (1976). Power is the great motivator. *Harvard Business Review, 54*(2), 100–110.

McDonald, P., Thorpe, K., & Irvine, S. (2018). Low pay but still we stay: Retention in early childhood education and care. *Journal of Industrial Relations, 60*(5), 647–668.

McMullen, M. B., Lee, M. S., McCormick, K. I., & Choi, J. (2020). Early childhood professional well-being as a predictor of the risk of turnover in child care: A matter of quality. *Journal of Research in Childhood Education, 34*(3), 331–345.

Rybnicek, R., Bergner, S., & Gutschelhofer, A. (2019). How individual needs influence motivation effects: A neuroscientific study on McClelland's need theory. *Review of Managerial Science, 13*(2), 443–482.

Sarver, S., Roberts, A. M., Gallagher, K. C., & Daro, A. M. (2018). *Early childhood teacher turnover in Nebraska*. Research Brief. Retrieved from https://buffettinstitute.nebraska.edu/-/media/beci/docs/early-childhood-teacher-turnover-in-nebraska-new.pdf?la=e.

Shahid, A. (2018). Employee intention to stay: An environment based on trust and motivation. *Journal of Management Research, 10*(4), 58–71.

Taormina, R., & Gao, J. (2013). Maslow and the motivation hierarchy: Measuring satisfaction of the needs. *The American Journal of Psychology, 126*(2), 155–177.

Thomas, L., Tuytens, M., Devos, G., Kelchtermans, G., & Vanderlinde, R. (2020). Transformational school leadership as a key factor for teachers' job attitudes during their first year in the profession. *Educational Management Administration & Leadership, 48*(1), 106–132.

Vroom, V. H. (1964). *Work and motivation*. New York: Wiley.

Wahba, M., & Bridwell, L. (1976). Maslow reconsidered: A review of research on the Need Hierarchy Theory. *Organizational Behavior and Human Performance, 15*, 212–240.

Whitebook, M., McLean, C., Austin, L., J., & Edwards, B. (2018). *Early childhood workforce index—2018*. Berkeley, CA: Center for the Study of Child Care Employment, University of California, Berkeley. Retrieved from https://www.fcd-us.org/early-childhood-workforce-index%e2%80%89-%e2%80%892018.

Wright, B., O'Halloran, P., & Stukas, A. (2019). Enhancing self-efficacy and performance: An experimental comparison of psychological techniques. *Research Quarterly for Exercise and Sport, 87*(1), 36–46.

Zhang, Y., Zhang, J., & Li, J. (2018). The effect of intrinsic and extrinsic goals on work performance: Prospective and empirical studies on goal content theory. *Personnel Review, 47*(4), 900–912.

ONLINE RESOURCES

GovLeaders.org: https://www.govleaders.org

Mind Tools (leadership & motivation): https://www.mindtools.com

Small Business Know How: https://www.businessknowhow.com

Workforce Management: https://www.workforce.com

APPLICATION SHEET 3-1

Employee Motivation Assessment Questions

1. *Maslow's Hierarchy of Needs*:

   (example) How safe do you feel in your workplace?   Very   Somewhat   Not at all

2. *Alderfer's ERG Theory:*

3. *Herzberg's Two-Factor Theory:*

4. *McClelland's Theory of Learned Needs:*

5. *Bandura's Theory of Self-Efficacy:*

6. *Vroom's Expectancy Theory:*

7. *Equity Theory:*

APPLICATION SHEET 3-2

The Internet address and summary of sites that I found most informative for understanding the concept of motivational leadership:

A.

B.

C.

D.

E.

Others:

APPLICATION SHEET 3-3A

The first administrator I interviewed: _____.

Name of program: _____

Date: _____

Summary of the interview results:

How effective do you think this administrator's strategies are for motivating staff members?

APPLICATION SHEET 3-3B

The second administrator I interviewed: _____ .

Name of program: _____

Date: _____

Summary of the interview results:

How effective do you think this administrator's strategies are for motivating staff members?

APPLICATION SHEET 3-4

Five incentives that would motivate me to change my eating and/or exercise habits:

1.

2.

3.

4.

5.

4

The Motivational Leader

OBJECTIVES

After reading this chapter, you will be able to do the following:

- Describe the concept of hybrid leadership and its relationship to early childhood programs.
- Discuss how individuals typically assume leadership positions in organizations.
- Explain why trait, attribute, and competency theories have not proven to be effective for identifying individuals who would be successful leaders.
- Identify several key functions that motivational leaders are expected to fulfill in an organization.
- Compare and contrast the autocratic and participative leadership styles, and discuss the advantages and limitations associated with each style.
- Describe how an individual can determine the best leadership style to follow.
- Identify four signs of stress and discuss the potential effects on leaders and their programs.
- Outline the steps an individual can take to become a motivational leader.

KEY TERMS

- traits
- attributes
- competencies
- autocratic leadership
- consultative leadership
- participatory leadership
- laissez-faire leadership
- transactional leadership
- transformational leadership
- charismatic leadership
- servant leadership
- authentic

■ ■ ■

I've learned that people will forget what you said, people will forget what you did, but people will never forget how you made them feel.

—Maya Angelou, American poet

INTRODUCTION

The leadership concept is the subject of this chapter. The terms *leadership* or *leader* are used throughout this chapter and book, but their use is not limited to an individual who holds a formal title or sits in a designated office. Rather, motivational leaders are found throughout an organization. They have many different titles (e.g., office managers, head teachers, directors, team leaders, program coordinators). In other words, anyone who makes decisions, mentors, or encourages another employee's performance is displaying leadership qualities.

Several key motivational theories were presented in chapter 3. Attention now shifts to the individuals who occupy leadership roles: how they often arrive at their position, their typical qualifications, responsibilities, leadership styles, and several unanticipated challenges they are likely to face. Finally, practices that will help you to become an effective motivational and empowering leader are discussed.

LEADER, MANAGER, OR DIRECTOR?

The terms *leader* and *manager* are often used interchangeably when referring to someone who occupies a position of authority in an organization. However, the two terms are not synonymous or equivalent.

Managers are typically individuals who receive top-down directives from leadership and, in turn, are responsible for coordinating and overseeing employee performance (McKale, 2019). Their primary role is to inform personnel about what and how things need to be done in order to accomplish certain expected outcomes. Thus, they tend to focus on project implementation, efficiency, and completion and are less concerned with encouraging employee creativity and development.

In contrast, leaders are individuals who occupy a position of influence. They embrace a relationship-oriented style and are passionate about inspiring and motivating others to work toward collaborative goals. They involve employees in decision-making processes and listen to what they have to say. Leaders create environments in which personnel are valued, their development is nurtured, and efforts are acknowledged.

Motivational leaders understand that building relationships with employees fosters improved job satisfaction, performance, and retention (Ergun & Yalcinkaya, 2018; Inceoglu et al., 2018). For example, Sims, Waniganayake, and Hadley (2019) noted that early childhood teachers more readily accepted change and were willing to implement new policies when their leaders employed a relationship-oriented approach. They understood that their leaders were continuously looking for ways to motivate improved performance and program quality.

Early childhood programs are typically administered by a director. In public school settings, directors work closely with the building principal. In many respects, they fulfill a role that encompasses the functions of both managers and leaders. They perform essential managerial tasks, such as assuring a program's fiscal well-being, training staff, maintaining required documentation, and monitoring adherence to required safety practices. They also play a pivotal leadership role in creating high-quality participatory environments, motivating independent thinking and performance, acknowledging accomplishments, and supporting personnel development. They recognize when change is needed and use their influence to guide programs in new directions. Researchers have described this combined style as hybrid leadership and noted that it is most often observed in community organizations, education, and health care fields (Bagley & Margolis, 2018; Croft, 2015; Giacomelli, 2019).

"WHO ME?" HOW PEOPLE BECOME LEADERS

Few individuals receive any formal leadership training, yet many find themselves in leadership positions for reasons that are often unrelated to their qualifications for the job (Figure 4.1). Some people are promoted to a leadership position because they have worked for an organization longer than anyone else, or because no one else wants to assume the responsibilities associated with the role. Others may actively seek leadership positions because they enjoy the recognition and a formal title. Still others may have won their colleagues' respect and admiration based upon prior demonstrations of their leadership abilities in responding to challenging situations, or they have a sincere interest in contributing to their organization.

Regardless of the pathway that has led an individual into a leadership position, it is their performance in the position that matters. A program's success or failure ultimately depends

FIGURE 4.1 Motivational and inspirational leaders occupy many positions throughout an organization.
SDI Productions

upon the quality of its leadership. Motivational leaders set the tone for an organization through their ability to inspire and empower others. They influence almost every function, including the following:

- communication
- the decision-making process
- use of power and authority
- resource allocation
- program quality and stability
- employee behavior and performance
- conflict resolution
- customer satisfaction
- advocacy

Dysfunctional leadership can contribute to organizational inefficiency, confusion, demoralized employees who may leave their jobs, decline in program quality, loss of consumers, and eventual failure (Kilic & Gunsel, 2019; Roter, 2017). Effective leadership enables an organization to run smoothly and to successfully accomplish its goals and objectives (Andersen et al., 2018; Bloom & Abel, 2015). Such leaders understand the "big picture" and are not as likely to get bogged down by small problems and minute details. They are able to assess situations efficiently, formulate a vision, develop responsive plans, and rally the resources necessary to achieve an objective. They build trust and loyalty among employees through their honesty, guidance, inspiration, and open communication.

Did You Know? ·

Most early childhood program directors have less than five years of leadership experience and limited formal training.

· ·

The leadership role has and continues to be the subject of numerous studies, popular articles, and books. Despite such efforts, significant questions remain. For example, is there a specific path one can follow to become a leader? Are people born to be leaders, or do they acquire leadership skills through training and experience? Which leadership style is most effective? Should a leader be people- or outcome-oriented or both? Is it more productive to share leadership responsibilities, or should one person be solely or primarily in charge? Although questions remain, researchers agree that motivational leadership plays an essential role in creating environments where employees enjoy working.

LEADERSHIP: TRAITS, ATTRIBUTES, OR COMPETENCIES?

For decades, researchers have been intrigued by the possibility that outstanding leaders possessed certain personality **traits** that distinguished them from non-leaders. They thought that certain qualities, such as masculinity, dominance, intelligence, tolerance, and sociability were inborn and responsible for an individual's leadership capabilities (Mann,

1959; Stogdill, 1948). Critics countered that trait identification was subjective and biased and, consequently, not a reliable method for predicting a person's leadership potential (Conger & Kanungo, 1998; Derue et al., 2011). They also concluded that study results did not account for trait effectiveness in various conditions or settings, nor could traits be easily taught to individuals.

If trait theories were not useful for identifying outstanding leaders, perhaps research focused on **attributes** would prove more beneficial. Attributes that were commonly examined ranged from a person's height, weight, eye color, gender, and age to intelligence, attractiveness, ethnicity, political orientation, religious affiliation, personality, popularity, and socioeconomic status. Would these characteristics unilaterally or collectively predict leadership capability conclusively?

Despite numerous efforts, a definitive list of characteristics that effective leaders have in common has never been established. An assumption that all great leaders possessed the same or similar personal characteristics that were equally applicable in all settings proved overly simplistic. Studies that would have continued to follow similar research paths were abandoned, thus ending speculation that gifted leaders are born with special leadership attributes.

Although clear reproducible evidence may be unavailable, some research results point toward the idea that successful leaders exhibit certain leadership **competencies** (Table 4.1). Competency lists appear in almost every book published on the topic of leadership. Although the lists are relatively consistent, differences among them may reflect the complex nature of a leadership role coupled with the diverse settings in which leaders typically function.

For example, competencies that a leader requires to oversee a large international company are understandably different from those needed to run a local school or early childhood education program. Variations in program goals and objectives, the nature of employees (e.g., training, experience, values, personalities), the scale of the organization, and customers' needs and expectations require different combinations of leadership abilities (Gardner, 1989; Hersey, 1984). It may also be true that leaders who possess various competencies are able to address similar problems, but in their own unique style. Finally, assessment of a person's leadership potential based upon competencies may be advantageous because these are skills that can be learned.

Table 4.1: Common Characteristics of Effective Leaders

Some characteristics often associated with being an effective leader are:	
integrity and honesty	self-confidence
respect	self-control
transparency	initiative and passion
dependability	sense of humor
empathy	ability to work with, and supervise, others
cognitive and emotional intelligence	adaptability
time management	visionary
risk-taker	effective communication skills

Connecting Points

Leaders and teachers share many qualities in common. Children often consider their teachers to be "special" people who seem to know everything about everything. Take a minute to recall your favorite teacher.

- Why did you consider this teacher to be special?
- What qualities did you find especially admirable about this person?
- Which of these qualities, if any, do you think would be important for a motivational leader to exhibit? Explain.
- Did this person have qualities that you believe were inappropriate for a motivational leader to use in the workplace? Describe.

LEADERSHIP ROLES

An examination of leadership functions provides another potential strategy for identifying exceptional leaders. For example, leaders are expected to attract and retain dedicated employees. Also assumed is that they will keep their organizations running smoothly based upon their ability to continually gather relevant information, maintain open lines of communication, and make critical decisions. Organizations also rely on leaders to recognize opportunities and mobilize resources necessary to improve the current organizational configuration and to move in new, promising directions.

Because effective leadership is so fundamental to an organization's success, vitality, improvement, and survival, much contemporary research focuses on key functions that leaders are expected to fulfill (Alchin, Arthur, & Woodrow, 2019; Kerns, 2020). Some of the responsibilities commonly cited in such studies include the following:

- facilitation
- communication
- organization
- inspiration
- motivation
- mentoring
- goal-setting
- hiring and retaining competent employees
- team-building
- diversity competence
- mediation
- delegation
- innovation
- serving as a role model

Initially, such lists may prove beneficial for the identification and evaluation of persons who are under consideration for leadership positions. It is generally assumed that leaders will be capable of performing certain routine responsibilities and responding to unexpected challenges, such as an injured child or cook who calls in sick. Thus, the greater their repertoire of skills, the more likely they are to be successful.

It is unlikely that an individual would be aware of, and proficient in, all aspects of leadership. However, it may not be necessary for every leader to have the same level of expertise because leadership functions at multiple levels within an organization. For example, a multi-site early childhood program may purposively seek out a director who has financial expertise or a coordinator who has special education training. Some leaders may work more effectively with a specific group or groups of employees. For example, a leader who has experience as a classroom teacher will have first-hand knowledge of teachers' responsibilities and, thus, can relate more directly to their concerns. Some leaders have a greater understanding of important cultural values and are able to communicate and respond to employees' unique needs in a sensitive and respectful manner.

Personality differences can also influence one's leadership effectiveness by enhancing, or interfering with, working relationships. For example, directors who consider themselves to be an expert on policy development may independently make all such decisions and, thereby, disenfranchise employees who are never consulted. Thus, a person's outstanding resume, experience, or charisma may not necessarily make them the best candidate for a job. The right fit depends upon the organization's needs coupled with a match of the leader's skills and ability to work with, and motivate, a program's employees.

CLASSICAL LEADERSHIP MODELS

The way in which an individual guides, shapes, and leads others toward an accomplishment or outcome is commonly referred to as one's leadership style. This topic has undergone extensive study for decades, and has been examined from multiple perspectives. For example, early twentieth-century research focused on a leader's role as a decision-maker who either showed greater concern for outcome achievement versus encouragement of employee input and autonomy.

Although several leadership theories and models resulted, most have been challenged on the basis of their limitations, including whether any one particular leadership style is consistently functional in most situations. Perhaps surprisingly, research designed specifically to study leadership models that are effective in early childhood settings is generally unavailable.

Authority and Control

An approach to understanding one's leadership style and its effect on an organization involves the consideration of who controls the power and decision-making authority, and how much support and involvement employees have in the process (Figure 4.2). Four classical styles are frequently identified:

- autocratic
- consultative
- participative
- laissez-faire

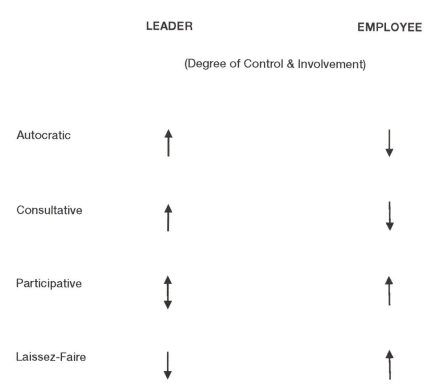

FIGURE 4.2 Leadership Styles and Employee Control and Involvement

Leaders who adopt an **autocratic leadership** style maintain full, personal control of all decision-making responsibilities (Lewin, Lippitt, & White, 1939). Employees are not consulted in this style. They are told how a task is to be performed and then closely monitored as they carry out their assigned work. Rewards and reprimands are used to motivate performance.

The autocratic leader essentially sets policy, generates all ideas, assigns tasks, and monitors results. There are no opportunities for constructive input or criticism by employees, either in the formulation of a task or in its completion. If the autocratic leader makes a mistake in defining a task or making a decision, employees are the ones likely to experience any negative consequences. For example, a licensing inspector may observe and cite a teacher who is not using the correct handwashing procedure with the children when he (the teacher) was only following the protocol set by his supervisor.

Although this leadership style limits employees' contributions and creativity, it can be an effective method to use with new employees or those whose skills or experiences are limited. The autocratic style is also frequently used when program leaders must make immediate decisions. Not surprisingly, this style is often identified as a major contributing factor to high employee absenteeism and turnover (Jing, 2018; Magbity, Ofei, & Wilson, 2020).

Leaders who practice a **consultative leadership** style tend to listen attentively to employee suggestions and comments, but always make the final decisions about what will be done, how it is to be completed, and who will be assigned to the task. The leader, in this case, also supervises employees' work closely. Again, there is essentially one person, the leader, who assumes responsibility for task formulation, assignment, and completion. Although employees contribute their ideas and feedback, none of the suggestions are likely to be implemented.

The **participative leadership** style reflects a teamwork approach and is generally considered to be more democratic than other leadership forms. Employees are encouraged to take part in decision-making and problem-solving processes, typically in a group setting. This team approach is characterized by

- considerable employee input and discussion;
- decisions that are reached collectively before presentation to leadership; and
- leadership that grants final approval, or accepts and supports the group's decision.

Employees receive minimal instruction and are relatively free to determine how and when a task can best be accomplished to achieve a stated and satisfactory outcome. The utilization of a team approach is a prime example of participative leadership. For example, a director may involve several teachers in policy formation, hiring decisions, or the establishment of the next year's tuition rates.

The participative form of leadership is beneficial in programs that place a premium on innovation and creativity. It is also most effective with employees who are skilled and experienced, and builds trust, self-confidence, self-esteem, and professional growth. The participative style improves retention efforts and can also be an effective strategy for developing the skills of future leaders (Chan, 2019).

Finally, the **laissez-faire leadership** style turns all decision-making responsibilities over to the employees. In this "hands-off" approach, decisions are reached and tasks performed with minimal-to-no direction or support from leadership. Brainstorming sessions encourage participants to express their ideas and concerns without constraint. For example, a director may ask the teaching staff to develop guidelines for use and maintenance of the playground, annual fundraising activities, or revision of the center's discipline policy. This style works well with highly skilled, self-motivated employees, and can be appropriate in situations where a program director wants to maximize employees' engagement, creativity, and problem-solving abilities (Wong, 2018).

There is a potential problem with this leadership approach. The lack of clear directions or a designated project leader may result in confusion, disorganization, tasks that may not be completed on time, and outcomes that may not meet original expectations. Team members may not understand their role and, therefore, lack commitment. Unless explicit guidelines are provided to ensure task completion and anticipated results, a leader may find that nothing significant is accomplished despite good intentions.

People- versus Task-Orientation

Leadership styles have also been studied from a behavioral perspective and characterized by the way in which leaders allocate their time, efforts, and resources (Blake & Mouton, 1964; Yukl, 1994). Some leaders may adopt a task-oriented approach. For example, they may set an enrollment goal or budget predictions and then measure their personal success against the program's ability to reach the metric.

The task-oriented leader views employees as a means to an end and shows limited concern about addressing their personal needs. For example, teachers may be assigned tasks or given directions and then expected to achieve predetermined goals, such as completing their in-service hours, arranging their classrooms a certain way, or meeting specific learning outcomes, all according to the leader's standards.

People-oriented leaders tend to show a greater concern and respect for employees as individuals. They are sensitive to how decisions will affect their employees and are, therefore, more likely to devote time and attention to coaching, mentoring, and building employee relationships than to goal attainment. By doing so, they make employees feel valued, appreciated, and more committed to the organization. As a result, employees are often more efficient and productive (Jing, 2018).

Most motivational leaders practice a style that falls somewhere between these two approaches. They adjust their responses and expectations to meet the demands of a particular situation. However, Sharma et al. (2019) noted that today's employees expect program leaders to be more people- than product-oriented and to focus on a team-building approach.

Did You Know? ·

More than ninety percent of employees identify leadership empathy as an important factor in their decision to leave or remain with an organization.

· ·

CONTEMPORARY LEADERSHIP MODELS

During the 1970s and 1980s, several new leadership models were proposed as part of attempts to better integrate workforce complexity with business environments. These models focused on leaders' intended objectives, the nature of their relationship with employees, and their effectiveness in retaining competent employees who could achieve an organization's goals.

Transactional and Transformational Leadership

Burns (1978) suggested that all leaders fit into one of two style categories, namely, **transactional** or **transformational leadership**. He concluded that transactional leaders are characterized by the efficient manner in which they accomplish an organization's goals. They establish and communicate clear objectives, provide extensive instructions and needed resources, and set deadlines that employees are expected to follow.

Transactional leaders use rewards and punishments to achieve organizational goals. Incentives, often monetary, are offered to gain employee cooperation and to reward performance. However, such extrinsic rewards seldom prove adequate to reduce long-term employee frustration or to motivate increased productivity (Kark, Van Dijk, & Vashdi, 2018). Leaders who use a punitive approach, such as intimidation, termination, or refusal to grant an anticipated promotion or pay raise, create anger and resentment among their employees. As a result, researchers have found that transactional leaders typically experience higher employee turnover rates in their organizations (Caillier, 2018).

Transformational leaders practice a creative and visionary approach in their leadership role (Lee et al., 2019). They are skilled communicators, exhibit high emotional intelligence, and appear to be less concerned about achieving specific goals for personal gain. Rather, their primary efforts are focused on creating change in an organization by fostering employee trust and participation in important decisions. Transformational leaders place a high value on mentoring, inspiring, motivating, and acknowledging employees' efforts and contributions. They create a workplace environment that boosts employees' self-confidence, appreciates their performance, and promotes their skill development (Figure 4.3).

Leaders seldom use one style to the exclusion of the other. Successful leaders typically practice a combination of transactional and transformational styles, which gives them maximum flexibility to respond to different circumstances. Both leadership styles offer advantages and disadvantages. For example, the transactional style may be effective for accomplishing things quickly, especially if a project is relatively simple, employees' skills are limited, or there is a short deadline. However, if this style is used exclusively, it can lead to poor employee morale, lack of commitment, and job dissatisfaction (Dishop et al., 2019). Transformational leaders are often instrumental in energizing employees and moving a program in new directions. However, they may become distracted by the process itself and experience limited success if this is the only leadership style they use.

FIGURE 4.3 Transformational leaders encourage employees' input and involvement. *SDI Productions, iStock / Getty Images Plus*

———————————————— Connecting Points ————————————————

Consider a recent situation in which someone else made a decision that affected your behavior.

- Did you feel the decision was appropriate given the circumstances?
- Were your needs and concerns taken into consideration?
- If you could reverse roles, how might your decision differ?

Charismatic Leadership

Robert J. House (1977) introduced the term **charismatic leadership** to describe leaders who possess unique personality traits, such as charm and likeability, which they use to persuade others to follow their ideas. These leaders are considered to have exceptional communication skills, engage in convincing rhetoric, and show compassionate support for their employees. Conger, Kanungo, and Menon (2000) noted that employees establish a close relationship with charismatic leaders based on reverence, trust, and a collective identity. Parry et al. (2019) described this association as an emotional connection that forms between charismatic leaders and their followers. In turn, the sense of belonging or unity creates an environment in which employees may well feel compelled to comply with the leader's expectations and performance standards (Lovelace et al., 2019).

Charismatic leaders are energetic visionaries who are confident in their ability to identify a challenge or an opportunity which they work to meet or to take advantage of, respectively. They are zealous, determined, diligent in their efforts to accomplish change. They use their own enthusiasm to convince individuals that each one is important for achievement of the organization's success. History is replete with many such charismatic leaders, including Winston Churchill, Martin Luther King Jr., Nelson Mandela, Angela Merkel, and Oprah Winfrey.

Charismatic and transformational leaders share similar leadership qualities. They focus on relationship-building and the creation of supportive environments to gain employees' trust and long-term commitment. They are people-oriented, concerned about employees' needs, and able to build a unifying team spirit.

Conversely, some charismatic leaders differ from transformational leaders with respect to their primary leadership objective. Their interest in accomplishing organizational change by building employee-leader relationships is not their only focus. Charismatic leaders are often more concerned with their personal image and may utilize their position to promote unethical programs or use employees in ways that advance their own personal gain (Fragouli, 2018; Judge, Piccolo, & Kosalka, 2009). They limit employee input and innovation as a result of the strong buy-in mentality that some charismatic leaders expect.

Vergauwe et al. (2018) noted that highly charismatic leaders are often ineffective due to their self-serving interests and self-perceived success in resolving challenging issues. They also observed that leaders who exhibited low charisma are unable to rally the level of employee support necessary to achieve their objectives and, as a result, were also ineffective in their role. Leaders who displayed a moderately charismatic approach were most successful in developing employee support and attaining the organization's goals.

Servant Leadership

The **servant leadership** model, introduced by Robert Greenleaf (1970), suggested that leaders occupy a privileged and altruistic position designed to serve the needs of others—employees, customers, and the community at-large. Their primary role should be devoted to empowering employees by supporting their career development and building a collaborative culture of trust for achieving program objectives. Servant leaders are expected to be good listeners, encouraging of others, and models of exemplary moral and ethical standards. Greenleaf promoted the idea that servant leaders can address social injustices by relinquishing some of their power and authority and giving employees a greater say in decision-making processes. He suggested that this was also an important step for developing new leadership.

Scholars have attempted to describe this leadership style in terms of attributes typically exhibited by successful servant leaders (Banks et al., 2018; VanMeter et al., 2016). Among these are honesty and integrity, humility, a genuine respect and concern for others, team-building, ability to inspire and motivate others' performance, and the promotion of another individual's development. Servant leaders have also been defined as people who encourage power and authority-sharing with their employees, but are also capable of assuming a directional role when decisions must be made.

Despite attempts, a precise definition of this conceptual model has not been developed. Critics have suggested that servant and transformational leadership styles are difficult to distinguish from each other, that the concept is overly idealistic and not practical in many organizations, and that servant leaders create a dependency among their followers (Banks et al., 2018; Eva et al., 2019).

The servant leadership approach decreased in use for a period of time but has attracted renewed attention because of its emphasis on a leader's ethical and moral standards and movement away from authoritarian control. Researchers have since found a strong correlation between servant leadership and employee commitment, job performance and satisfaction, and trust in leaders (Allen et al., 2018; Kiker, Callahan, & Kiker, 2019). Furthermore, von Fischer & De Jong (2017) noted that although teachers' extrinsic and intrinsic satisfaction increased when their principal practiced a servant leadership style, the effect was most significant on extrinsic satisfaction. Teachers cited improved working conditions, such as implementation of school policies, higher salaries, reduced workload, greater recognition, and better opportunities for advancement as notable extrinsic rewards.

IS THERE A RIGHT LEADERSHIP STYLE?

Effective leaders understand that no one best leadership style works is all situations. Early childhood leaders who practice a single leadership style often find that their ability to respond to program needs is not successful and may have a negative effect on their relationship with employees. Differences in program structure, goals, objectives, employees, geographical location, and customers, among other factors, require different types of leadership. Leaders must also consider their own personality, values, strengths and weaknesses, and motivation when determining which leadership style they are most comfortable implementing.

As the early childhood field continues to undergo change, it becomes increasingly important that leaders develop a repertoire of skills and competencies rather than reliance on a singular leadership style. This approach allows flexibility in responding to different audiences and situations that they are likely to encounter.

Several criteria can also be used to determine which style may be most appropriate and effective in a given situation, including the following:

- the nature of the task or problem to be addressed
- employees' strengths, limitations, values, qualifications, and competencies
- how quickly a decision must be made
- which players possess the information necessary for making a sound decision
- the leader's personality: how comfortable they are in turning control or decision-making responsibilities over to others

Choosing and implementing an effective leadership style requires leaders to carefully assess a situation, gather information, modify their behavior if required, and involve employees whenever it is appropriate. For example, a program director might rely on an autocratic style when dealing with an unannounced visit from state licensing agents. The task and immediacy of the situation, combined with the director's firsthand knowledge, may support the decision to assume full leadership control. However, the same director may employ a participative style when formulating an employee dress code or purchasing new classroom equipment.

--------------------- *Connecting Points* ---------------------

Wanda began as a classroom teacher in a small neighborhood center soon after finishing her degree at the local community college. Three years later, she was asked to take over as the director. Although Wanda had no leadership experience, she was willing to learn and appreciated the advisory board's vote of confidence in her abilities. Fifteen years later, Wanda was ready for a change. She applied for a director position at a large corporate early childhood program and was hired.

Wanda prides herself in making all of the decisions and providing detailed information that informs the teachers how they are to be implemented. She considers this approach a more efficient use of her time and effort. Last week, two head teachers who had been with the center for many years quit. Several younger teachers have complained to Wanda that they no longer have opportunities to participate in decisions that affect their jobs and lack the autonomy they were accustomed to having with the previous director.

- How would you describe Wanda's leadership style?
- Why do you think her staff is upset?
- What changes would you advise Wanda to make in this situation?
- If Wanda is unable to change her leadership style, what suggestions would you have as a member of the advisory board?

UNANTICIPATED LEADERSHIP CHALLENGES

A private office and a title on the door may be trophies that some leaders desire. However, symbols are inevitably accompanied by challenges and expectations that even the most experienced leaders must address.

Advanced Preparation

Leaders who take time to learn about an organization and thoroughly understand the requirements of a new position are more effective from day one. Such an effort also applies to individuals who may be promoted from within, which is often the case in early childhood programs. Even though a new director may have excellent credentials and familiarity with the program, there will always be much to learn.

Steps that can make the transition to a new position smoother and less stressful include

- becoming familiar with the organization's values, mission, goals, employees, customers, and resources;
- engaging in self-awareness; assessing your personal attributes (e.g., strengths, weaknesses, emotional makeup) and leadership skills (e.g., communication, problem-solving, decision-making, style); working on those that may need improvement;
- meeting and communicating with individual employees early and often; learning about their unique interests, concerns, talents, goals, strengths, and feelings about the organization (e.g., what is working, what is not working, what could be improved);
- recognizing that it will take time for you to feel comfortable in your new role and for others to accept your leadership and authority; and
- being yourself and a good role model for others to follow.

The business world has long understood the importance of having trained, competent motivational leaders to oversee their organizations (DePass, Ehrlich, & Leis, 2019; Sims, Waniganayake, & Hadley, 2019; Subramony et al., 2018). Only recently has the early childhood field begun to address this issue through the development of formal coursework, certification, and credentialing of program administrators (Abel, Talan, & Magid, 2018; Goffin & Daga, 2017). This trend continues to gain momentum and national attention as the field moves toward professionalization and recognizes the impact that administrator preparation has on teacher recruitment, teacher retention, and the quality of education that children receive (De-Souza, Galuski, & Pollock, 2019; Hylton & Vu, 2019). (Additional information about early childhood administrator credentialing in the United States is presented in chapter 9.)

Trust and Acceptance

New leaders often face an unanticipated challenge in terms of gaining employees' respect and acceptance. They are inevitably viewed with caution and skepticism relative to their personality, leadership style, and intended changes. Establishing a trusting relationship with employees, as a prelude to gaining their acceptance, is an essential first step that occurs gradually through a leader's many actions and decisions (Textbox 4.1).

BUILDING TRUST WITH EMPLOYEES

Motivational leadership is built on a foundation of trust and integrity.

- Be friendly and make yourself approachable. Introduce yourself and share some personal information about your interests, hobbies, travels, family, etc. Social exchanges help employees begin to form an emotional connection and to see you as "one of them," not just as their leader.
- Be transparent. Communicate often and be a good listener. For example, ask teachers for their ideas and keep them informed, especially when making changes.
- Solicit feedback often from your employees. Ask employees about what they believe is working, important to them, or problematic and needs to be addressed. This shows that you respect and value their knowledge and opinions.
- Establish and communicate clear expectations to avoid employee confusion, stress, and uncertainty. Follow through in a consistent manner to discourage questions about your loyalty and integrity.
- Be honest and direct with employees. Keep them informed about your goals and rationale for implementing any change. Uninformed employees are more likely to form their own assumptions and resist change, especially if their conclusions are inaccurate.
- Demonstrate trust in your employees by delegating responsibilities that they are qualified to handle or willing to learn. Explain what needs to be done and let employees use their creativity when performing new tasks. Employees are more likely to form a trusting relationship with leaders who empower their personnel, even when risk is involved.
- Let employees know that you care about them as a person, not only as an employee. Acknowledge their efforts and ask for their input often.

DIRECTOR'S SHOWCASE

The research tells us that it is important to establish a culture of trust in the workplace. Do you agree, and how do you create this type of environment?

Yes, I believe that trust is fundamental to running a quality program. I must have trust in my teachers, and they must be able to trust me. I always try to be honest with them and to encourage two-way communication so they are aware of what is occurring or needs to be addressed and I am aware of their concerns. Whenever possible, I also involve them in making group decisions because this is empowering and builds trust and respect. Sometimes they even surprise me by coming up with suggestions or solutions that I had not considered. We also make time to socialize and have fun together as friends, not just co-workers.

—Tim A., director

Researchers have noted that trust in leadership has a direct effect on employee engagement, performance, and job satisfaction (Haque, Fernando, & Caputi, 2019). A recent Gallup report (2017), *State of the American Workplace*, confirmed that the primary reason people leave a position is because of their leader's or director's actions, not the job or organization itself. This result underscores the significant role that leaders play in establishing a trusting relationship with employees and creating a workplace culture and environment in which they feel supported, empowered, and engaged (Meng & Berger, 2019; Yue, Men, & Ferguson, 2019).

Authenticity and Accountability

New leaders may be eager to make decisions that will increase their "likeability" among employees. However, researchers have found that employees trust leaders who are genuine, **authentic**, and exhibit integrity (Mehdad & Sajadi, 2019; Oh, Cho, & Lim, 2018). They value leaders' honesty in establishing meaningful rapport and caring relationships (Figure 4.4).

Employees also expect new leaders to communicate and implement consistent expectations and to be accountable for their mistakes. Moore et al. (2019) noted that authentic leaders exert a significant influence on employees' ethical behavior when they assume responsibility for their own actions and, in turn, create a culture in which honesty and integrity are valued.

These findings have important implications for new leaders. Mistakes are expected during the early months in a new position. However, leaders can begin to establish credibility

FIGURE 4.4 Effective leaders trust, respect, and listen carefully to their employees. *fizkes, iStock / Getty Images Plus*

by acknowledging when events do not proceed or turn out as intended. Furthermore, those who view failure as a learning opportunity often become more effective sooner in achieving their desired outcomes. Motivational leaders who practice this approach create a psychological environment in which blame and hostility are avoided and there is less leader-employee tension. As a result, their employees are more likely to exhibit a strong work ethic and enjoy greater job motivation and satisfaction (Feng et al., 2018; Osibanjo et al., 2018).

Stress and Burnout

Leaders who assume a new position often find the first few months invigorating and an opportunity to exercise their skills and creativity. However, when the novelty wears off, the associated pressures may begin to affect an individual's productivity. Leaders must be able to juggle multiple roles and resolve unforeseen challenges on a daily basis. They must interact with diverse audiences and carry out difficult decisions that are unlikely to please everyone. Loneliness and stress may gradually develop. Both are often unanticipated challenges seldom addressed in the literature, especially as they relate to early childhood directors.

An overwhelming workload or deadline may cause short-term stress that is usually resolved once the project is completed. Taking short breaks (e.g., a walk outside, eating a snack, listening to quiet music, daydreaming about a favorite vacation) can temporarily alleviate work tedium and help to refocus one's attention. Short-term stress can also be managed by reframing the way in which a workload or project is viewed. For example, rather than dreading the hours required to conduct job interviews, consider the benefits associated with hiring an outstanding candidate who can relieve some stress by assuming a portion of your responsibilities.

Chronic and unmanaged stress can lead to burnout and have an adverse effect on a leader's performance as well as the organization and its employees (Textbox 4.2). Harms

---

TEXTBOX 4.2

WARNING SIGNS OF LEADERSHIP BURNOUT

Signs of chronic stress and burnout:

- feeling overwhelmed
- physical and emotional exhaustion
- difficulty concentrating
- poor decision-making
- procrastination
- loss of interest or enthusiasm in one's job
- irritability and tendency to overreact
- loss of happiness and motivation
- increased or decreased appetite; frequent indigestion
- head-, back-, stomach-, and/or muscle aches
- anxiety disorders; frequent illness

et al. (2017) found that the quality of leader-employee communications and relationships were negatively affected when leaders experienced significant stress and, in turn, increased employee burnout and job departure. Similarly, Tafvelin et al. (2019) noted that employee burnout and turnover rates were lower when leaders experienced less stress and had more "vigor and peer support." These findings reinforce the importance of addressing stressors that can potentially contribute to burnout and reduce leaders' resilience (Textbox 4.3).

TEXTBOX 4.3

BURNOUT PREVENTION STRATEGIES

Developing a repertoire of effective coping skills builds resilience and affords leaders protection against burnout.

- Recognize the signs of stress (e.g., increased heart rate, feeling cold/hot, headache, stomachache, jaw clenching).
- Identify potential stressors.
- Take periodic breaks.
- Delegate responsibilities when appropriate.
- Avoid procrastination; practice time management; prioritize tasks and tackle difficult matters first to get them out of the way; reward yourself when they are finished.
- Manage perfectionism (reworking a report or project multiple times may not make it better); accept that there are some things you cannot control.
- Develop a strong professional network and social support system; spend time with friends.
- Make time to have fun, relax, and laugh. Laughter significantly reduces cortisol (stress hormone) levels (Fujisawa et al., 2018).
- Maintain a healthy lifestyle; consume a nutritious diet; get seven to eight hours of uninterrupted sleep; engage in at least thirty minutes of physical activity several times each week.
- Unplug and unwind; use vacations (e.g., few days, week) to recharge and refresh mentally; leave work-related projects at home; turn off your phone and Internet (except for personal use).

Did You Know? •

More than half of all employees report that they experience high levels of stress and burnout in their jobs.

• •

PUTTING IT ALL TOGETHER: BECOMING A MOTIVATIONAL LEADER

The question now becomes, what can we take away from these various leadership models to become more effective early childhood leaders? How can we apply this knowledge to create environments that inspire, motivate, and support employees in their work with children and families?

Motivational leaders distinguish themselves through their ability to connect with employees and influence their behavior (Textbox 4.4). They inspire performance through an acknowledgment of employees' efforts and contributions, regardless of their significance. For example, a kind word offered to a teacher who has stayed late to meet with an upset parent, or a thoughtful note left on a new teacher's desk congratulating him on an engaging science activity are simple, but meaningful acts. They convey a powerful message of gratitude that can boost an employee's self-confidence and reinforce the potential for similar or improved performance in the future.

TEXTBOX 4.4

CHARACTERISTICS OF MOTIVATIONAL LEADERS

Motivational leaders

- try to see the positive side of situations
- compliment others frequently
- encourage others to share their ideas and opinions
- are patient, and good listeners
- set a good example for others to follow
- are supportive and encourage others, especially those who may have limited experience with a new task or role
- believe that a pleasant work environment improves working relationships and productivity
- look for ways to continually improve their own leadership skills
- avoid blaming others
- understand that people make mistakes, and try to use the experience as a learning opportunity
- are sensitive to and respect individual differences with regard to personal needs, concerns, and values

---

Motivational leaders invest time and effort getting to know individual employees and their capabilities, limitations, work styles, needs, backgrounds, and comfort levels. They achieve a collaborative spirit by building on individual strengths, encouraging creativity, welcoming employee input, providing constructive feedback, and leading by positive example. Successful early childhood leaders maintain open lines of communication, and are available for consultation and assistance. They also recognize that employees are in various stages of their own professional careers, and modify the nature and intensity of their mentoring accordingly.

The art of creating an enjoyable workplace environment is also a trademark of motivational leaders. They continually monitor employee morale and are sensitive to changes in their attitudes, appearance, commitment, and work habits. Motivational leaders support and encourage their employees to experiment, create change, and develop their unique potentials. They establish an atmosphere where appreciation is shown, initiative is acknowledged, and learning from mistakes is expected. In addition, they recognize that making excessive demands is unlikely to have positive, long-term outcomes and may contribute instead to employees' dissatisfaction and eventual departure.

Motivational leaders dedicate themselves to helping employees develop their own personal motivators, thereby increasing self-efficacy and reducing dependency on others for encouragement and reinforcement (Vieira, Perin, & Sampaio, 2018). This transition is accomplished gradually by helping employees to set personal goals, take advantage of continued learning opportunities, seek and receive constructive feedback, and accept new challenges and responsibilities. Collectively, these efforts represent a critical step in fostering employees' self-esteem and career development.

Early childhood leaders often overlook the fact that they must be equally motivated before they can successfully motivate others. This may not be an easy task to maintain, but it is essential to their continued performance effectiveness. There are several steps that leaders can take to maintain their energy and job-related passion:

- *Self-evaluation:* Ask yourself if you continue to feel fulfilled by the work you are doing; solicit evaluation feedback often.
- *Self-improvement:* Keep learning; improve existing skills and develop new ones by attending conferences or enrolling in a class.
- *Self-involvement:* Create a social network of individuals who share similar positions or interests and can serve as mentors.
- *Self-fulfillment:* Maintain a healthy work-personal life balance; reward yourself after working hard (e.g., visit a museum, read a good book, go shopping, paint a picture, play golf, take a walk, see a movie, attend a concert).

Early childhood leaders must continuously examine their personal and professional goals and objectives, leadership style, and accomplishments if they are to remain committed and passionate about their role. Only then can they be effective role models and serve as an inspiration to their employees.

SUMMARY

- Effective leadership is essential to an organization's quality and success.
- Early childhood program directors often engage in a blend of managerial and leadership roles for which they may have limited or no prior formal training.
- Successful leaders have many personal qualities or traits, attributes, and/or competencies in common.
- Leaders influence almost every functional operation within an organization, from communication to innovation and team-building.
- Some leaders show greater concern for accomplishing tasks than building employee relationships.

- The autocratic, consultative, participative, and laissez-faire leadership styles reflect differences in the source of authority and degree of control and decision-making efforts.
- Contemporary leadership models place a high priority on fostering positive, engaging employee relationships versus task completion.
- No single leadership style works effectively in all situations.
- Motivational leaders are able to bring out the best in their employees; they create a pleasant work environment and support, encourage, inspire, and acknowledge employees' efforts.

APPLICATION ACTIVITIES

1. Identify an employer whom you consider to be an outstanding motivational leader. Prepare a list of their personal leadership qualities, and record your responses on Application Sheet 4-1.
2. Interview the directors of four early childhood education centers (e.g., private, community-based, public school, home-based). Learn what they consider to be their most challenging employee motivational needs. What strategies do they use to engage and motivate employees so they feel appreciated? Record your results on Application Sheet 4-2.
3. Read one of the following books: *Random acts of kindness*, by D. Kingma and D. Markova; *Attitudes of gratitude*, by M. J. Ryan; *The 5 languages of appreciation in the workplace: Empowering organizations by encouraging people*, by G. Chapman and P. White; *The 7 habits of highly effective people*, by S. R. Covey. Summarize the principles described in the book, and discuss their application for early childhood leaders on Application Sheet 4-3.
4. Use Application Sheet 4-4 for this activity. List your leadership strengths (traits) in one column, and your perceived limitations in the other. Select two limitations and develop at least one improvement goal for each. Next, identify several strategies that will help you to achieve each of your goals.

REVIEW POINTS

1. React to the statement, "Good leaders are made, not born."
2. What leadership style would you most likely choose if your objective was to involve the teaching staff in redesigning an outdoor play area? Support your decision by describing the advantages, limitations, and effectiveness of this approach.
3. When might it be appropriate for a motivational leader to use an autocratic style? Identify two situations and analyze the potential effect(s) that an autocratic style is likely to have on the outcome.
4. Describe the ways in which transactional and transformational leaders differ.
5. Discuss why relying on a single leadership style is often not effective.
6. Explain what it means to be accountable, and why this quality is important for leaders to possess.
7. In what ways can burnout affect a leader's health? The organization?
8. What characteristics are often associated with a motivational leader?

KEY TERMS DEFINED

traits—characteristics unique to an individual

attributes—personal qualities or characteristics (e.g., sincere, helpful, patient, reliable)

competencies—a combination of knowledge, skills, and abilities

autocratic leadership—leaders who maintain full control of all decisions and limit employee input

consultative leadership—leaders who listen to employees' suggestions before making decisions

participative leadership—leaders who encourage, involve, and respect employee participation in decision-making activities

laissez-faire leadership—leaders who grant employees full decision-making control and provide little or no guidance

transactional leadership—a style characterized by the outcomes or accomplishments resulting from a leader's efforts; task or product orientation

transformational leadership—a style that reflects a leader's concern with building employee relationships to achieve desired outcomes; process orientation

charismatic leadership—leaders who use their charm, communication skills, and convincing personalities to attract and influence followers

servant leadership—a style characterized by a leader's devotion to meeting employees' needs and developing their abilities to achieve organizational goals

authentic—sincere; genuine

REFERENCES

Abel, M. B., Talan, T. N., & Magid, M. (2018). *Closing the leadership gap. 2018 status report on early childhood program leadership in the United States.* Retrieved from https://mccormick-assets.floodlight.design/wp-content/uploads/2019/02/2018-LEAD-Clearinghouse-webbook_04.pdf.

Alchin, I., Arthur, L., & Woodrow, C. (2019). Evidencing leadership and management challenges in early childhood in Australia. *Australasian Journal of Early Childhood, 44*(3), 285–297.

Allen, S., Winston, B., Tatone, G., & Crowson, H. (2018). Exploring a model of servant leadership, empowerment, and commitment in nonprofit organizations. *Nonprofit Management & Leadership, 29*(1), 123–140.

Andersen, L., Bjørnholt, B., Bro, L., & Holm-Petersen, C. (2018). Achieving high quality through transformational leadership: A qualitative multilevel analysis of transformational leadership and perceived professional quality. *Public Personnel Management, 47*(1). Retrieved from https://journals.sagepub.com/doi/full/10.1177/0091026017747270.

Bagley, S. S., & Margolis, J. (2018). The emergence and failure to launch of hybrid teacher leadership. *International Journal of Teacher Leadership, 9*(1), 33–46.

Banks, G. C., Gooty, J., Ross, R. L., Williams, C. E., & Harrington, N. T. (2018). Construct redundancy in leader behaviors: A review and agenda for the future. *The Leadership Quarterly, 29*(1), 236–251.

Blake, R. R., & Mouton, J. S. (1964). *The managerial grid.* Houston: Gulf Publishing.

Bloom, P. J., & Abel, M. (2015). Expanding the lens—Leadership as an organizational asset. *Young Children, 70*(2), 8–13.

Burns, J. M. (1978). *Leadership.* New York: Harper & Row.

Caillier, J. G. (2018). Can changes in transformational-oriented and transactional-oriented leadership impact turnover over time? *International Journal of Public Administration, 41*(12), 935–945.

Chan, S. (2019). Participative leadership and job satisfaction. *Leadership & Organizational Journal, 40*(3), 319–333.

Conger, J. A., & Kanungo, R. N. (1998). *Charismatic leadership in organizations.* Thousand Oaks, CA: Sage.

Conger, J. A., Kanungo, R., & Menon, S. (2000). Charismatic leadership and follower effects. *Journal of Organizational Behavior, 21*(7), 747–767.

Croft, C. (2015). A new approach to hybrid leadership development. In S. B. Waldorff, A. R. Pedersen, L. Fitzgerald, & E. Ferlie (Eds.), *Managing change: Organizational behavior in health care series* (pp. 170–185). London: Palgrave Macmillan.

DePass, M., Ehrlich, V., & Leis, M. (2019). *Accelerating school success: Transforming K–12 schools by investing in leadership development.* Center for Creative Leadership. Retrieved from https://files .eric.ed.gov/fulltext/ED596159.pdf.

Derue, D. S., Nahrgang, J. D., Wellman, N., & Humphrey, S. (2011). Trait and behavioral theories of leadership: An integration and meta-analytic test of their relative validity. *Personnel Psychology, 64*(1), 7–52.

De-Souza, D., Galuski, T., & Pollock, B. (2019). Educating the child care administrator. *Journal of Early Childhood Teacher Education, 40*(3), 1–11.

Dishop, C., Green, A., Torres, E., & Aarons, G. (2019). Predicting turnover: The moderating effect of functional climates on emotional exhaustion and work attitudes. *Community Mental Health Journal, 55*(5), 733–741.

Ergun, E., & Yalcinkaya, K. (2018). The effects of leadership behaviors on employees' change capacity: A research study. *Business and Economics Research Journal, 9*(3), 681–696.

Eva, N., Robin, M., Sendjaya, S., van Dierendonck, D., & Liden, R. (2019). Servant leadership: A systematic review and call for future research. *The Leadership Quarterly, 30*(1), 111–132.

Feng, J., Zhang, Y., Liu, X., Zhang, L., & Han, X. (2018). Just the right amount of ethics inspires creativity: A cross-level investigation of ethical leadership, intrinsic motivation, and employee creativity. *Journal of Business Ethics, 153*(3), 645–658.

Fragouli, E. (2018). The dark-side of charisma and charismatic leadership. *Business and Management Review, 9*(4), 298–307.

Fujisawa, A., Ota, A., Matsunaga, M., Li, Y., Kakizaki, M., Naito, H., & Yatsuya, H. (2018). Effect of laughter yoga on salivary cortisol and dehydroepiandrosterone among healthy university students: A randomized controlled trial. *Complementary Therapies in Clinical Practice, 32*, 6–11.

Gallup. (2017). *State of the American Workplace.* Retrieved from https://www.gallup.com/ workplace/238085/state-american-workplace-report-2017.aspx.

Gardner, J. (1989). *On leadership.* New York: Free Press.

Giacomelli, G. (2019). The role of hybrid professionals in the public sector: A review and research synthesis. *Public Management Review.* Retrieved from https://doi.org/10.1080/14719037.2019.16 42952.

Goffin, S. G., & Daga, E. (2017). *2017 early childhood education leadership development compendium: A view of the current landscape.* (3rd Ed.). Washington, DC: Goffin Strategy Group.

Greenleaf, R. K. (1970). *The servant as leader.* Newton Centre, MA: Robert K. Greenleaf Center.

Haque, A., Fernando, M., & Caputi, P. (2019). The relationship between responsible leadership and organizational commitment and the mediating effect of employee turnover intentions: An empirical study with Australian employees. *Journal of Business Ethics, 156*(3), 759–774.

Harms, P. D., Credé, M., Tynan, M., Leon, M., & Jeung, W. (2017). Leadership and stress: A meta-analytic review. *Leadership Quarterly*, 28(1), 178–194.

Hersey, P. (1984). *The situational leader*. New York: Warner.

House, R. J. (1977). A 1976 theory of charismatic leadership. In J. G. Hunt & L. L. Larson (Eds.), *Leadership: The cutting edge* (pp. 189–207). Carbondale, IL: Southern Illinois University Press.

Hylton, N. R., & Vu, J. A. (2019). Creating a work environment that supports staff retention. *Young Children*, 74(4), 34–38.

Inceoglu, I., Thomas, G., Chu, C., Plans, D., & Gerbasi, A. (2018). Leadership behavior and employee well-being: An integrated review and a future research agenda. *The Leadership Quarterly*, 29(1), 179–202.

Jing, F. (2018). Leadership paradigms and performance in small service firms. *Journal of Management & Organization*, 24(3), 339–358.

Judge, T. A., Piccolo, R. F., & Kosalka, T. (2009). The bright and dark sides of leadership traits: A review and theoretical extension of the leader trait paradigm. *The Leadership Quarterly*, 20(6), 855–875.

Kark, R., Van Dijk, D., & Vashdi, D. (2018). Motivated or demotivated to be creative: The role of self-regulatory focus in transformational and transactional leadership processes. *Applied Psychology*, 67(1), 186–224.

Kerns, C. D. (2020). Managing organizational culture: A practice-oriented framework. *International Leadership Journal*, 12(1), 77–101.

Kiker, D. S., Callahan, J. S., & Kiker, M. B. (2019). Exploring the boundaries of servant leadership: A meta-analysis of the main and moderating effects of servant leadership on behavioral and affective outcomes. *Journal of Managerial Issues*, 31(2), 172–197.

Kilic, M., & Gunsel, A. (2019). The dark side of the leadership: The effects of toxic leaders on employees. *European Journal of Social Sciences*, 2(2), 51–56.

Lee, A., Legood, A., Hughes, D., Tian, A., Newman, A., & Knight, C. (2019). Leadership, creativity, and innovation: A meta-analytic review. *European Journal of Work & Organizational Psychology*. Retrieved from https://doi.org/10.1080/1359432x.2019.1661837.

Lewin, K., Lippitt, R., & White, R. K. (1939). Patterns of aggressive behavior in experimentally created social climates. *Journal of Social Psychology*, 10, 271–301.

Lovelace, J., Neely, B., Allen, J., & Hunter, S. (2019). Charismatic, ideological, & pragmatic (CIP) model of leadership: A critical review and agenda for future research. *The Leadership Quarterly*, 30(1), 96–110.

Magbity, J. B., Ofei, A. M., & Wilson, D. (2020). Leadership styles of nurse managers and turnover intention. *Hospital Topics*, 98(2), 45–50.

Mann, R. D. (1959). A review of the relationships between personality and performance in small groups. *Psychological Bulletin*, 56, 241–270.

McKale, L. (2019). *Leaders vs. managers: 17 traits that set them apart*. Retrieved from https://www.resourcefulmanager.com/leaders-vs-managers.

Mehdad, A., & Sajadi, M. (2019). Mediating role of psychological capital in the relationship of authentic leadership and work engagement. *International Journal of Psychology*, 13(1), 133–156.

Meng, J., & Berger, B. K. (2019). The impact of organizational culture and leadership performance on PR professionals' job satisfaction: Testing the joint mediating effects of engagement and trust. *Public Relations Review*, 45(1), 64–75.

Moore, C., Mayer, D. M., Chiang, F. T., Crossley, C., Karlesky, M. J., & Birtch, T. A. (2019). Leaders matter morally: The role of ethical leadership in shaping employee moral cognition and misconduct. *Journal of Applied Psychology*, 104(1), 123–145.

Oh, J., Cho, D., & Lim, D. (2018). Authentic leadership and work engagement: The mediating effect of practicing core values. *Leadership & Organization Development Journal*, *39*(2), 76–90.

Osibanjo, A. O., Akinbode, J. O., Falola, H. O., & Oludayo, O. O. (2018). Work ethics and employees' job performance. *Journal of Leadership, Accountability and Ethics*, *12*(1), 107–117.

Parry, K., Cohen, M., Bhattacharya, S., North-Samardzic, A., & Edwards, G. (2019). Charismatic leadership: Beyond love and hate and toward a sense of belonging? *Journal of Management & Organization*, *25*(3), 398–413.

Roter, A. (2017). *Understanding and recognizing dysfunctional leadership*. New York: Routledge.

Sharma, G. D., Aryan, R., Singh, S., & Kaur, T. (2019). A systematic review of literature about leadership and organization. *Research Journal of Business Management*, *13*(1), 1–14.

Sims, M., Waniganayake, M., & Hadley, F. (2019). What makes good even better? Excellent EC leadership. *International Journal of Educational Management*, *33*(4), 573–586.

Stogdill, R. M. (1948). Personal factors associated with leadership. A survey of the literature. *Journal of Psychology*, *25*, 35–71.

Subramony, M., Segers, J., Chadwick, C., & Shyamsunder, A. (2018). Leadership development practice bundles and organizational performance: The mediating role of human capital and social capital. *Journal of Business Research*, *83*, 120–129.

Tafvelin, S., Nielsen, K., Schwarz, U., & Stenling, A. (2019). Leading well is a matter of resources: Leader vigour and peer support augments the relationship between transformational leadership and burnout. *Work & Stress*, *33*(2), 156–172.

VanMeter, R., Chonko, L. B., Grisaffe, D. B., & Goad, E. A. (2016). In search of clarity on servant leadership: Domain specification and reconceptualization. *AMS Review*, *6*(1–2), 59–78.

Vergauwe, J., Wille, B., Hofmans, J., Kaiser, R., & De Fruyt, F. (2018). The double-edged sword of leader charisma: Understanding the curvilinear relationship between charismatic personality and leader effectiveness. *Journal of Personality and Social Psychology*, *114*(1), 110–130.

Vieira, V. A., Perin, M. G., & Sampaio, C. H. (2018). The moderating effect of managers' leadership behavior on salespeople's self-efficacy. *Journal of Retailing and Consumer Services*, *40*(1), 150–162.

von Fischer, P., & De Jong, D. (2017). The relationship between teacher perception of principal servant leadership behavior and teacher job satisfaction. *Servant Leadership: Theory & Practice*, *4*(2), 53–84.

Wong, S. (2018). The thin line between empowering and laissez-faire leadership: An expectancy match perspective. *Journal of Management*, *44*(2), 757–783.

Yue, C. A., Men, L. R., & Ferguson, M. A. (2019). Bridging transformational leadership, transparent communication, and employee openness to change: The mediating role of trust. *Public Relations Review*, *45*(3), 101799.

Yukl, G. A. (1994). *Leadership in organizations*. (3rd Ed.). Englewood Cliffs, NJ: Prentice Hall (pp. 53–75).

ONLINE RESOURCES

Association for Supervision and Curriculum Development (ASCD): https://www.ascd.org

Business News Daily: https://www.businessnewsdaily.com/lead-your-team

Free Management Library: https://managementhelp.org

MindTools: https://www.mindtools.com

APPLICATION SHEET 4-1

Initials of the leader you consider to be outstanding: _____.

The personal leadership qualities this person possesses include the following:

APPLICATION SHEET 4-2

Director A:

Director B:

Director C:

Director D:

APPLICATION SHEET 4-3

The title of the book I read was _____.

The major themes and leadership principles presented in this book:

Briefly describe how these principles can be applied in an early childhood program:

APPLICATION SHEET 4-4

My leadership strengths:

My leadership limitations:

The two limitations I would like to improve:

a.

b.

Strategies that will help me achieve my goals include the following:

a.

b.

5

The Art of Effective Communication

OBJECTIVES

After reading this chapter, you will be able to do the following:

- Explain how effective communication contributes to a program's success.
- Define the term *communication*.
- Describe how downward, upward, and grapevine communications differ.
- Discuss why active listening is essential to the communication process.
- Identify barriers that may interfere with mutual understanding.
- Role-play how to provide effective feedback.

KEY TERMS

- communication competence
- transactional
- encode
- perception checking
- decode
- synchronous communication
- asynchronous communication
- two-way communication
- one-way communication
- downward communication
- upward communication
- horizontal communication
- grapevine communication
- constructive feedback

■ ■ ■

The art of communication is the language of leadership.
—James Humes, author

The single biggest problem in communication is the illusion that it has taken place.
—George Bernard Shaw, playwright, Nobel Prize in Literature

INTRODUCTION

Communication is the "glue" that holds an organization together and allows it to function smoothly and efficiently. Leadership sets the tone and determines the quality of communication that takes place. Many successful leaders will tell you that it is one of their most challenging daily tasks and a skill they are often unprepared to perform effectively. Leaders who are poor communicators may fail to understand how their ineffective skills contribute to the organization's struggles. For example, an accreditation visit is unlikely to go well if the program director does not give her teachers advanced notice about documents they need to prepare.

Organizational leaders spend approximately seventy to eighty percent of their day engaged in various communication forms, such as reading reports, writing memos, responding to emails, providing instructions, explaining a policy change, or listening to an employee's concerns (Klemmer & Snyder, 2006; Miller, 2012). In each instance, communication is employed to gather or convey information, express feelings, achieve a goal, and/or influence another person's behavior.

A continuous, open, and transparent flow of information among all participants, including directors, employees, families, and community members, is fundamental to an early childhood program's ability to support its staff and provide high-quality education for children. Motivational leaders quickly realize that communication involves more than simply telling people what to do and how things should be done. Rather, they are able to build trust and positive working relationships by creating a culture that encourages employee input and open communication (Kelly & MacDonald, 2019).

Motivational leaders are good listeners and able to alter their communication style so that it is effective and appropriate for different situations, such as face-to-face, written, emails, telephone, and video communications. They understand and respect the ways in which gender, culture, and other forms of diversity influence communication and an individual's expectations. Failure to master any of these skills will interfere with a leader's **communication competence** and have a direct effect on employees' job satisfaction, engagement, and retention (Brown, Paz-Aparicio, & Revilla, 2019; Kang & Sung, 2017). For example, informing a lead teacher via email that she is being permanently reassigned to another classroom would not be an appropriate method for communicating this change. It is also likely to cause the teacher to feel anger and resentment unless she had previously requested the transfer. Arranging a face-to-face meeting with the teacher is likely to result in a more effective outcome and allow both parties to discuss the reasons for the reassignment, check for understanding, and respond to any other concerns.

WHAT DOES IT MEAN TO COMMUNICATE?

The term *communication* can best be defined as the **transactional** process involved in transmitting a message to another individual or individuals that results in a mutual understanding (Figure 5.1). The key element in this definition is the mutual understanding achieved between sender and recipient(s) when they each interpret a message and arrive at the same intended conclusion. However, this process is not always successful. Say that Teacher A is busy setting the children's tables for lunch. Teacher B, who is across the room, is about to prepare materials for an art project that the children will work on later that afternoon. Without looking up, Teacher A tells Teacher B, "I have everything ready." Teacher B is confused because she does not understand that Teacher A is referring to the lunch tables and not to the art materials that she was to get ready. In other words, the two teachers have not achieved a mutual understanding because they each have interpreted the message differently. Teacher A can eliminate any potential misinterpretation by simply rephrasing her statement to be more explicit. "I have the children's tables set and ready for lunch."

Effective communication involves a multi-step process. The sender first decides who should receive the message and then **encodes** her thoughts into words, symbols, voice tone, facial expressions, gestures, or other communication forms that are most likely to achieve a mutual understanding. Terms that are technical, offensive to some groups, or may have multiple meanings that could potentially be misinterpreted should be avoided:

- "That idea is over the moon."
- "Any imbecile could figure that out."
- "Her decision could put us in a jam."

FIGURE 5.1 Effective communication is essential to a program's success. *Weekend Images Inc.*

The sender must also determine the best time for transmitting the message to an intended recipient(s). For example, it would not be prudent to distribute an important memo at 5:30 p.m. when employees are anxious to go home. If you expect them to read the memo and take action, it would be more effective to deliver the message early the next morning unless a time constraint exists.

The sender must also consider the nature of information to be transmitted when deciding on an appropriate delivery method. For example, informing a teacher of subpar performance in an email may be open to misinterpretation and lead to hostile feelings. In contrast, discussing the matter in a face-to-face meeting with the employee permits clarification, **perception checking**, and an improved chance for achievement of mutual understanding.

When an incoming message is detected, the recipient **decodes** it to the best of his or her ability. This process involves analyzing and interpreting the information in an effort to comprehend its meaning. Ideally, the message is understood as the sender intended, but this is not always the case. Many factors (discussed later in this chapter) can interfere with the communication process and result in an understanding that is different from the sender's vision. Recall that communication is a transactional process. A sender constructs a message (encoding), which is sent to a recipient(s), who interprets it (decoding) and provides verbal and nonverbal feedback in return. The sender is then able to use this information to determine if the communication has been a success or failure.

How We Communicate

Humans communicate through a combination of verbal and nonverbal methods. Verbal communications consist of words or symbols that are used in oral and written interactions. Conversations that take place in real time are referred to as **synchronous communications,** such as face-to-face meetings, telephone calls, video or audio conferencing, FaceTime, live chat, and virtual gaming, either multi-user dimensions [MUDs] or multi-oriented objects [MOOs]. **Asynchronous communications** are described as information exchanges that do not occur in person or simultaneously, such as a memo, handbook, voice mail, text or instant messaging, email, chat room, blog, or other Internet posting.

Nonverbal communications refer to a range of behaviors, including facial expressions, gestures, posture, touch, voice quality (e.g., tone, pitch, rate, volume), eye contact, handshakes, and personal attire that convey information without the use of words. This information provides additional clues about an individual's intentions, level of engagement, understanding, and/or emotional reactions to a message. For example, a person who shows up to a job interview in casual workout clothes does not convey a sense of serious commitment or interest in the position. A weak, timid voice quality may be mistaken for a person's lack of confidence.

In some cases, a person's body language may not be consistent with their comments and reveal more about their true feelings. For example, a teacher who is told that he has not been adhering to an important school policy may nod and utter a verbal agreement while displaying negative behaviors that suggest otherwise, such as frowning, folding his arms across his chest, fidgeting, and/or sighing in displeasure. Consequently, it is important to always engage in perception checking when delivering instructions or feedback. This step provides an opportunity for the sender to ask questions, have the recipient repeat what they have heard, clarify any potential misunderstandings that could lead to distress or job dissatisfaction, and achieve a mutually understood outcome. Although perception checking is easier to conduct during face-to-face (**two-way**) conversations, it can also be achieved in **one-way communications** by noting word choices and the tone of a person's response.

Did You Know? . . . .

Nonverbal communication accounts for more than half of the information relayed in a verbal message.

. . . .

Motivational leaders are sensitive to individual differences that can interfere with effective communications. Personality characteristics, such as shyness and a lack of self-confidence, or cultural values that discourage individuals from challenging authority may restrict an individual's ability to ask questions. Perceptive leaders can initiate steps to overcome these limitations by restating points that are most likely to be misunderstood. For example, individuals whose cultural values discourage the questioning of authority can be encouraged to request clarification at a later time, either in person or through an alternative communication format that he or she may find more comfortable or less intimidating, such as texting, emailing, or talking on the telephone.

COMMUNICATION CHANNELS

A variety of communication channels or formats, including everything from face-to-face meetings, telephone calls, and memos to email, text messages, and video conferencing, are commonly used in today's workplace settings. The sender must consider several factors when determining which of these formats is best suited for disseminating information (Textbox 5.1). If the correct channel is chosen, communication is more likely to be successful and meaningful to the intended recipient(s). Delivering information through a channel that is ineffective for achieving a desired outcome can result in misunderstanding and a loss of trust in leadership.

Face-to-face meetings and telephone calls have a distinct advantage over the use of written media. These formats allow the sender an opportunity to evaluate the recipient's body language and engage in perception checking. Braun et al. (2019) noted that most employees prefer to receive information during face-to-face interactions and that they experience greater job satisfaction as a result. However, conducting in-person meetings to distribute the same information to multiple employees may also not be the most efficient use of a leader's time.

Written communications, such as memos, texts, emails, and blogs, can be an effective, efficient, and, at times, indispensable means to inform employees about an event, policy change, or situation that requires their attention. This format also allows the sender to construct and review a thoughtful message and produces a document that can be retrieved for future reference.

HOW TO DETERMINE THE BEST
COMMUNICATION CHANNEL

Each factor should be weighed carefully to determine which channel is most efficient, effective, and meaningful for achieving successful communications:

- intended audience (e.g., individual, team, or large group; age; cultural and linguistic preferences)
- nature of information to be transmitted (e.g., general, technical, confidential, persuasive)
- time and urgency involved (e.g., brief message versus lengthy instruction; urgent versus no specific hurry)
- importance of maintaining a permanent record
- expense associated with using different formats

However, there are also disadvantages associated with written communications. They must be composed carefully to avoid word choices or a tone that recipients may misinterpret. Unless a timely reply is required, the sender will not know if the message reached the intended recipient(s), if the message was actually read, or if the recipient understood the message as it was originally intended. Who has not observed employee mailboxes—physical and electronic—filled with numerous unopened messages? Written communications also limit opportunities for perception checking and observing the recipient's body language. For these reasons, thoughtful planning must go into composing written communications that are focused, explicit, and meaningful. Once a document has been sent, any misspellings, grammatical errors, or unclear statements cannot be retracted (Textbox 5.2).

In the end, the sender must weigh the advantages and disadvantages of each delivery method to determine the most efficient and appropriate channel for communicating a particular message. For example, sending an announcement to an employee who seldom checks his email may not be the most effective option for informing him about a weekly team meeting. Knowing your target audience and their preferences for receiving and responding to information are essential communication considerations. Senders must also give serious consideration to the most efficient use of their time and communication resources for creating a strong organization.

Communication Pathways

The nature and directional flow of communication in an organization is typically determined by its leadership. For example, a director who maintains an open-door policy and involves employees in policy development sends a strong message that two-way conversation is welcomed and valued. This leader is also more likely to create an organizational culture that is strong and resilient when faced with adversity. In contrast, an administrator who

---

TEXTBOX 5.2

KEYS TO PRODUCING EFFECTIVE WRITTEN COMMUNICATIONS

Well-written documents are more likely to be read and to get results. The ability to produce effective written communications requires the writer to do the following.

- Plan the message. Consider what information to include, the audience for whom the document is intended, and the most effective communication channel for achieving your goal.
- Provide a clear, concise title and purpose statement. Be sure to also date the document.
- Prepare a draft. Use clear and concise sentences to increase the likelihood that the message will be read. Use language that is appropriate for the intended purpose (e.g., instructional, informational, persuasive) and recipient(s); avoid jargon, euphemisms, clichés, and terms that may be unfamiliar to the audience.
- Include a summary statement. Describe any specific action(s) that recipients are expected to take, encourage their questions, and let them know that you appreciate their time and efforts.
- Proofread the document for spelling, grammar, punctuation, sentence structure, and content errors. Ask another person to review the document and provide constructive feedback.
- Revise and distribute the document.

---

keeps her office door closed most of the day or controls all program communications creates quite a different environment that discourages employee commitment.

Several communication pathways are utilized in most organizations. **Downward communications** refer to information, such as messages, policies, handbooks, and requests, that flows from leadership or administration down to employees. This approach can be an efficient and timely way for leaders to deliver some types of information to employees. However, there is also a potential for misinterpretation, conflict, or resentment that may develop among employees who have not been given an opportunity to contribute or respond.

Upward communications describe a pathway whereby employee-generated information, such as grievances, reports, data, and suggestions, is forwarded to leadership. This communication style tends to foster improved employee trust, creativity, productivity, and morale. Researchers have also found that employees experience greater job satisfaction and feel valued, respected, and less frustrated when leadership solicits their contributions (Kremer, Villamor, & Aguinis, 2019; Sadiartha & Sitorus, 2018).

Although upward communication offers several advantages, it also has limitations. Leadership may be confronted with an overabundance of ideas or information that can slow the decision-making process. Additionally, failure to acknowledge or implement employees' suggestions can have a negative effect on morale and their willingness to contribute in the future. Motivational leaders must also help employees to understand that situations will arise from time to time that require an immediate executive decision. Such instances may not permit their involvement or feedback or negate the culture of upward communication that is typically the norm.

Horizontal communications are common in most organizations and represent a third information exchange pathway. In this approach, information is transmitted laterally among similarly ranked employees, as in teacher-to-teacher, paraprofessional-to-paraprofessional, or administrator-to-administrator communications. These interactions can be formal, such as team meetings or memos, and informal, such as hallway conversations and text messages. For example, several teachers may arrange to meet and plan for an upcoming open house, or a child's paraprofessionals may decide to get together and discuss how they can best support his interest in learning to read.

Horizontal communications are ideal for fostering collaboration, creativity, and efficiency when addressing challenging issues. However, they can also create situations in which the group has difficulty agreeing or reaching an acceptable solution and, thus, necessitate a leader's intervention. An effective leader may be able to help the group reach a consensus by providing additional information, clarifying the pros and cons of a solution under consideration, or offering alternative suggestions. In contrast, leaders who are unwilling to get involved or express frustration over the group's failure to achieve a successful outcome convey a lack of empathy and support for their employees.

The term **grapevine communication** is used on occasional to describe impromptu hallway or "watercooler" conversations, rumors, or gossip among employees or supervisors and employees. Gossiping is a common occurrence in workplace settings and serves positive and negative purposes. Sharing information, influencing behavior, fostering or maintaining friendships, relieving stress, and boosting one's own morale can be positive aspects associated with gossip (John et al., 2019). In some situations, a hallway conversation may be the most efficient and timely way to inform other teachers about an important matter, such as finding a wasp nest on the playground or an approaching storm.

However, grapevine communications can also be malicious and a source of misinformation about an individual employee or program. Sudhir (2018) noted that employees engaged in more negative rumor-spreading behavior when they distrusted management, became anxious or felt threatened due to uncertainty in the organization, or lacked self-esteem or self-confidence. Motivational leaders can use this knowledge to foster more dialogue with employees and to discover concerns that may have prompted the rumor(s). They can also improve their own communication quality by being open, honest, and encouraging of employee input.

ACTIVE LISTENING

Listening plays a crucial role in interpersonal communications and is a task that both sender and recipient must engage in to achieve successful information exchange. Active listening involves attending carefully to a speaker's message, evaluating the information (decoding), organizing one's thoughts, and then responding based upon a perceived understanding (Figure 5.2).

Active listening requires the recipient to focus on words that are spoken (including voice quality) as well as to observe the sender's body language, such as facial expressions, posture,

FIGURE 5.2 Active listening.

gestures, and mood for additional clues (Textbox 5.3). Studies have shown that listeners form a "first" impression of the speaker, based on nonverbal cues, within the first few seconds of contact. This appears to be an automatic and unconscious process that may account for more than fifty percent of an interpreted message (Hall, Horgan, & Murphy, 2019).

An active listener must concentrate on the message being delivered. However, remaining focused can be challenging given that humans are able to process information four times faster than a person speaks. The listener must also reserve judgment until the sender has finished delivering his or her message. This reduces the potential for becoming distracted by thoughts about what is or is not being said. It also encourages the listener to hear all that a speaker has to say (Itzchakov et al., 2018; Spataro & Bloch, 2018).

TEXTBOX 5.3

IMPROVE YOUR LISTENING SKILLS!

With practice, you can improve your listening skills with these methods:

- Devoting your full attention to the speaker. Save daydreaming, distracting thoughts, texting, and checking your watch until you are alone.
- Being courteous and allowing the speaker to finish without interruption.
- Keeping your emotions in check until the speaker has finished.
- Showing genuine interest by maintaining eye contact. Also note the speaker's mannerisms, voice tone, and word selection—all convey subtle, but important messages.
- Trying to understand the speaker's perspective and agenda.
- Reserving preconceived judgments about the topic or speaker's intentions until you have had a chance to clarify your interpretations.
- Restating what you have heard during the conversation to determine if your understanding is accurate and what the speaker envisioned. Use reflective statements such as, "If I understand correctly, you are suggesting . . ." or "My understanding is that we will be . . ."
- Asking open-ended questions after the speaker has finished talking. This is an opportunity to correct any potential misunderstandings and conveys a genuine interest in what the speaker had to say. "What outcomes do you anticipate?" "How soon would you like to have us implement this policy change?"

DIRECTOR'S SHOWCASE

What are some of the ways you try to maintain good communication with your staff?

I make a point of walking around the building at different times during the day to talk with the teachers, even if it is just a quick "hello, is there anything I can do for you" inquiry. This helps me to stay in touch with things going on in the classrooms. It also lets my employees know that I am interested in what they are doing and appreciate their efforts. Sometimes I can retrieve a book from another classroom or make a phone call to help out a busy teacher. We also hold weekly staff meetings because I believe it is important for everyone to be up-to-date and on the same page with things that are happening. I know that good communication is the reason our program continues to be successful.

—Rosa R., director

Did You Know? ·

Seventy-five to eighty percent of all employee-related problems in the workplace are due to ineffective communication.

· ·

—————————— *Connecting Points* ——————————

Your dentist scheduled you in for an emergency appointment over the lunch hour. Before you leave, you and your assistant teacher set the tables for lunch and make sure the children wash their hands so they are ready to eat when the substitute arrives. As you head out, you stop by the director's office to let her know that you are leaving and to report a minor incident that occurred earlier in the day. She is talking on the telephone, but motions for you to come in and sit down. When the call ends, she smiles, asks if everything is okay, and then turns to her computer to answer an email while you explain the incident.

- What direct or indirect message(s) is the director's nonverbal behavior conveying?
- How would this experience make you feel?
- What effect is the director's behavior likely to have on the quality of communication that occurs?
- What suggestions would you have to improve the director's active listening skills?

COMMUNICATION BARRIERS

It is easy to assume that communication is a simple and straightforward process. A sender composes a meaningful message, determines an appropriate time and method for delivery, and then forwards it to an intended recipient or recipients. However, several barriers can act as filters that disrupt the successful exchange of information. Recognizing this potential in advance enables participants to take steps that can improve the quality of all communications (Figure 5.3).

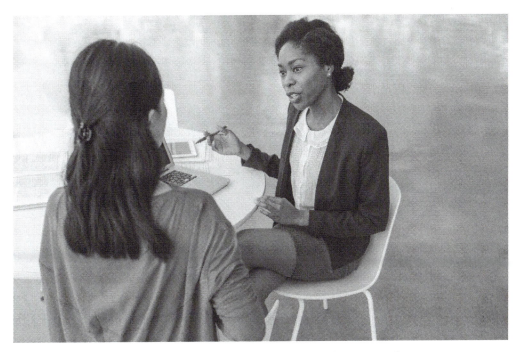

FIGURE 5.3 Many barriers can interfere with the effectiveness of information exchanges.
kate_sept2004, E+

Environmental Barriers

Environmental conditions, including setting and location, are known to affect the quality of communication exchanges (Shannon et al., 2019). For example, background noise emanating from a ringing telephone, children's laughter, music, or people talking nearby can be distracting and interfere with the receiver's ability to hear and understand what is being said. Distractions, such as these, can easily be eliminated by closing an office door, moving to a quiet room, or temporarily muting a telephone until the conversation is over (unless this is the delivery method being used). A cluttered room or uncomfortable furniture (e.g., a broken chair spring, a chair that is too soft or too hard, an unpleasant odor) may also interfere with active listening. Room temperature (e.g., too warm, too cold) may cause an individual to focus on personal comfort and not on the message being conveyed. Timing is also important to consider. An employee who is preoccupied by fatigue, hunger, discomfort, or illness will have difficulty concentrating and recalling conversation details. Neuroscientists have found that these conditions trigger biochemical changes that can increase impatient behavior, negative emotions, and irrational decision-making (Orquin & Kurzban, 2016; Verhulst et al., 2019).

Stans et al. (2017) noted that the quality of client attention and frequency of interactions improved significantly when simple steps were taken to provide comfortable surroundings. Examples of such measures included providing adequate lighting, quiet acoustics, comfortable temperature and humidity, careful furniture placement, and the availability of paper and pen. Their results suggest that leaders give careful consideration to the room environment, especially if they are presenting employees with information that is complex, unexpected, critical, or likely to arouse questions or an emotional response.

Perceptual Barriers

Personal values and life experiences also influence the ways in which an individual interprets and responds to information. For example, certain words or phrases may trigger positive or negative feelings associated with a former experience. Topics such as religion, politics, racism, and sexuality that many people find offensive or emotionally laden can also form a perceptual or psychological barrier that causes the receiver to make assumptions about the speaker and stop listening to what the person has to say.

Although it is preferable to avoid discussing sensitive topics in the workplace, they may come up in casual conversation from time to time. When they do, it is important that strong personal opinions and persuasive efforts be kept out of the conversation. If individuals feel harassed or threatened by such comments, they should express their discomfort and step away from the conversation. Leadership should be made aware if these situations continue so that the inappropriate behavior can be stopped. It is also important that programs develop workplace policies regarding issues such as solicitation, religious and political expressions, and holiday celebrations and include them in their employee handbook.

Negative interactions or prior conflict with a colleague can also serve as perceptual barriers. For example, a teacher who been subjected to these behaviors is likely to have difficulty remaining nonjudgmental and communicating effectively with this person in the future. For some individuals, a speaker's appearance, mannerisms, or voice quality may also serve as a perceptual barrier or distractor that causes them to focus on the behavior and fail to listen to what is being said. In each case, the individual's internal emotional response to a situation results in a perceptual barrier or preconceived bias that interferes with their ability to remain objective. As a result, effective communication is diminished because the recipient is no longer able to engage in active listening.

Semantic Barriers

Words, language, or symbols that have multiple meanings can create a semantic barrier, which may cause the recipient to misinterpret a message that is being conveyed. Semantic barriers are especially problematic for nonnative speakers because countless English words sound alike but have quite different meanings (Figure 5.4). For example, many word pairs share the same pronunciations but their spelling differs (homophones): here/hear, write/right, jeans/genes, bale/bail, and die/dye. Words that are spelled and pronounced the same but have distinctly different meanings (homonyms), such as nail (a fingernail or nails used in construction), present (to be in a certain place or a gift), or tear (a torn paper or fabric or a drop of moisture from a person's eye), can also be confusing. When these words are spoken quickly, nonnative listeners may not have enough time to put the word into its proper context. Is it any wonder that a message can so easily be misunderstood?

Technical jargon and the use of clichés can also lead to semantic confusion, especially if an individual or audience does not share a common background with the sender. Unfamiliar or potentially confusing words should be explained when they are first used. This approach mitigates a recipient's distraction from active listening as the conversation progresses. Jokes

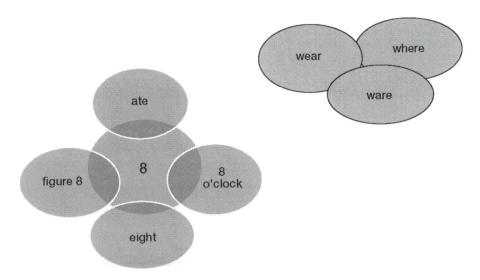

FIGURE 5.4 Semantic confusion.

and humorous comments can also result in semantic confusion. Although some people may find them funny, cross-cultural and gender differences in humor styles may hurt or offend some people. These situations can be avoided altogether by simply refraining from their usage, especially in the workplace.

Cross-Cultural Barriers

Cultural variations in language, communication styles, and tradition can also serve as barriers to effective communication. Words that do not exist or may have quite different meanings in another language can interfere with an employee's ability to fully comprehend information presented in a memo or conversation (Kemp, Xu, & Regier, 2018). A speaker's dialect may distort word pronunciations or sentence order, making it difficult for a listener to remain focused on the conversation. In some instances, listeners may nod their head in agreement to simply avoid embarrassment even though they do not understand what is being said (Maneze et al., 2016).

Silence is another communication form that can create a cross-cultural barrier unless its purpose is fully understood. Prolonged pauses are not typical in most Western conversations and may be mistaken for an individual's disinterest or lack of anything substantial to say. However, silence is considered a sign of respect, politeness, and contemplation in many Asian cultures (Cai, 2019; Wells, 2018). Similarly, interrupting a person while they are speaking or not maintaining eye contact may be considered rude in Western cultures, but is considered customary in others. Additionally, a failure to respect cultural norms that govern the concept of personal space may cause a person to feel uncomfortable and stop listening (Sorokowska et al., 2019). For example, Russians and Middle Easterners prefer to stand in close proximity to one another when conversing and consider a person who maintains a greater distance as being cold and unfriendly. In contrast, the Japanese are protective of their personal space. They typically do not engage in touching one another and will stand two to three feet away from an individual with whom they are speaking.

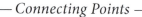
Connecting Points

Numerous studies have shown that humor, when used appropriately in the workplace, can reduce stress, increase employees' productivity and positive emotions, build trust, and bring individuals closer together. In fact, a good sense of humor is considered to be a highly desirable leadership trait. Southwest Airlines actually encourages its flight attendants to use humor for entertaining passengers and putting them at ease.

- How can motivational leaders use humor to promote and enhance communication within their organization?
- What are some potential risks associated with the use of humor?
- What qualities are likely to make an intentional joke appropriate or inappropriate?

There are obviously many linguistic and cross-cultural variations that influence communication styles and expectations (Textbox 5.4). Leaders who educate themselves about these individual differences are able to communicate more effectively with a workforce and family population that is becoming increasingly diverse. However, leaders must also avoid making assumptions based upon a person's presumed country of origin. Immigrants who have been naturalized and their children may gradually adapt communication patterns of the country in which they are now living. It should also be remembered that information about communication styles reflects generalities and may not be applicable to all individuals or regions of a specific country. Additionally, long-held communication customs in many countries are gradually changing as a result of social media exposure and worldwide travel.

Communication misunderstandings are less likely to occur if steps are taken to respect cross-cultural and linguistic differences, empathize with the participants, use uncomplicated language, talk slowly (not louder), listen carefully, summarize, and encourage questions. However, remember that communication errors are inevitable despite these efforts, but that listeners will appreciate and respect a leader's best efforts.

Gender Barriers
Language and communication styles, both verbal and nonverbal, are known to differ among men and women. For example, females in Western cultures are often thought to talk more frequently than males, engage in longer discussions, ask more questions, and interrupt more often during conversations (Chan & Hardono, 2018; Coates, 2015). Similarly, men employ a communication style (oral and written) that tends to be brief, direct (to-the-point), and somewhat impersonal, whereas women are more likely to use language that is descriptive, caring, and personal (e.g., feelings, thoughts, beliefs) (Park et al., 2016; Wainwright, 2019). Women are also more likely than men to be affected by comments and to read unintended meanings into a message (Magee & Upenieks, 2019).

A SAMPLING OF CROSS-CULTURAL DIFFERENCES IN BODY LANGUAGE CUSTOMS

Gestures commonly used in one culture may be viewed differently in another. Awareness is essential to avoiding behaviors that could be interpreted as rude or offensive.

- "Thumbs up"—often used as a sign of approval or for hitchhiking; considered offensive, rude, and an insult in the Middle East, Australia, Germany, Nigeria, and Bangladesh.
- "Okay" sign (fingertip to thumb)—indicates approval or that things are acceptable in many English-speaking countries; viewed as rude in Brazil and Argentina, or that you consider the person to be homosexual in Greece and Turkey.
- "V" or peace sign—conveys a message of peace or goodwill; when used with back of hand facing the recipient, it is considered extremely insulting in the United Kingdom, Australia, New Zealand, and South Africa.
- Hands in pocket—may indicate comfort or at ease; considered rude in countries such as Mexico, Thailand, Switzerland, Poland, and the Netherlands.
- Pointing—often considered an innocuous gesture in the United States; however, viewed as impolite and rude in many countries including Korea, Japan, China, Germany, Russia, Italy, and Latin America.
- Checking your watch—may be interpreted as a signal that you are in a hurry; this act would be considered rude in many Spanish and Middle Eastern cultures.
- Handshake—expected to be offered with a firm grip in many Western cultures; tend to last longer among Middle Easterners; a bow is often preferred in China and Japan.
- Sitting with legs crossed—given little thought in many countries; however, considered to be disrespectful in Japan, especially if the conversation participants are older.

Researchers have determined that many gendered communication patterns are learned through early socialization processes (Knothe & Walle, 2018). These findings reinforce the importance of supporting young children's development of cross-gender communication skills and the early elimination of communication biases (Xiao et al., 2019).

Gender differences are also evident in the display of nonverbal communications. Women are inclined to speak in a higher and softer voice tone, touch or move near the person with whom they are speaking, maintain eye contact, and display emotions through a range of facial expressions (Grebelsky-Lichtman & Katz, 2019; Hall, Horgan, & Murphy, 2019). In contrast, men tend to speak in a tone that is lower and strong or forceful. They also display fewer facial expressions than women, typically face the person directly with whom they are speaking, and often offer a firm handshake or pat on the back. Such observations have been reported in studies that are focused on Western nonverbal communication styles and are not present in all cultures.

Cultural norms often define the way in which some nonverbal behaviors, such as touch or eye contact, are also communicated among genders. For example, in many Asian and Middle Eastern societies it is considered improper to touch a person of the opposite gender who is not a family member (International Institute of Minnesota, 2019). In contrast, a pat on the back, handshake, or kiss on both checks are greeting practices commonly displayed among Italians. Maintaining eye contact is expected in many Western cultures. However, some Native American, Latin American, African, and Asian groups consider it impolite to gaze directly at a person of the opposite gender or someone who is in a position of authority.

Clearly, it is important that motivational leaders be familiar with the different ways in which genders communicate in their own and other cultures. This effort conveys respect, improves the effectiveness of information exchanges, and avoids making stereotypical assumptions that may be incorrect. Leaders should also take time to examine job descriptions, interview questions, performance reviews, program policies, and other documents for signs of unintentional gender bias in language that is used.

Generational Barriers

Stereotypical assumptions about the communication preferences associated with each generational employee cohort are common (Table 5.1). However, such assumptions should be regarded with caution because they often are not representative of all individuals within a designated age group. Empirical research results have shown that cohort groups actually have more communication usage and preferences in common than was originally thought (Glazer, Mahoney, & Randall, 2019; Van Rossem, 2019). Younger generations have grown up with technology, are tech savvy, and rely heavily on electronic devices for most communications. However, studies have shown that Baby Boomers and Gen Xers also embrace and are adept at using it for multiple purposes.

Although employees in all generational cohorts may use various electronic communication forms, they still prefer face-to-face, direct, and frequent interactions with their colleagues and supervisors (Braun et al., 2019; Stanton, 2017). For example, Braun et al. (2019)

Table 5.1: Suggested Generational Communication Preferences

Communication Preferences	
➢ Baby Boomer (born 1944 to 1964)	Person-to-person, written document; telephone conversation or voice mail. Prefers periodic feedback and face-to-face interactions.
➢ Generation X (born 1965 to 1980)	Person-to-person; email; texting. Prefers email and brief, to-the-point messages.
➢ Millennials (born 1981 to 1996)	Social media; text messaging. Relies on smartphone and apps for researching and texting.
➢ Generation Z (born after 1997)	Instant messaging; video chat. Prefers information that is immediate, brief, and to-the-point.

noted that employees perceive in-person communication to be of a higher quality than email or telephone messages and, thus, preferred having more information delivered in this form. Such research results are not surprising because they underline the value attached to open, high-quality communication, opportunities for perception checking, and personal interaction. An organizational shift from a top-down management style toward a more collaborative team approach has also contributed to an employee preference for frequent, transparent, and in-person communication.

Successful leaders are able to look beyond age stereotypes and recognize that communication differences among employees will always exist to some extent in any workplace. However, those who understand the fundamental communication process, including barriers that can interfere with information transmission, will be able to implement strategies that create an effective and collaborative work environment (Textbox 5.5).

TEXTBOX 5.5

STRATEGIES FOR IMPROVING INTERGENERATIONAL COMMUNICATION

Steps that leaders can take to promote effective communication among employees of all ages include the following:

- Meeting with individual employees to learn about their communication preferences. Note when a person indicates a favorite method or has a special need, such as a hearing loss or language deficiency, that may require information to be provided in an alternative format.
- Accepting and respecting individual employees' communication differences. For example, a Baby Boomer may expect a performance review to be conducted in a formal manner whereas a Gen X employee may be more comfortable with a relaxed conversational style.
- Being open and receptive to change. Your preferred mode for communicating with employees may not be their preferred way to receive information. Remember the goal is to achieve mutual understanding. It may be necessary and easier for you to alter your style than to expect others to change theirs.
- Mentoring or providing training for employees who may not be familiar with or comfortable using various communication technologies, such as file-sharing, video-conferencing, digital business management tools, or instant messaging.
- Listening to employees' most recent comments and feedback. An employee's communication preference stated two years ago may no longer be relevant.

Information Overload

Early childhood leaders and program personnel spend a majority of their day communicating with different audiences. They read, write, listen, and interact with children, parents, administrators, colleagues, and community leaders continuously. Although sharing and receiving information are essential to performing their job, exposure to too much information can become a barrier to accomplishing it effectively (Roetzel, 2019).

Neuroscience has shown that the human brain is able to process and store only so much information in working memory at any given time before it essentially shuts down (Byyny, 2016; Reutskaja et al., 2018). At this point, a person begins to lose focus, stops listening or only hears a portion of what is being said, becomes anxious, or feels overwhelmed. When this occurs, a person's thought-processes slow down, and their ability to make sound decisions is diminished.

Information overload can be avoided by limiting the amount of material provided at any one time (e.g., reducing the extensive instructions often presented during a new employee orientation). Delivering information slowly and in clear, concise terms allows the recipient time to process what is being heard and to ask for clarification if necessary. Encouraging recipients to take notes or providing them with a written copy of any instructions or feedback also improves understanding and recall.

PROVIDING EFFECTIVE FEEDBACK

Motivational leaders play a major role in inspiring employee performance and job satisfaction. One way they accomplish this is by maintaining open communication and creating an environment in which employees feel comfortable seeking and receiving feedback (Figure 5.5). Time taken to acknowledge employees' efforts and to identify things that may require

FIGURE 5.5 Information provided in clear, concise terms is more likely to be understood and remembered. *SDI Productions*

improvement can significantly enhance trust, morale, and self-efficacy (Chordiya, Sabhar-wal, & Battaglio, 2019; Szeto & Cheng, 2018).

When **constructive feedback** is provided regularly, versus once or twice a year during the often-dreaded performance review, employees are able to address problematic behaviors and improve their skills in a timely manner. Feedback that is provided more often also eliminates prolonged concerns about an employee's unacceptable performance that may affect other personnel and program quality. However, providing corrective feedback too often can have a negative effect on employee self-esteem and performance (Pichler, Beenen, & Wood, 2018).

Leaders who have limited administrative experience may find it difficult to discuss unacceptable performance with employees. Some are reluctant to draw attention to performance that requires improvement because they fear that doing so may be upsetting and cause the individual to leave. These conversations generally become easier and less uncomfortable with time and practice. Also, keep in mind that employees want to know how they are doing and that withholding appraisal information can be detrimental to their performance, job satisfaction, and personal growth (Cappelli & Conyon, 2018).

Motivational leaders understand that two-way communication and active listening are essential if feedback is to be meaningful and constructive. They know that a positive outcome also requires mutual respect and trust. Thus, to be effective, constructive feedback should be

- *timely*—positive and negative comments should be provided soon after a specific behavior or event has occurred. Praising an employee's success in calming an upset parent will have limited meaning if it is delayed until an annual performance review six months later. Similarly, an employee's failure to wash her hands before serving food may continue for months if it is not addressed immediately. Employees prefer to receive feedback shortly after an event has occurred so they understand the relationship between their behavior and its consequence and can take steps to address any deficiency (Kuvaas, Buch, & Dysvik, 2017).

- *objective and nonjudgmental*—feedback is, in essence, an evaluation of an employee's performance and whether it meets or fails to meet expected standards. Feedback must be based on observational data, not hearsay or assumptions. Conclusions formed on impressions may be judgmental and inaccurate. For example, you notice that the center's cook has arrived late to work twice this week. Although it would be easy to accuse her of tardiness, you decide to stop by the kitchen and ask if everything is okay. She apologizes for being late but explains that she had to pick up several lunch items from the grocery store that were not available when she shopped earlier in the week. In other words, she was trying to be conscientious in performing her job and was not being disrespectful of program policies. Feedback must also be presented in a communicative manner that is respectful of individual employees' culture and gender differences and makes them feel included.

- *descriptive*—feedback should always include a clear statement that describes the specific behavior in question. For example, "I noticed that three children did not wash their hands before sitting down for lunch today" instead of "You failed to notice that several children did not wash their hands today." The first statement focuses on the problem and is not directed at the person per se. Framing statements from an "I" perspective eliminates an accusatory tone and, thus, reduces the tendency for the individual to feel threatened or to react defensively to negative feedback. The same approach should be used when providing positive feedback. For example, "I noticed how quickly you responded and were able to calm Kami down after she threw the book at Ayana," rather than "You did a great job today." Focusing on a specific behavior informs the employee about actions that may need improvement or reinforces things they are already doing well.

- *reasonably frequent*—constructive feedback is important to provide for all employees but especially for those who may be new to the job, learning a new skill, or working under challenging circumstances (Ansley, Houchins, & Varjas, 2019). Frequent suggestions offered in a constructive manner can accelerate the learning process and help an employee from repeating the same mistakes. However, all employees value and need leadership's support. Hearing that you are on the right track or doing quality work is motivating and satisfies fundamental human psychological needs for belonging and self-actualization (Olencevicius & Dilling-Hansen, 2019).

Feedback should always be delivered in private and during a time that is mutually convenient. Unless there is an immediate safety risk involved, an employee should never be singled out, criticized, or reprimanded in a public area. This also holds true for praising an employee who might otherwise be embarrassed by unsolicited attention. The meeting should take place in a quiet, comfortable area that is conducive to a two-way conversation.

A few positive comments about the employee's performance to date can be offered before stating the meeting's intended purpose. Ample time should then be devoted to discussing the event or behavior that is of concern and allow for the employee's questions. The employee should also be involved in identifying specific suggestions to improve their future performance. This often-overlooked step is important because it conveys the leader's trust in the employee and supports their continued development. Offering constructive feedback also ends the discussion on a positive note and is more likely to motivate an employee to follow through with recommendations. Before the meeting ends, the employee should receive a copy of the evaluation so that any misunderstandings can be corrected (perception checking), and be reassured that continued mentoring and support will be provided. It is also important to place a dated copy of the evaluation form along with any additional comments from the meeting in the employee's file.

SUMMARY

- Communication involves a successful flow of information between a sender and intended recipient(s). Communication is only effective if it results in a mutual understanding.
- Various channels can be used to deliver information to other individuals. Choosing the most effective method depends upon several basic factors, including the recipient audience, type of information to be disseminated, time factor, whether a permanent record or response is desired, and expense involved in distributing the message.

- Active listening is an essential component of successful communications. The listener must focus on the speaker's words and body language, interpret the message being delivered, ask questions to clarify any potential misunderstandings, and respond appropriately if required.
- Factors such as environmental noise, semantics, gender, culture, and generational differences can serve as barriers that interfere with communication quality. Motivational leaders must be aware of these possibilities and take steps in advance to address them.
- Employees want and expect their leaders to provide feedback. When feedback is timely, relatively frequent, objective, descriptive, and constructive, it builds trust and allows employees to improve their performance.

APPLICATION ACTIVITIES

1. In two sentences, describe on Application Sheet 5-1 what you believe is occurring in the following scenario and explain how you think the director should respond to achieve successful communication: Li Min's parents smile and nod their heads several times when the program director asks them to bring in their child's notarized health forms. A week later, they still have not provided the requested materials.
2. Set a timer for three minutes and take the quiz on Application Sheet 5-2 to test your decoding skills.
3. Create a written set of step-by-step instructions for how to tie a shoe (use Application Sheet 5-3). Exchange your paper with another student or colleague and follow their instructions *exactly* as they are written. Evaluate the outcome, and comment on the quality of instructions that were communicated. Were the instructions clear, easy to follow, and meaningful? What did this activity teach you about communication? If the outcome was not satisfactory, revise the instructions that you were given.
4. Rewrite the following as "I" statements (use Application Sheet 5-4):
   - That isn't the way to mix the tempera paints.
   - You always put the children's toothbrushes in the wrong cabinet.
   - Why do you always ask to leave early on Fridays?
   - You forgot to fill out the medication administration form.

   Explain why "I" statements are a more effective way to provide constructive feedback.

REVIEW POINTS

1. Recall the game "telephone" that you may have played as a child. (A short statement is whispered from one person to another, with the last person repeating out loud what they have heard.) Explain why the final version is usually quite different from the original statement.
2. If you were blind or visually impaired, what nonverbal sources could you utilize to obtain additional clues or information about a verbal message that is being communicated?
3. What are communication barriers? Identify two different barrier categories and describe how each can potentially interfere with communication quality.

4. Review the following memo that was delivered to the staff at a local early childhood program: "An hour-long training session will be held on Thursday to review the use of epinephrine auto-injector pens and their potential adverse effects. If you are unsure about how to use this device, you should attend." Critique and discuss the memo's effectiveness in communicating the director's intentions. Finally, revise the memo so that it is meaningful.

KEY TERMS DEFINED

communication competence—knowledge of effective and appropriate communication (e.g., language, grammar, rules, styles, barriers) to achieve meaning that is mutually understood

transactional—a give-and-take exchange of information between a sender and recipient

encode—the process used to translate thoughts or ideas into words or expressions that another individual will understand

perception checking—a strategy used to determine another person's understanding of information that has been communicated

decode—the mental process used to translate what is heard into thoughts or ideas

synchronous communication—a face-to-face or real-time exchange of information between sender and recipient(s)

asynchronous communication—information exchanges that do not occur in person or simultaneously (e.g., memo, voice mail, text message, blog, email)

two-way communication—a back-and-forth exchange of information between sender and recipient

one-way communication—information that is only transmitted from sender to recipient

downward communication—information that flows from leadership to subordinates

upward communication—information that flows up the administrative hierarchy, from subordinates to administration

horizontal communication—information that flows laterally among individuals on a similar hierarchy level

grapevine communication—informal hallway or "watercooler" conversations, rumors, or gossip that take place among employees or supervisors and employees

constructive feedback—information that is specific, nonjudgmental, and meaningful regarding an employee's performance and opportunities for improvement

REFERENCES

Ansley, B., Houchins, D., & Varjas, K. (2019). Cultivating positive work contexts that promote teacher job satisfaction and retention in high-need schools. *Journal of Special Education Leadership, 32*(1), 3–16.

Braun, S., Bark, A., Kirchner, A., Stegmann, S., & van Dick, R. (2019). Emails from the boss—Curse or blessing? Relations between communication channels, leader evaluation, and employees' attitudes. *International Journal of Business Communication, 56*(1), 50–81.

Brown, O., Paz-Aparicio, C., & Revilla, A. J. (2019). Leader's communication style, LMX and organizational commitment: A study of employee perceptions in Peru. *Leadership & Organization Development Journal, 40*(2), 230–258.

Byyny, R. (2016). Information and cognitive overload. How much is too much? Retrieved from https://pdfs.semanticscholar.org/8a20/267e9d262ee2ef8ffd227b16d7574769f375.pdf.

Cai, M. (2019). Reflection of cultural difference of the East and the West in nonverbal communication. 1st International Symposium on Education, Culture and Social Sciences (ECSS 2019). *Advances in Social Science, Education, and the Humanities Research, 311*, 288–296. Retrieved from https://doi.org/10.2991/ecss-19.2019.59.

Cappelli, P., & Conyon, M. J. (2018). What do performance appraisals do? *ILR Review, 71*(1), 88–116.

Chan, N., & Hardono, S. (2018). Difference between women's speech and men's speech in a conversation. *Asian Journal of Technical Vocational Education and Training, 5*, 50–54.

Chordiya, R., Sabharwal, M., & Battaglio, R. P. (2019). Dispositional and organizational sources of job satisfaction: A cross-national study. *Public Management Review, 21*(8), 1101–1124.

Coates, J. (2015). *Women, men and language: A sociolinguistic account of gender differences in language.* (3rd Ed.). United Kingdom: Routledge.

Glazer, S., Mahoney, A., & Randall, Y. (2019). Employee development's role in organizational commitment: A preliminary investigation comparing generation X and millennial employees. *Industrial and Commercial Training, 51*(1), 1–12.

Grebelsky-Lichtman, T., & Katz, R. (2019). When a man debates a woman: Trump vs. Clinton in the first mixed gender presidential debates. *Journal of Gender Studies, 28*(6), 699–719.

Hall, J., Horgan, T., & Murphy, N. (2019). Nonverbal communication. *Annual Review of Psychology, 70*(1), 271–294.

International Institute of Minnesota. (2019). Body language and personal space. Retrieved from https://iimn.org/publication/finding-common-ground/culture-at-work/body-language-personal-space/.

Itzchakov, G., DeMarree, K., Kluger, A., & Turjeman-Levi, Y. (2018). The listener sets the tone: High-quality listening increases attitude clarity and behavior-intention consequences. *Personality and Social Psychology Bulletin, 44*(5), 762–778.

John, A., Bakar, A., Nayan, L., Rosli, M., & Rashid, A. (2019). Relationship between quality and gossiping behavior at workplace. *Proceedings of the Regional Conference on Science, Technology, and Social Sciences* (RCSTSS 2016). Springer, Singapore.

Kang, M., & Sung, M. (2017). How symmetrical employee communication leads to employee engagement and positive employee communication behaviors: The mediation of employee-organization relationships. *Journal of Communication Management, 21*(1), 82–102.

Kelly, S., & MacDonald, P. (2019). A look at leadership styles and workplace solidarity communication. *International Journal of Business Communication, 56*(3), 432–448.

Kemp, C., Xu, Y., & Regier, T. (2018). Semantic typology and efficient communication. *Annual Review of Linguistics, 4*(1), 109–128.

Klemmer, E., & Snyder, F. (2006). Measurement of time spent communicating. *Journal of Communication, 22*, 142–158.

Knothe, J. M., & Walle, E. A. (2018). Parental communication about emotional contexts: Differences across discrete categories of emotion. *Social Development, 27*(2), 247–261.

Kremer, H., Villamor, I., & Aguinis, H. (2019). Innovation leadership: Best-practice recommendations for promoting employee creativity, voice, and knowledge sharing. *Business Horizons, 62*(1), 65–74.

Kuvaas, B., Buch, R., & Dysvik, A. (2017). Constructive supervisor feedback is not sufficient: Immediacy and frequency is essential. *Human Resource Management, 56*(3), 519–531.

Magee, W., & Upenieks, L. (2019). Gender differences in self-esteem, unvarnished self-evaluation, future orientation, self-enhancement and self-derogation in a U.S. national sample. *Personality and Individual Differences, 149*, 66–77.

Maneze, D., Everett, B., Kirby, S., DiGiacomo, M., Davidson, P., & Salamonson, Y. (2016). "I have only little English": Language anxiety of Filipino migrants with chronic disease. *Ethnicity & Health*, *21*(6), 596–608.

Miller, P. (2012). Leadership communication: The three levels. *SIM Today's Manager* (February–March), 19–21.

Olencevicius, S., & Dilling-Hansen, M. (2019). Relation between proper management, feedback frequency and employee age. *Journal of Organizational Psychology*, *19*(2), 111–122.

Orquin, J. L., & Kurzban, R. (2016). A meta-analysis of blood glucose effects on human decision making. *Psychological Bulletin*, *142*(5), 546–567.

Park, G., Yaden, D., Schwartz, H., Kern, M., Eichstaedt, J., Kosinski, M., Stillwell, D., Ungar, L. H., & Seligman, M. (2016). Women are warmer but no less assertive than men: Gender and language on Facebook. *PLoS ONE*, *11*(5): e0155885.

Pichler, S., Beenen, G., & Wood, S. (2018). Feedback frequency and appraisal reactions: A meta-analytic test of moderators. *The International Journal of Human Resource Management*, *2017*(1), 10366–10372.

Reutskaja, E., Lindner, A., Nagel, R., Andersen, R. A., & Camerer, C. R. (2018). Choice overload reduces neural signatures of choice set value in dorsal striatum and anterior cingulate cortex. *Nature Human Behaviour*, *2*, 925–935.

Roetzel, P. G. (2019). Information overload in the information age: A review of the literature from business administration, business psychology, and related disciplines with a bibliometric approach and framework development. *Business Research*, *12*, 479–522.

Sadiartha, A. A., & Sitorus, S. (2018). Organizational culture, communication and leadership style on job satisfaction. *International Journal of Research in Business and Social Science 7*(4), 1–9.

Shannon, M., Elf, M., Churilov, L., Olver, J., Pert, A., & Bernhardt, J. (2019). Can the physical environment itself influence neurological patient activity? *Disability and Rehabilitation*, *41*(10), 1177–1189.

Sorokowska, A., Sorokowski, P., Hilpert, P., Cantarero, K., Frackowiak, T., Khodabakhsh, A., Alghraibeh, A. M., Aryeetey, R., Bertoni, A., Bettache, K., Blumen, S., Blazejewska, M., Bortolini, T., Butovskaya, M., Castro, F., Cetinkaya, H., Cunha, D., David, D., David, O. A., Pierce, J. (2019). Preferred interpersonal distances: A global comparison. *Journal of Cross-Cultural Psychology*, *48*(4), 577–592.

Spataro, S., & Bloch, J. (2018). "Can you repeat that?" Teaching active listening in management education. *Journal of Management Education*, *42*(2), 168–198.

Stans, S., Dalemans, R., de Witte, L., Smeets, H., & Beurskens, A. (2017). The role of the physical environment in conversations between people who are communication vulnerable and health-care professionals: A scoping review. *Disability and Rehabilitation*, *39*(25), 2594–2605.

Stanton, R. (2017). Communicating with employees: Resisting the stereotypes of generational cohorts in the workplace. *IEEE Transactions on Professional Communication*, *60*(3), 256–272.

Sudhir, S. (2018). Rumors in organizational communication: A nightmare for HR managers. *Human Resource Management International Digest*, *26*(5), 18–21.

Szeto, E., & Cheng, A. (2018). Principal–teacher interactions and teacher leadership development: Beginning teachers' perspectives. *International Journal of Leadership in Education*, *21*(3), 363–379.

Van Rossem, A. (2019). Generations as social categories: An exploratory cognitive study of generational identity and generational stereotypes in a multigenerational workforce. *Journal of Organizational Behavior*, *40*(4), 434–455.

Verhulst, N., De Keyser, A., Gustafsson, A., Shams, P., & Van Vaerenbergh, Y. (2019). Neuroscience in service research: An overview and discussion of its possibilities. *Journal of Service Management*, *30*(5), 621–649.

Wainwright, A. (2019). Gender differences in the narrative productions of African American adults. *American Journal of Speech-Language Pathology*, *28*(2), 623–638.

Wells, A. (2018). Communication is culture. In *The tech professional's guide to communicating in a global workplace*. Berkeley, CA: Apress.

Xiao, S., Cook, R., Martin, C., Nielson, M., & Field, R. (2019). Will they listen to me? An examination of in-group gender bias in children's communication beliefs. *Sex Roles*, *80*(3–4), 172–185.

ONLINE RESOURCES

Institute for Public Relations: https://instituteforpr.org/organizational-communication-research

McCormick Center for Early Childhood Leadership: https://mccormickcenter.nl.edu/

Society for Human Resource Management: https://www.shrm.org/resourcesandtools/tools-and -samples/toolkits/pages/managingorganizationalcommunication.aspx

The Community Toolbox (see chapter 15, section 4): https://ctb.ku.edu/en/table-of-contents

APPLICATION SHEET 5-1

What may be the source of miscommunication with Li Min's parents?

APPLICATION SHEET 5-2

Read through all the instructions carefully before completing the exercise.

1. Print your name in the upper right-hand corner of the paper.

2. Circle the word *corner* in number 1.

3. Draw three small circles in the upper left-hand corner of the paper.

4. Put an *X* in each circle.

5. Draw a square around the center circle.

6. Put an *X* in the lower left-hand corner of the page.

7. Draw a box around the *X*.

8. Turn the page over and multiply 85×40.

9. Draw a circle around the word *paper* in number 3.

10. Call out your first name loudly when you reach this point in the test.

11. If you think you have carefully followed the directions, say "I have."

12. Add 115 and 209 together on the reverse side of the page.

13. Circle your answer to the math problem presented above.

14. Count out loud from 15 to 1 backwards in a quiet voice.

15. Fold your paper in half horizontally.

16. Sign your name in cursive at the bottom of the page, in the middle.

17. When you reach this point, call out loudly, "I am the leader in following directions."

18. Open your paper and underline all of the odd numbers on the left-hand side of the page.

19. When you have finished reading carefully, only complete line 1.

(Adapted from G. Kroehnert (1991), 100 training games. Sydney, Australia: McGraw-Hill Book Company.)

APPLICATION SHEET 5-3

Step-by-step shoe-tying instructions.

APPLICATION SHEET 5-4

Rewrite the following as "I" statements:

That isn't the right way to mix tempera paints.

You always put the children's toothbrushes in the wrong cabinet.

Why do you always ask to leave early on Fridays?

You forgot to fill out the medication administration form.

Problem-Solving and Conflict Management

OBJECTIVES

After reading this chapter, you will be able to do the following:

- Describe four common sources of conflict in organizations.
- Discuss why it is imperative that motivational leaders acknowledge and address workplace conflict.
- Identify and summarize the six-step problem-solving process.
- Describe five strategies for managing organizational conflict.
- Discuss a motivational leader's role in addressing workplace conflict.

KEY TERMS

- conflict
- emotional intelligence
- competing
- collaborating
- compromising
- avoiding
- accommodating
- individualist
- collectivist
- incivility

■　■　■

If we manage conflict constructively, we harness its energy for creativity and development.

—Kenneth Kaye, American psychologist

INTRODUCTION

This chapter addresses conflict, a common workplace occurrence that is usually viewed unfavorably. Although some conflicts can be ignored, most require intervention to prevent them from producing a negative effect on employee productivity, morale, and retention (Obiekwe & Eke, 2019).

Should motivational leaders do everything in their power to avoid conflict in their programs? Most researchers and business authorities would disagree. Conflict presents organizations with an opportunity for innovation, improvement, and growth. When leaders manage conflict effectively, they also create environments in which employees are engaged, feel appreciated and empowered, and are more likely to remain working.

WHY DOES CONFLICT OCCUR?

The term **conflict** refers to a disagreement or incompatible viewpoint. Conflict may be limited to an individual experience (intrapersonal) or ensue among members of the same group (intragroup) or between groups (intergroup). It describes the negative feelings that individuals experience when there is a discrepancy between what, when, or how they expected something to be done and what actually occurs. For example, a team may become upset with one of its members who fails to complete her assigned responsibilities or contribute equally to a joint project. The resulting tension that develops among the individuals may be expressed as anger, disgust, frustration, discouragement, or a host of other unproductive emotions.

Conflicts arise because people often perceive the same issue in various ways. Individual differences in values, needs, goals, and past experiences collectively shape a person's interpretation of a situation as either manageable or problematic. It also influences the way in which a person is likely to respond. For example, some employees may choose to avoid a conflict because they do not consider it significant, or they conclude that it does not affect them personally. Others become frustrated or upset when they encounter people with whom they disagree and may spend substantial time trying to convince them that their own idea is correct. Still others may consider the situation beneficial and support change.

Most conflict in programs can be traced to four primary sources (Figure 6.1). Ineffective communication is consistently identified as the most significant and common cause. Leaders who fail to provide employees with the information needed to perform their jobs and meet expectations should anticipate the development of interpersonal friction (Hill, Offermann, & Thomas, 2019). Poor communication also increases gossip and rumors among employees as they attempt to draw conclusions based upon incomplete or inaccurate information. Schad (2019) noted that teachers frequently reported limited communication with their supervisors as a significant reason for job dissatisfaction and poor morale. When leaders encouraged upward and downward communication in their organizations, employees experienced less interpersonal conflict and greater job satisfaction (Kelly & MacDonald, 2019).

Competition for limited resources is another major cause of organizational conflict (Pai & Bendersky, 2020; Zia & Syed, 2013). Internal struggles most often center around things that may be or thought to be in short supply, such as personnel, status, space, materials, and information. For example, conflict may likely occur if several teachers discover that only two will have their fees paid to attend a required in-service program, or that a teacher with less experience and seniority has been chosen over other teacher applicants to become the new assistant director.

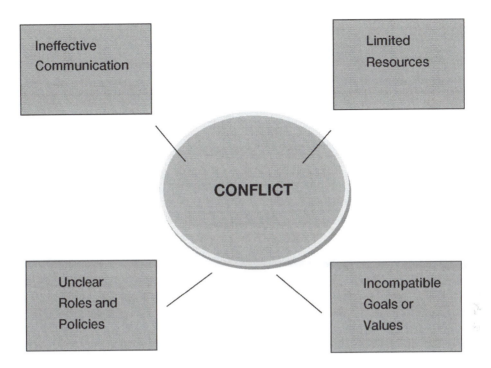

FIGURE 6.1 Common sources of organizational conflict.

Such examples illustrate why open and frequent communication plays an important role in reducing frustration, resentment, and conflict. Employees expect to be treated fairly and may perceive a leader's actions as unjust unless they understand the reasoning behind the decisions. However, not all leaders make communication a priority. Sherf, Venkataramani, and Gajendran (2019) found that managers often cited work and time pressures as reasons for not devoting more attention to issues of fairness and communication when making decisions.

Vague, poorly communicated, or nonexistent job descriptions and/or policies are another common cause of organizational conflict. Friction is inevitable when employees are unclear about their expected roles and responsibilities. For example, a teacher who was not informed that he is responsible for ordering consumable classroom materials (e.g., paper, paint, crayons) every six months is likely to be confronted by upset colleagues when supplies run out. Or angry feelings may erupt when a colleague oversteps her role and completes a task that was assigned to another teacher. In each scenario, a combination of ambiguous guidelines and poor communication led to employee discord.

Perceived discrepancies related to an employee's conduct often become apparent during performance reviews. Although it may appear that an employee has not performed according to expectations, it may be that the individual was never given a clearly defined job description or copy of personnel policies.

Conflict may also develop as the result of incompatible goals or values. These differences can occur at several levels. Leaders may feel pressured by their administrators to do things differently, employees may disagree with a new policy that is to be enforced, or individual members may consider team goals as incompatible with their own professional values. For example, teachers may vehemently disagree with their director's belief that infants should be taught sign language, or that a different assessment instrument is better than the one they are currently using. What is important to understand is that tension may develop when a program's goals or values conflict with an individual's personal beliefs.

Did You Know? ·

More than eighty percent of employees report that they have experienced conflict in their workplace.

· ·

THE LEADER'S ROLE IN CONFLICT MANAGEMENT

Motivational leaders play a pivotal role in keeping their programs running efficiently and effectively and creating environments where employees enjoy working. However, conflicts can be expected to occur from time to time despite a leader's best intentions. The results of several large-scale surveys conducted by organizations, such as the American Management Association among others, suggest that leaders spend approximately fifteen to twenty percent of their time engaged in conflict resolution.

Conflict management is a skill that few leaders are taught but one that is vital for maintaining a friendly, productive workplace (Figure 6.2). An ability to successfully identify, manage, and resolve conflict requires an understanding of the fundamental leadership skills that have been discussed in previous chapters. Continuous self-awareness and **emotional intelligence** must also be practiced if motivational leaders are to achieve positive outcomes for their employees and programs.

Effective leaders understand the importance of identifying workplace conflict in its early stages. They are sensitive to changes in employees' behavior, performance, and/or conversations that may indicate underlying tensions. Depending upon the circumstances, motivational leaders may decide to simply remain vigilant and assume a wait-and-see approach. At other times, they may be more proactive and intervene before a conflict intensifies and has a detrimental effect on employee trust, commitment, and well-being (Caesens et al., 2019; Kuriakose et al., 2019). Researchers have noted that prolonged or repeated exposure to conflict can interrupt sleep quality and increase the risk for cardiovascular diseases (Demsky et al., 2019; Felix et al., 2019; Jacob & Kostev, 2017).

Motivational leaders must also be mindful of the way their behavior establishes the tone and dynamics that others are likely to follow when managing conflict (Kay & Skarlicki, 2020; Zhao, Thatcher, & Jehn, 2019). For example, a leader who approaches conflict in an open, calm, and confident manner may inspire others to assume a similar demeanor. In contrast, a leader's angry, terse, or accusatory responses may increase hostilities and compromise chances for achieving a constructive resolution.

How well workplace conflict is ultimately managed also depends upon a leader's knowledge of the problem-solving process. Effective leaders recognize if and when a problem exists, and they know how to proceed to resolve it. They are familiar with conflict management

FIGURE 6.2 Leaders must be able to identify and resolve workplace conflict. *SDI Productions*

strategies and understand the advantages and disadvantages associated with each. They also are aware of their confidence and competence in implementing the various approaches (Cemaloğlu & Duykuluoğlu, 2019; Tehrani & Yamini, 2020). They listen to all sides of a conflict, are open-minded and respectful of individual differences, remain focused on the facts, and guide the process to reach an acceptable resolution.

A satisfactory outcome requires that all parties involved in a dispute come together to discuss the rationale for their decisions. Collective problem-solving encourages the sharing of ideas and contributes to an improved understanding of what each person considers to be important. During this process, individuals often discover that they have more in common with regard to their values and goals than they may have initially thought. For example, the teachers in the earlier example who did not support the teaching of sign language to infants may all agree that promoting children's language development is indeed an important goal.

THE PROBLEM-SOLVING APPROACH

Conflicts are inevitable in any early childhood program. However, the way in which motivational leaders manage workplace conflicts determines whether the outcome will have a beneficial or detrimental effect on employees and the program. Ignoring problems or engaging in hasty decisions may increase hostilities among employees, disrupt their performance, or cause them to eventually leave (Choi & Junghee, 2018; Van Gramberg et al., 2020). Valuable opportunities for program improvement may also be lost if conflict is not addressed in a constructive manner (Textbox 6.1).

CONFLICT AND ITS POTENTIAL BENEFITS

Conflict presents programs with opportunities for:

- identifying and addressing misunderstandings, assumptions, and differences of opinion that can interfere with employee productivity and commitment if not resolved;
- examining creative alternative solutions to existing operations (e.g., policies, procedures, communication patterns);
- minimizing differences and improving collegiality, trust, and cooperation among employees by acknowledging areas of potential disagreement and conflict; and
- acquiring new skills and improving one's expertise in managing conflict.

Achievement of a successful resolution requires motivational leaders to use fundamental problem-solving and decision-making skills. Lahana et al. (2019) found that nurses experienced improved job satisfaction and working relationships with co-workers when hospital managers employed a problem-solving approach to address conflict. They also believed that managers gained a clearer understanding of the issues involved and were able to resolve matters in a more efficient and effective manner.

Problem-solving involves a multi-step process that can be used by an individual or a team (Figure 6.3). It includes the following steps:

- *Identifying the problem*—Conflict must be defined in specific and objective terms: what has occurred, who is involved, and/or what actions led up to the conflict. Pinpointing the underlying problem requires a separation of personal emotions and opinions from the issue in question.
- *Gathering information*—During this step, objective information is collected through thoughtful observation and active listening. This process contributes to an understanding of the conflict, the needs and concerns of all individuals who are involved, and potential solutions. For example, a teacher stops by your office to report that someone "has broken the copy machine again." Your immediate response might be to call for a service repairman or determine who was responsible for causing the repeated malfunctions. However, if you had asked the teacher to explain what she meant by "broken" or examined the copier yourself, you would have discovered that a simple paper jam had caused the copier to stop functioning.
- *Developing alternative solutions*—This step offers leaders and/or team members an opportunity to generate a list of creative solutions. Because individuals often perceive conflict differently, they may also offer divergent resolutions that others had not considered. Therefore, all suggestions that address the underlying cause of a conflict should be encouraged, even if they may not seem to be practical at the time.

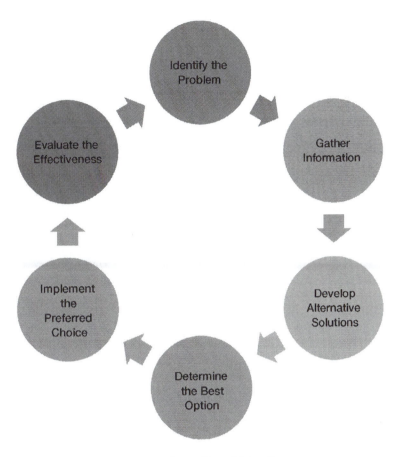

FIGURE 6.3 The Problem-Solving Process

- *Determining the best option*—The advantages and disadvantages of alternative resolutions should be carefully analyzed. Those that are likely to fail or are impractical can be eliminated so that attention is focused on those most likely to achieve the desired outcome. An analysis of the remaining solutions should weigh their potential impact(s) on the program, employees, budget, required resources, fairness, and time constraints.

   Motivational leaders may choose to make the final decision or to solicit a group vote depending upon the nature of the conflict involved. For example, a budget submission may require a director's immediate decision whereas a staff meeting could be called to address a scheduling concern. However, researchers have found that employees are generally more satisfied and willing to follow through with a resolution when they are given a voice in the final decision (Nechanska, Hughes, & Dundon, 2020).

- *Implementing the preferred choice*—This step centers around the development of a workable action plan. It should spell out how the chosen solution is to be implemented, the roles and responsibilities that individuals are expected to fulfill, specific timelines, and evaluation criteria. Once a plan is finalized, all aspects must be explained clearly to those who are responsible for its implementation.

During this process, it may become apparent that a solution has unanticipated consequences or is not feasible. For example, a center's advisory board agrees to increase enrollment numbers in response to parents' frustrations over long waiting lists. However, the board's directive is met with an angry response from teachers who argue that they are already short-handed and overworked. After considerable deliberation, the advisory board approves the hiring of two additional teachers, but they must eliminate planned building improvements from the budget to make this solution work.

- *Evaluating the effectiveness*—An important step in the problem-solving process involves the monitoring of a solution's effectiveness in resolving conflict (Textbox 6.2). Some leaders may overlook this crucial stage and consider a problem solved once a plan is in place. Follow-up is always necessary to ensure that the plan is being implemented correctly and is achieving the intended result. Monitoring should be continued until all involved parties are satisfied that the conflict has been successfully resolved.

TEXTBOX 6.2

EVALUATING THE EFFECTIVENESS OF A CONFLICT RESOLUTION PLAN

Questions to determine if a conflict resolution plan has been effective:

- What indicators suggest that the resolution plan is working?
- Are there parts of the plan that have not proven to be effective and, if so, what changes are needed?
- Has this process built mutual trust and respect among the involved parties?
- What have you learned that will be helpful in preventing similar situations in the future?
- How has this experience improved your ability to resolve organizational conflict?

Connecting Points

Teachers are upset with the program's cook. He often refuses their requests to borrow baking pans and utensils to use for classroom cooking projects.

- What should be your first step in addressing this conflict?
- What are some optional solutions to this dilemma?
- What process would you use to decide on a workable resolution?
- How will you determine if the chosen solution is effective in satisfying the needs of the cook and the teachers?

Common Barriers to Effective Problem-Solving

Resolving workplace conflicts would seem to be a relatively easy task if leaders simply followed the problem-solving process step-by-step. However, there are times when intentional or unintentional decisions can create barriers that prevent achievement of a successful outcome. Some errors can be avoided if motivational leaders are aware of obstacles that often prove to be most problematic, including these:

- *Amount and type of information*—A leader's misdiagnosis or misunderstanding of circumstances that led up to a conflict may divert attention away from the real issue. As a result, the information gathered may not be relevant and, thus, may lead to erroneous conclusions and ineffective solutions. The opposite can also occur. Too much information solicited over an undefined time period may cause a leader to feel overwhelmed, distracted, and unable to reach a conclusive decision.

  The type of information needed to make a sound decision becomes apparent when the problem is clearly defined. Establishing a specific time frame also assures that the process will continue to move forward by reducing the tendency to gather unnecessary information or delay a resolution.

- *Personal biases*—A leader's personal beliefs shape the way in which conflict is perceived, defined, and managed. As a result, the information gathered may be misdirected by the leader's biased point of view. For example, a director who considers most parent complaints as frivolous may listen but take no action. Or, a program director who believes that women are better cooks may overlook job applications for the center's cook position that are submitted by men.

  Personal biases may also cause some leaders to use the same management strategy in every conflict situation. They may erroneously believe that because a resolution strategy has worked for them in the past it will be effective again. This is a risky approach and unlikely to achieve the desired result. For example, a director who believes that teachers should work out their own disagreements may choose to ignore the complaints of several assistant teachers who were recently reassigned to different classrooms. Although this approach may have proven successful in other conflict situations, it does not respect or resolve the teachers' present concerns.

- *Poor communication*—Workplace conflict and failed problem-solving can often be traced to poor communication (Kelly & MacDonald, 2019). Leaders may become distracted by the emotional aspects of a conflict and fail to engage in effective communication practices, such as active listening, perception checking, respecting individual differences, and avoiding information overload. A successful resolution outcome requires that all involved parties participate in a mutual exchange of information and receive explanations about expectations, time schedules, and their individual roles and responsibilities. Participants should also be kept apprised frequently and formally of the progress that is being made throughout the resolution process.

- *Too many participants*—Leaders must determine how many individuals to involve in the problem-solving process. If too few are included, the amount of information and number of solutions generated may be limited. Involving too many people in the process may make it difficult to focus on the issues, yield more information than is needed, and slow the decision-making process.

Factors that motivational leaders should consider when determining the appropriate number of individuals to involve in a problem-solving exercise include the:

- nature of the conflict (e.g., confidential, personal, general); if the decision should be made by the leader or involve other employees.
- amount of time before a final decision must be made.
- knowledge and experience an individual will need to make an informed decision.
- ability of individuals to work together in a collegial manner.

Did You Know? •••

Most U.S. leaders and employees never receive any conflict management training.

•••

CONFLICT MANAGEMENT STRATEGIES

Thomas and Kilmann (1974) developed a model to help leaders understand when and how different management styles can be used to address conflict (Figure 6.4). They proposed five basic strategies:

- competing
- collaborating
- compromising
- avoiding
- accommodating

Each strategy is described in terms of the effect it has on interpersonal dynamics (the degree of cooperation needed to satisfy one's personal interests or those of others) and the consequences for participants (the degree of personal gain or desire to satisfy another individual's interests). The authors do not suggest that one approach is better than another. Rather, the structure provides leaders with options that are determined by the type of conflict situation and desired outcome.

Competing. This strategy is considered a win-lose proposition and is about power and control. Leaders who use this strategy are highly assertive and low on cooperation. They set out to win at all costs, including their relationship with employees or other involved parties. They tend to be defensive, certain that they are correct, and unwilling to compromise. As a result, conflicts may end in a standoff without any satisfactory resolution.

Although the competitive approach may have negative overtones, there are times when it may be appropriate and effective, such as in an emergency or when a difficult, unpopular, or non-concessional decision must be made.

Misuse or too frequent use of this strategy can create a hostile work environment, job dissatisfaction, and strained relationships with and among employees (Zhao, Thatcher, & Jehn, 2019). It should never be used to humiliate, disrespect, or exert strict authoritarian control over employees. Exclusive use of this conflict management style can also limit creativity and innovation in programs.

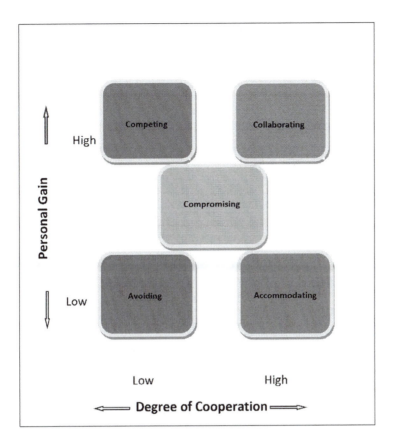

FIGURE 6.4 Thomas-Kilmann Conflict Management Model. Modified from Thomas, K. W., & Kilmann, R. H. (1974). *Thomas-Kilmann conflict mode instrument.* Tuxedo, NY: Xicom

Collaborating. A collaborating management strategy is considered a win-win approach. It requires a high level of cooperation and, as a result, everyone usually gains and loses some of what they initially desired. The results are similar to a compromise and typically increase participants' trust, buy-in, and commitment (Weaver et al., 2019). When leaders use collaboration to address conflict, they must devote time and effort to build relationships, understand each other's position, and reach a solution that everyone, or almost everyone, involved finds acceptable.

The downside of the collaborative strategy is that some innovative ideas may be overlooked because both sides involved in the conflict must make concessions. Leaders must also recognize that some conflict situations are not amenable to a collaborative outcome, especially if a quick or difficult decision must be made.

Compromising. A compromising conflict management strategy is considered moderate in terms of personal gain, cooperativeness, and fairness. Everyone involved in the dispute wins and relinquishes a portion of what they originally wanted in order to reach a resolution (Figure 6.5). Compromising may be an effective approach when leaders want a temporary and expedient solution, or when the involved parties cannot agree.

FIGURE 6.5 A compromising approach may not work when conflict requires a quick response.
Wavebreakmedia, iStock / Getty Images Plus

On the surface, this strategy appears to be a highly desirable way to resolve disagreements. However, not everyone will consider the outcome fair, equitable, or one with which they are willing to comply. In addition, compromising may not achieve an effective solution or address the specific needs that caused the initial conflict.

Avoiding. Leaders use avoidance more often than any other conflict management style (Patton, 2020). Those who are uncomfortable dealing with conflict issues tend to ignore or postpone efforts to address discord, hide or distract attention from disagreements, or hope that someone else will step in and assume the responsibility (Lahana et al., 2019; Tehrani & Yamini, 2020). This strategy results in a lose-lose proposition in which there is no cooperation or personal gain, and the conflict usually remains unresolved.

However, an avoidance approach may be effective if conflicts are likely to have minimal impact on employees or the program, or a conflict is likely to resolve itself over time. Leaders may simply adapt a "wait and see" approach and continue to monitor the situation. It may be prudent to refrain from taking immediate action in conflicts that are intense or highly emotional and to allow time for all individuals to regain control. An avoidance style also allows leaders more time to gather pertinent information so that a sound decision can be made.

Failure to address conflict in a timely manner can also have negative consequences for leaders and their programs. Leaders who ignore conflict may be perceived as weak, uncaring, or incompetent. Disagreements may escalate and become more complicated. Unresolved conflict can also have a negative effect on employee morale and productivity (Rezvani, Barrett, & Khosravi, 2019; Zhao, Thatcher, & Jehn, 2019).

Accommodating. Leaders may also choose to address conflict by limiting any discussion and simply accommodating or giving in to employees' demands. For example, a director may decide to back down from imposing a new uniform dress code in order to avoid further employee opposition. In other words, she may consider it more important to maintain a positive working relationship with her staff (lose-win proposition) than to enforce a directive. Accommodation may also be a preferable option when conflict involves relatively minor issues, more time is needed to explore an issue, or leaders realize they have made a judgment error.

Accommodation may leave leaders feeling frustrated and unable to implement change or to move an organization in a preferred direction. Frequent use may create an environment that reinforces employees' demanding or complaining behavior while weakening leader's respect, power, and authority. Leaders should use an accommodating approach cautiously to maintain a healthy balance among goal attainment and meeting employees' and organizational needs.

DIRECTOR'S SHOWCASE

How would you describe your approach to managing conflict?

We are fortunate not to experience many serious conflicts that require leadership intervention right now. However, this wasn't always the case. When I accepted this position, it was my first job as a program director. When I look back on those early years, I realize that my lack of leadership experience probably contributed to some of the friction that developed. I was really uncomfortable dealing with conflict issues and would ignore them or tell the teachers to work it out among themselves.

Now, I am more confident in my ability to deal with conflict in a positive way. I have worked hard to create a collaborative work environment where we respect and appreciate one another. When disagreements arise, we meet as a group to discuss a possible solution. Usually the result is a compromise that everyone can accept. I believe this approach empowers the teachers to think creatively, solve their own problems, and develop leadership skills in the process. I consider myself a guide and not the decision-maker.

—Hannah B., program co-owner, director

—————————— *Connecting Points* ——————————

Gina and Kiki have both asked to take the afternoon off. Gina suffered an injury to her foot last night and needs to see a doctor to find out if it is broken. Her doctor has an appointment opening at 1:30 p.m. today. Kiki just realized that her driver's license expires tomorrow. She wants to renew it today because the county transportation office is closed for the rest of the week. If you were their director:

- What would your initial reaction be to the teachers' requests?
- How would you resolve this conflict?
- What management strategy would you be most likely to use?
- What advantages and disadvantages might be associated with your decision?

Choosing a Conflict Management Style

Effective motivational leaders are familiar with the potential benefits and limitations associated with each conflict management strategy (Table 6.1). They understand that a single approach is unlikely to be successful in managing all conflict situations. They recognize that each instance requires a thoughtful assessment of the circumstances, desired outcome, and confidence to achieve a successful resolution (Tehrani & Yamini, 2020). For example, a director may decide to use an accommodating style if preserving harmony and employee relationships are priorities. Or a team leader may decide to avoid involvement in a conflict that has developed between two teachers. If given time, they may be able to resolve their own problems.

Table 6.1: Conflict Management Strategies

Leaders should be familiar with the five basic conflict management strategies and understand when they are most effective to use.

	When Effective	*When Not Effective*
Competing	■ an immediate or unpopular decision must be made ■ an administrative decision is involved (e.g., hiring, firing, financial) ■ there is no room for negotiation	■ others have information needed to make a sound decision ■ the intention is to use one's authority to achieve a personal goal or objective
Accommodating	■ the outcome is more important to others than yourself ■ maintaining a working relationship is more important than achieving a desired outcome ■ a leader realizes he/she is wrong ■ the consequences of a decision are relatively minor and employees can learn from their mistake	■ in situations where others are reluctant to speak up or state their position ■ if the resolution may cause the conflict to escalate ■ a decision is likely to affect an organization's reputation or ability to function
Avoiding	■ conflict is minor or unimportant ■ the solution creates more negative consequences than it resolves ■ conflict is highly emotional and a cool-down time is needed ■ the involved parties may be able to resolve their own dispute ■ conflict is symptom of a larger issue ■ time is needed to gather more information	■ a quick decision is needed to resolve an issue ■ a conflict may escalate if ignored
Collaborating	■ the needs or concerns of participants are too important or vital to compromise ■ there is too much animosity for parties to overcome in achieving a resolution ■ provides an opportunity to gain a better understanding of each other's views	■ conflict is minor ■ resources are limited ■ a quick decision is needed
Compromising	■ a decision provides a temporary resolution to a complex conflict ■ other strategies have proven ineffective ■ other strategies may have resolved the conflict but created more negative consequences in the process ■ both sides can agree on a workable solution	■ a resolution may not be in everyone's best interest ■ in situations where strong leadership is needed, a leader may be seen as weak and indecisive ■ when overused by some parties to obtain their desires ■ if demands are too great or parties are too divided to reach an acceptable agreement

Motivational leaders give careful consideration to the individuals who are involved in a conflict when determining an appropriate management strategy to use. Culturally competent leaders recognize that workplace conflicts may be attributable to misperceptions and miscommunications (Caputo et al., 2019; Gomez & Taylor, 2018). Stereotypical assumptions about people's behavior and expectations may be incorrect and work against an otherwise successful outcome (Caputo et al., 2019; Marin, Olekalns, & Adair, 2019). For example, attributing a teacher's direct and confrontational manner to her **individualist** cultural background may fail to recognize that she is experiencing considerable stress due to her mother's terminal illness. Or it may be a mistake to believe that an employee's **collectivist** heritage causes her to tolerate a colleague's **incivility**. Because she does not complain, the conflict is likely to go undetected and unresolved.

Motivational leaders are often able to achieve a constructive resolution when they understand employees' unique personalities, beliefs, values, and needs. Time spent in frequent interactions with individual employees fosters an awareness and ability to respond in a sensitive and respectful manner. Culturally competent leaders also consider it important to provide sensitivity training for their employees. This effort helps to reduce cross-cultural misunderstandings and increase employee commitment and resilience to conflict (Azevedo & Shane, 2019).

Selecting an effective conflict management strategy also requires motivational leaders to engage in self-reflection. The process often reveals personal biases that may prevent a leader from remaining neutral and focused on important issues. It also allows leaders to examine their strengths and limitations, past successes and failures, and their degree of confidence in using management strategies to address conflict. For example, a director may decide that a compromising strategy was not the most effective way to resolve a conflict with the program's teachers over reduced benefits. As a result, she may decide to try a different approach if faced with a similar employee-administration conflict in the future.

Reducing the incidence of workplace conflict is always the desirable goal. Motivational leaders who establish meaningful relationships with their employees and maintain open lines of communication are often successful in doing so. They also become more proficient in recognizing the early signs of conflict and achieving constructive resolutions as they continue to gain experience.

SUMMARY

- Conflict is a common occurrence in organizations and should be anticipated. Workplace conflicts are often due to ineffective communication, competition for resources, unclear guidelines, and incompatible goals or agendas.
- Early recognition and management of conflict is an essential leadership skill that is typically learned through experience.
- Successful conflict management requires motivational leaders to use the problem-solving process for identifying the issue, gathering relevant information, generating alternative solutions, selecting and implementing the best option, and evaluating the outcome.
  o Irrelevant or incomplete information, personal biases, poor communication, and too few or too many participants can interfere with a successful resolution outcome.

- Fundamental conflict management strategies include competing, collaborating, avoiding, accommodating, and compromise. Each has advantages and limitations that motivational leaders must consider when determining the best approach to use.
- Leaders' ability to manage conflict plays a significant role in creating an environment in which employees enjoy working, are productive, and are more likely to remain.

APPLICATION ACTIVITIES

1. Interview three individuals from different cultures to learn how conflict is typically viewed, expressed, and resolved between males and females, among siblings, and among employees. Prepare a summary of your findings and discuss how they compare/contrast with your beliefs and experiences. Record your interview results and personal summary on Application Sheet 6-1.

2. Identify a conflict (or disagreement) in which you were recently involved. Use the problem-solving process to analyze the experience. What factors triggered the conflict? What was your initial reaction? What were some of the potential solutions? How was the conflict ultimately resolved? Were you satisfied with the outcome or were there other solutions that may have proven to be more effective? Record your responses on Application Sheet 6-2.

3. Participants' body language yields important clues about what they are feeling and can be useful in identifying and resolving conflict. List three or four nonverbal behaviors that you would expect to observe if an individual was angry or upset, uninterested, skeptical, disappointed, confused, or elated. Record your responses on Application Sheet 6-3.

REVIEW POINTS

1. In what ways can poor or inadequate communication contribute to conflict?
2. What is emotional intelligence? Provide an example.
3. Describe several negative consequences that may result when the problem-solving process is not followed step-by-step.
4. What criteria can a leader use to determine which conflict management style may be best to use?
5. How do personal biases influence the problem-solving process?
6. How do the competing and compromising management strategies differ in terms of their use and potential outcomes?
7. What negative consequences may a program experience if the director is ineffective in managing conflict?

KEY TERMS DEFINED

conflict—a difference of opinion or perceived incompatibility of interests, goals, or needs

emotional intelligence—the ability to recognize and understand emotions (personal and those of others) and to use the information to guide one's decisions

competing—a conflict management style in which one individual controls and makes the decisions

collaborating—a conflict management style in which an agreement or solution is reached that satisfies the desires of everyone involved

compromising—a conflict management style in which both parties relinquish some of their demands to achieve a mutually acceptable resolution

avoiding—a management style in which a leader ignores or chooses not to become involved in conflict

accommodating—a conflict management style in which one party gives up their demands in order to satisfy the wishes of others

individualist—cultures that encourage and value individual effort and achievement. Individualism is predominant in many European and American countries

collectivist—a political or cultural philosophy that emphasizes group welfare over individual or personal gain. Collectivist cultures are represented in many Asian and Latino countries

incivility—disrespectful or offensive treatment directed toward another individual

REFERENCES

Azevedo, A., & Shane, M. J. (2019). A new training program in developing cultural intelligence can also improve innovative work behavior and resilience: A longitudinal pilot study of graduate students and professional employees. *The International Journal of Management Education, 17*(3), 1–20.

Caesens, G., Stinglhamber, F., Demoulin, S., De Wilde, M., & Mierop, A. (2019). Perceived organizational support and workplace conflict: The mediating role of failure-related trust. *Frontiers in Psychology, 9*, 2704.

Caputo, A., Ayoko, O. B., Amoo, N., & Menke, C. (2019). The relationship between cultural values, cultural intelligence and negotiation styles. *Journal of Business Research, 99*, 23–36.

Cemaloğlu, N., & Duykuluoğlu, A. (2019). Relationship between teachers' workplace friendship perceptions and conflict management styles. *International Education Studies, 12*(9), 42–53.

Choi, Y., & Junghee, H. (2018). Job satisfaction and work productivity: The role of conflict-management culture. *Social Behavior and Personality, 46*(7), 1101–1110.

Demsky, C. A., Fritz, C., Hammer, L. B., & Black, A. E. (2019). Workplace incivility and employee sleep: The role of rumination and recovery experiences. *Journal of Occupational Health Psychology, 24*(2), 228–240.

Felix, A. S., Lehman, A., Nolan, T. S., Sealy-Jefferson, S., Breathett, K., Hood, D. B., Addison, D., Anderson, C. M., Cené, C. W., Warren, B. J., Jackson, R. D., & Williams, K. P. (2019). Stress, resilience, and cardiovascular disease risk among Black women. *Circulation: Cardiovascular Quality and Outcomes, 12*(4), e005284. https://doi.org/10.1161/CIRCOUTCOMES.118.005284.

Gomez, C., & Taylor, K. A. (2018). Cultural differences in conflict resolution strategies: A US–Mexico comparison. *International Journal of Cross-Cultural Management, 18*(1), 33–51.

Hill, N. S., Offermann, L. R., & Thomas, K. (2019). Mitigating the detrimental impact of maximum negative affect on team cohesion and performance through face-to-face communication. *Group & Organization Management, 44*(1), 211–238.

Jacob, L., & Kostev, K. (2017). Conflicts at work are associated with a higher risk of cardiovascular disease. *German Medical Science, 15*. Doi: 10.3205/000249. Retrieved from https://www.ncbi.nlm.nih.gov/pmc/articles/PMC5406615/.

Kay, A. A., & Skarlicki, D. P. (2020). Cultivating a conflict-positive workplace: How mindfulness facilitates constructive conflict management. *Organizational Behavior and Human Decision Processes, 159*, 8–20.

Kelly, S., & MacDonald, P. (2019). A look at leadership styles and workplace solidarity communication. *International Journal of Business Communication, 56*(3), 432–448.

Kuriakose, V., Sreejesh, S., Wilson, P. R., & Anusree, M. R. (2019). The differential association of workplace conflicts on employee well-being. *International Journal of Conflict Management, 30*(5), 680–705.

Lahana, E., Tsaras, K., Kalaitzidou, A., Galanis, P., Kaitelidou, D., & Sarafis, P. (2019). Conflicts management in public sector nursing. *International Journal of Healthcare Management, 12*(1), 33–39.

Marin, J. R., Olekalns, M., & Adair, W. (2019). Normatively speaking: Do cultural norms influence negotiation, conflict management, and communication? *Negotiation and Conflict Management Research, 12*(2), 146–160.

Nechanska, E., Hughes, E., & Dundon, T. (2020). Towards an integration of employee voice and silence. *Human Resource Management Review, 30*(1), 1–13.

Obiekwe, O., & Eke, N. U. (2019). Impact of employee grievance management on organizational performance. *Economics and Business Management, 5*(1), 1–10.

Pai, J., & Bendersky, C. (2020). Team status conflict. *Current Opinion in Psychology, 33*, 38–41.

Patton, C. M. (2020). Breaking the health-care workplace conflict perpetuation cycle. *Leadership in Health Care, 33*(2), 147–162.

Rezvani, A., Barrett, R., & Khosravi, P. (2019). Investigating the relationships among team emotional intelligence, trust, conflict and team performance. *Team Performance Management, 25*(1–2), 120–137.

Schad, E. (2019). No time to talk! Teachers' perceptions of organizational communication: Context and climate. *Educational Management Administration & Leadership, 47*(3), 421–442.

Sherf, E. N., Venkataramani, V., & Gajendran, R. S. (2019). Too busy to be fair? The effect of workload and rewards on managers' justice rule adherence. *Academy of Management Journal, 62*(2), 469–502.

Tehrani, H. D., & Yamini, S. (2020). Personality traits and conflict resolution styles: A meta-analysis. *Personality and Individual Differences, 157*. Available online, https://doi.org/10.1016/j.paid.2019.109794.

Thomas, K. W., & Kilmann, R. H. (1974). *Thomas-Kilmann conflict mode instrument*. Tuxedo, NY: Xicom.

Van Gramberg, B., Teicher, J., Bamber, G. J., & Cooper, B. (2020). Employee voice, intention to quit, and conflict resolution: Evidence from Australia. *ILR Review, 73*(2), 393–410.

Weaver, S. H., Hessels, A. J., Paliwal, M., & Wurmser, T. A. (2019). Administrative supervisors and nursing unit-based managers: Collaboration and job satisfaction. *Nursing Economic$, 37*(2), 67–76.

Zhao, E. Y., Thatcher, S. M., & Jehn, K. A. (2019). Instigating, engaging in, and managing group conflict: A review of the literature addressing the critical role of the leader in group conflict. *Academy of Management, 13*(1), 112–147.

Zia, Y. A., & Syed, P. H. (2013). An exploratory study into the causes of conflict and the effect of conflict management style on outcome in a competitive workplace. *Journal of Managerial Sciences, 33*(2), 299–315.

ONLINE RESOURCES

Association for Conflict Resolution: https://acrnet.org/

Free Management Library: https://managementhelp.org/personalproductivity/problem-solving.htm

Harvard Law School: https://www.pon.harvard.edu/free-reports/

The Balance Careers: https://www.thebalancecareers.com/workplace-conflict-resolution-1918675

APPLICATION SHEET 6-1

The three individuals from different cultures whom I interviewed:

Individual A:

Individual B:

Individual C:

Summary of findings:

How these findings compare and contrast with my personal beliefs/experiences:

APPLICATION SHEET 6-2

A recent conflict or disagreement that I was involved in:

Factors that caused the conflict or disagreement:

My initial reaction:

Potential solutions:

How the conflict was resolved:

I thought the resolution was:

APPLICATION SHEET 6-3

Three or four nonverbal behaviors that would be observable if a person was

a) angry or upset about a situation—

b) uninterested in the discussion—

c) skeptical that a solution would resolve the conflict—

d) disappointed with a suggested resolution—

e) confused about a proposed solution—

f) elated about the resolution—

7

Promoting Effective Teamwork

OBJECTIVES

After reading this chapter, you will be able to do the following:

- Describe two advantages and two disadvantages associated with the team concept.
- Identify three factors that motivational leaders must consider when assembling a team.
- Discuss the five stages of a team's development.
- Explain how motivational leaders can create a culture that supports team productivity.
- Describe three responsibilities that team members are expected to meet.
- Identify two organizational and two individual barriers to effective team performance.

KEY TERMS

- psychological safety
- social loafing
- homogeneous
- heterogeneous
- norms
- shared leadership

■ ■ ■

Coming together is a beginning, staying together is progress, and working together is success.

—Henry Ford, founder, Ford Motor Company

INTRODUCTION

Five-star chefs may select the freshest ingredients, but the way in which they assemble them can result in a dish that is delicious, unappetizing, or somewhere in between. Similarly, orchestra maestros may recruit highly gifted musicians, but they will only be successful in producing an outstanding performance if they are able to coordinate the players' individual efforts. The same principle also holds true in small and large organizations, including early childhood programs. Program directors may hire talented individuals, but it is their ability to form a cohesive team that determines whether the organization's quality and goals will be achieved.

WHY TEAMS?

Teams exist everywhere—debate, marketing, athletics, game shows, military, cooking, sales, schools, and so on. They are comprised of two or more individuals who are brought together to accomplish a specific task or purpose. Their collective efforts generally outperform those of an individual in terms of efficiency, innovation, and productivity (Clark, 2019; Neto et al., 2020). Michael Jordan described the team concept as, "There is no I in team, but there is in win."

Workplace teams are typically formed to serve different purposes. Some teams have an informal arrangement and develop around a common interest or cause. Others are organized to solve a problem or address a specific task, such as the planning of an upcoming event or development of a new admission policy. Once the project has been completed, the team may disband. There are also teams that have a permanent status and designated responsibilities. For example, a human resource team may be established to oversee an organization's hiring processes or to deal solely with staff development.

Interdisciplinary or cross-functional teams represent another type that brings together individuals with different expertise to tackle complex problems. Interdisciplinary teams are common in education (e.g., early intervention, literacy, STEM, STEAM), medicine and public health, technology, and research fields (Dinh et al., 2020; Larson & DeChurch, 2020).

In early childhood settings, *team* often refers to a conceptual framework that views all employees as members who are united in their commitment to a program's goals and principles (Figure 7.1). Team members communicate frequently among themselves and provide support and encouragement for one another. Each person contributes unique skills, ideas, and perspectives that help to create a rich productive work environment (Page & Eadie, 2019).

Benefits and Limitations

Teams are commonly found in many organizations today (Benishek & Lazzara, 2019). They have distinct advantages, but also limitations that most often are attributed to poor communication and leadership.

Teamwork provides an efficient and effective strategy for achieving results from an organizational perspective. Team-generated outcomes tend to be well-thought out and of a higher quality than what individuals can accomplish on their own (Bouwmans et al., 2019; Clark, 2019). Researchers note that teams are likely to produce results that are more creative because they can capitalize on members' collective intellect, talents, and experiences (Wang et al., 2019). Team decisions are also advantageous because they relieve an individual from shouldering a heavy commitment or having to make emotionally difficult choices.

Organizations that rely on a team approach also benefit from lower employee absenteeism and improved retention rates (García et al., 2019; Pérez-Vallejo & Fernández-Muñoz, 2020). Researchers note that teams provide employees with opportunities for social interaction and

FIGURE 7.1 Teamwork creates an environment where employees feel appreciated and valued.
SDI Productions

the formation of meaningful friendships. These experiences satisfy important fundamental human needs for belonging, recognition, and self-actualization. As a result, employees report feeling happier and more satisfied with their job when they work together as a team with colleagues.

Employees who enjoy their work environment are also more likely to be engaged, productive, and loyal to their organization (Avis, 2019). However, Rutishauser and Sender (2019) noted that cultural values play an influential role in an individual's intention to remain with or to leave an organization. For example, team members from collectivist cultures showed a stronger commitment to remain with an organization when they were unhappy. Those with a stronger individualist background were more inclined to leave.

Team participation also offers employees opportunities for collaboration, which builds trust and collegiality among members. Maloney et al. (2019) noted that team members tend to form strong emotional bonds with one another, especially individuals of the same gender, and that these relationships often endure long after the team has disbanded. Team members also appreciated opportunities to learn from one another and were motivated by their exposure to new ideas and perspectives.

Team membership also provides an element of **psychological safety** that allows individuals to contribute ideas or make decisions without fear of reprisal (Appelbaum et al., 2020; Han, Lee, & Beyerlein, 2019). It also offers social support and shared responsibility, which have been shown to reduce the stress that an individual may otherwise experience

(Espedido, Searle, & Griffin, 2019; Zaheer et al., 2019). For example, teachers reported less stress with respect to their work performance, interactions with parents and staff, and relationship with students when a team approach was in place (Rodríguez et al., 2019). The reduction in stress was especially notable when they were collaborating on complex or highly challenging tasks.

Undoubtedly, everyone reading this chapter can relate to an unpleasant experience they have had while participating in a class-, sport-, or work-related team project. The discontent can often be traced to one or more common sources (Trent, 2019). For example, large teams can be difficult to coordinate and small teams may create a heavy workload for a few individuals. Teams that include members who are incompatible, fail to fulfill their assigned responsibilities, or lack the requisite skills needed to perform a task often cause the team to become dysfunctional. Team productivity may also suffer when individuals lack trust in one another, impose their opinions on the group, or attempt to undermine the team's efforts (Breuer et al., 2020). Poor planning, guidance, and communication provided by weak leadership can also contribute to team failure.

WHOM TO INVITE?

Assembling a functional team requires motivational leaders to consider three basic elements:

- purpose
- group size
- team composition

Team Purpose

The initial step in team formation involves the identification of a specific task or reason for assembling a group. Teams are more effective when they understand the purpose and the outcome(s) they are expected to achieve. A defined purpose also has a direct bearing on membership selection. It serves as a guide for determining the preferred member attributes and role(s) they will be expected to fulfill. It also helps to identify the type of leadership (e.g., self-managed, designated leader, shared leadership) that will enable the group to be successful.

Team Size

How many members should ideally be included on a team usually depends upon its purpose. For example, the number of players on various sport teams, such as basketball, lacrosse, or softball, is established by official rules. However, similar specific numbers do not exist for most public and private organizations. For example, a school or early childhood program may refer to their collective staff as a team. In this case, the number of employees required to be on their "team" is based on teacher-child ratios established by state agencies.

The effect of group size on team outcomes has been the subject of numerous studies. Many researchers suggest that teams consisting of five or six individuals achieve the most efficient and effective results (Amir et al., 2018; Mueller, 2012; Steiner, 1972). Smaller teams may lack the resources (e.g., people, expertise, time) needed to accomplish challenging tasks. Larger teams (eight or more individuals) can be more difficult to manage in terms of coordination, communication, and cohesion. Also, participants have fewer opportunities to contribute with each added team member.

Researchers have also reported that large teams are generally less productive than those with fewer members (Amir et al., 2018; Mueller, 2012). Individuals have a tendency to reduce their effort and contributions as the group size increases (Czyz et al., 2016; Naicker & Parumasur, 2018). This psychological phenomenon is commonly referred to as "**social loafing**." It is thought to occur when individuals experience less accountability, intrinsic motivation, opportunity, control, and recognition for their performance. Social loafing can be detrimental to a team's cohesiveness, effectiveness, and productivity. Tok (2019) noted that males and individuals younger than age twenty-three exhibited lower levels of conscientiousness and compatibleness and, thus, were more likely to engage in social loafing. He recommended that this behavior could be reduced by providing clear task descriptions, assigning tasks based on individual skills, and engaging in continuous monitoring and feedback.

Weiss and Hoegl (2016) suggested that relative team size should not be only about numbers but also take into account the nature of tasks to be addressed. They argue that there are times when small teams may be most effective, such as during the early stages of project development or when completing a specialized task. However, restricting group size also diminishes the range of a team's creative and perspective resources while increasing the responsibilities that a few individuals must assume. A large team may be needed if the project is complex and long-term.

Team Composition

Program leaders are usually responsible for identifying individuals to serve on teams. Careful thought should be given to recruiting members who possess the requisite skills, experience, and expertise needed to achieve the group's objectives. Individuals who are selected should be willing and motivated to serve, share the organization's core values, and work collaboratively in a group. These are also important factors for program administrators to consider when hiring new employees to add to the team.

Consideration should also be given to the compatibility or fit of an individual's personality with that of other team members. Different personality traits can have a positive or negative influence on a team's mood, working relationships, and, ultimately, its effectiveness (Bell et al., 2018; Stipelman et al., 2019). For example, an individual who is consistently unprepared, domineering, or critical of others can quickly disrupt a team's best efforts. Agreeableness, outgoingness, and perfectionism might be considered valuable qualities to have in a team member, but they also may have a negative effect on team performance (Curseu et al., 2019). Individuals who always agree may have little to contribute; perfectionists may focus on details and delay the team's progress. Personality traits that are conducive to team unity, positive interactions, and group productivity are identified in Textbox 7.1.

The question is whether all team members should possess similar competencies and/ or personalities or whether there advantages to including more diverse representation.

PERSONALITY TRAITS THAT HAVE A POSITIVE TEAM EFFECT

Personality traits considered to be desirable in a team member include the following:

honesty	accountability
self-confidence	cooperativeness
adaptability	outgoingness
openness	self-control
trustworthiness	empathy
dependability	persistence
thoughtfulness	curiosity

For example, Yam et al. (2018) assigned the same task to teams with **homogeneous** and **heterogeneous** subgroups and found that both team types produced equivalent results. Sanz-Martínez et al. (2019) noted that homogenous groups were more likely to complete a task, experience higher rates of peer interaction, and report greater personal satisfaction with the experience. In another study, Anderson et al. (2019) observed that although homogenous student teams were initially more productive, heterogeneous teams (e.g., personality and cultural differences) produced higher quality results over time. As individuals became more familiar with their teammates and gained confidence working in a collaborative relationship, their unique contributions ultimately produced a superior product.

Although scholars have not reached a consensus about whether homogeneous or heterogeneous teams perform best, most would suggest that it depends upon the nature of the assigned task. Well-rounded teams comprised of individuals who are competent, task-oriented, and committed to working collaboratively are most likely to achieve success (Aggarwal & Woolley, 2019; Mitchell, Boyle, & Von Stieglitz, 2019).

Diversified team membership (e.g., age, gender, culture, ethnicity, socioeconomic, tenure) offers several advantages. Individuals from varied backgrounds bring unique experiences, insight, and competencies that add versatility and innovation to a team. Van Veelen and Ufkes (2019) also noted that team diversity contributes to increased innovation and productivity. Improved performance was linked to increased sharing of knowledge and skills. Researchers have also suggested that diversified teams often achieve superior results because members learn from one another and examine problems from a broader perspective (Emich & Vincent, 2020; Wang et al., 2019).

Team diversity is especially important today given the increasingly diverse population. Teachers who share similar racial, ethnic, linguistic, and/or cultural backgrounds with the children in their classrooms often have different expectations. They understand the ways in which children's behavior, learning styles, and motivations may differ and are able to respond to them in meaningful ways (Kaiser & Rasminsky, 2020; Rasheed et al., 2020; Zinsser et al., 2019). Diversification also encourages the development of greater tolerance, acceptance, and understanding among staff and the children and families a program serves. For example, Markowitz, Bassok, and Grissom (2020) found that parent engagement and involvement improved when teachers' race and/or ethnicity mirrored that of the children and their families. Researchers have also noted significant educational benefits and a reduction in behavioral challenges and absences when children had teachers of a similar gender, race, and/or ethnicity (LaSalle et al., 2020; Ramírez, López, & Ferron, 2019; Redding, 2019).

—————————— *Connecting Points* ——————————

The local school board recently voted to incorporate your early childhood program into the elementary school system. The building's principal is appointing a team to review the school's current policies in preparation for this move.

- How many individuals should be on this team in your view?
- Whom would you invite as a member?
- What qualifications should these individuals possess?

Did You Know? ·

Thirty-two percent of U.S. children under five years of age speak a language other than English at home. More than half of all U.S. children under age fifteen are from diverse racial/ethnic backgrounds.

· ·

HOW TEAMS DEVELOP

The focus to this point has been on the identification of team purpose and membership. The challenge now becomes how to assure that the pieces will function as a cohesive unit.

Group assembly does not necessarily create a team that performs as expected. It takes time for each member to understand their role and the **norms** that govern the group's behavior. Team members must become familiar with one another's strengths, preferences, and working style before a modicum of trust can be established (Aggarwal & Woolley, 2019). As team members continue to work together, they often develop a stronger sense of belonging, unity, and personal satisfaction (Maynard et al., 2019).

Tuckman (1965; Tuckman & Jensen, 1977) proposed a five-step model to explain how teams mature from the time they are formed until they complete their task and disband (Figure 7.2). He suggested that members' behavior and team productivity improve as the group progresses through each sequential stage:

Forming—During this initial stage, members convene and are introduced to one another. They are friendly and polite, but remain somewhat cautious in their interactions. They begin to form an opinion about other team members by inquiring about their background, experiences, and current interests. They may also share some of their own ideas about the upcoming project and what they hope the team will accomplish.

Storming—During this stage, individuals are becoming more comfortable with the group. Interpersonal frictions (subtle and not so subtle) may develop as individuals attempt to establish their dominance, different personalities and working styles start to emerge, or cliques begin to form among members who have a particular agenda. The team leader's plan and management style also become evident and determines whether the group will support or disagree with the approach.

Norming—Team members are now beginning to bond and unite around the stated agenda. They understand the norms, rules, and goals they are expected to address. At this point, individuals decide if they are willing to continue participating in the group or wish to withdraw.

Performing—All members have now formed a culture of teamwork. They have developed feelings of belongingness and trust in one another, and they are eager to begin working on the task for which they were assembled. They are aware of each team member's expertise and may form small subgroups to work on components of the team project.

Adjourning—Temporary teams usually disband when their project is complete. It is always important that a team's successes and members' contributions are celebrated before the group adjourns.

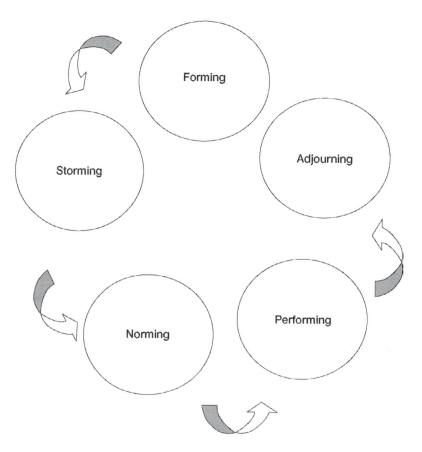

FIGURE 7.2 Stages of Team Development

Teams typically advance from one stage to the next in a relatively brief and linear manner. However, forward progress may be temporarily halted or even regress to a previous stage when a member leaves the team or a new person is added (Gonzalez-Mulé et al., 2020). When this occurs, teams briefly repeat the initial developmental stages (e.g., forming, storming, norming) before they continue to make progress. Leaders who understand how teams develop recognize that it takes them time to achieve unity and to reach peak effectiveness.

Did You Know? . . . .

Oxytocin, a hormone, is produced when a person feels safe, happy, and accepted by others. It creates trust and social bonding.

. . . .

THE TEAM LEADER'S ROLE

No athletic team would achieve its goals without thoughtful planning, guidance, commitment, and cooperation on the part of all of its members. Players and coaches alike must know how they fit into the organizational plan and understand what they must do to fulfill their individual roles and responsibilities. Perhaps Babe Ruth summed it up the best when he said, "The way a team plays as a whole determines its success. You may have the greatest bunch of individual stars in the world, but if they don't play together, the club won't be worth a dime."

Strong motivational leadership is essential to ensure a team's effectiveness. How team leaders arrive at their position can occur in one of several ways. Some occupy a permanent position within their organization (e.g., program director, principal, administrator, consultant). Others are appointed temporarily to oversee a specific project, or they may emerge from the membership after a team has been formed and begins to work together.

The nature of a team leader's authority may also vary. For example, some team leaders assume an autocratic or directive role in overseeing the group's performance. In contrast, collaborative teams, such as those common in early childhood programs, schools, health care settings, and the sciences, often use a **shared leadership** approach (Eckert, 2019; Wu, Cormican, & Chen, 2020). In these situations, team members participate in decision-making and task-completion processes.

Effective teams depend upon their leaders to fulfill several important roles and responsibilities (Textbox 7.2):

Establishing clear goals and a vision—Team members must understand why they have been assembled and specifically what the group is expected to accomplish. Leaders should provide a clear direction and purpose, which includes problem definition, goal establishment and prioritization, identification of expected outcomes, and creation of an anticipated timeframe.

Setting the tone—A team leader's actions and expectations send powerful signals that influence individual and group dynamics. They create a positive working environment by modeling core values, such as trust and respect, empathy, and fairness. Their encouragement, responsiveness, and acknowledgment of members' contributions fosters and strengthens team spirit.

Building and sustaining commitment—Motivational leaders strengthen and maintain members' commitment to the team by assigning roles or recruiting volunteers to assist with various tasks. Involving members in team activities builds a sense of ownership and empowerment. Individuals are also more likely to remain invested when their role appeals to their personal interests and talents or promotes new skill development.

Maintaining open and transparent communication—A continuous exchange of information between leaders and members is fundamental to a team's success. Motivational leaders are accessible and willing to listen whenever necessary. Frequent interactions reduce the potential for rumors and misunderstandings. Regularly scheduled meetings provide valuable opportunities for the team to brainstorm, plan, coordinate efforts, and socialize (Textbox 7.3).

Securing resources—Team leaders are in a position to identify, obtain, and/or assist team members in securing the resources needed to successfully conduct their activities.

Managing conflict—Tensions may develop among members from time to time and should be expected. Effective leaders understand that conflict is a beneficial aspect of the problem-solving process and must not be discouraged when it occurs. They recognize that it is important to remain neutral and intervene only when members are not successful in resolving their own disagreements or when conflict impedes team progress.

Celebrating successes—Successful leaders acknowledge team and individual efforts, not just favorable outcomes (see chapter 8). Their gratitude strengthens team unity and motivates a team's continued work toward goal achievement. Accomplishments should be celebrated periodically, not only when a project has been successfully completed. Sometimes it is nice to take a break from hard work and just have fun as a group!

TEXTBOX 7.2

CREATING A SUPPORTIVE TEAM ENVIRONMENT

Team productivity, creativity, and commitment are optimized when leaders create a supportive environment by

- communicating clearly defined goals and expectations;
- demonstrating trust and respect in team members;
- refraining from micromanaging team efforts;
- encouraging members to contribute by listening to, and valuing, their questions and ideas;
- empowering individuals by involving them in planning and decision-making activities;
- assigning roles that take advantage of individuals' respective skills and expertise;
- fostering cohesion by keeping members informed through frequent and meaningful communication; and
- building camaraderie and team spirit by acknowledging individuals' efforts and celebrating group successes.

GUIDELINES FOR CONDUCTING EFFICIENT AND EFFECTIVE TEAM MEETINGS

Leaders can take steps to make meetings interesting, run smoothly, and be productive by:

- distributing an agenda at least one day in advance so individuals can prepare accordingly.
- beginning the meeting on time. Start off with a few minutes of fun (e.g., playing a quick game, completing a sentence ["____ day this week was my favorite because ____"; "I'm looking forward to ____"], or sharing an accomplishment).
- assigning a notetaker so the meeting information can be distributed to team members and accessed for future reference.
- sticking to the agenda. Leaders should guide the discussion (but speak less than one-third of the time), encourage participation, and minimize digressions to stay on task.
- assessing participants' level of engagement (e.g., are they listening, reading email?).
- setting aside five to ten minutes before adjourning to review progress, make assignments, answer questions, and address any last-minute items.
- ending on a positive note and on time.
- establishing a time and date for the next scheduled meeting.

Babe Ruth's observation underscores the essential role that motivational leaders play in promoting cohesiveness, engagement, and guiding a team's performance. Numerous studies have shown that teams are more likely to be successful when leaders create a positive and collaborative environment. For example, Tremblay, Gaudet, and Vandenberghe (2019) noted that organizational culture has a direct influence on team participation, performance, and member satisfaction. When team leaders engaged in task-oriented behaviors (e.g., planning, establishing team goals, coordinating activities), showed concern, and supported employees' efforts, their productivity and goal attainment improved significantly.

DIRECTOR'S SHOWCASE

Why do you consider it important to foster collegiality and cohesiveness among the members of your teaching team?

For one thing, it helps us to set goals and agree on those that we want to accomplish. It also brings us closer together so that we become a family of problem-solvers. The teachers understand that they can disagree with one another but may have to negotiate and compromise to reach a solution that everyone can accept. In the end, we are always there to support one another regardless of the outcome. I also believe that our families have more confidence in their children's teachers when they see them working well together as a team.

—Manisha K., public school, pre-K director

TEAM MEMBERS' ROLES AND RESPONSIBILITIES

The online advertisement read: "Looking for experienced teachers to fill full-time positions in our early childhood program. All applicants considered." Administrators may be successful in recruiting and hiring highly qualified individuals to work in their programs. However, they must also be cautious in assuming that all of these teachers will necessarily be effective team members (Textbox 7.4).

TEXTBOX 7.4

CHARACTERISTICS OF AN EFFECTIVE TEAM MEMBER

Successful teams rely on members who possess positive characteristics like these:

- displays trust and respect for team members
- is encouraging and supportive of others
- shows genuine commitment to team values
- is dependable and accountable
- is a good listener and communicator
- maintains an open and flexible attitude
- is tolerant of opinions and ideas that differ from their own

---

Effective teamwork requires individual members to fulfill important roles and responsibilities (Wu, Cormican, & Chen, 2020). In some cases, these are assigned to team members whereas at other times they may be assumed by individuals who volunteer for a task. Belbin's (1981) observational research led him to conclude that teams were effective only when their members undertook certain roles. He suggested that individuals tend to gravitate toward, and assume, one or more of the nine fundamental team roles based on their personality, perceived strengths, and expectations:

Action-oriented roles—"Shaper, Implementer, and Completer-Finisher." These individuals encourage innovation, put plans into action, and see projects through to completion.

People-oriented roles—"Team Worker, Coordinator, and Resource Investigator." These individuals take on the role of team leadership, rally team spirit and cooperation, clarify goals, and locate resources that the team requires to achieve its objective.

Thought-oriented roles—"Planter, Monitor-Evaluator, and Specialist." These individuals are highly creative problem-solvers, are able to thoughtfully analyze the pros and cons of an idea, and contribute specialized knowledge and skills that make a solution viable.

It is important that team members fulfill their respective roles and responsibilities so the team functions smoothly. Members must be committed to the team's mission and willing to dedicate time to accomplishing its goals. Assignments must be completed on time, reflect a quality effort, and meet the expected requirements. Members must share information in a timely, open, and civil manner. Highly opinionated, argumentative, or hostile exchanges should be avoided to prevent the disruption of team performance, progress, and interpersonal relationships (Hill, Offermann, & Thomas, 2019). Team members must also remain unbiased and able to work with diverse audiences in a cooperative and collaborative capacity. In other words, team members have a professional and ethical responsibility to support the team's efforts.

BARRIERS TO EFFECTIVE TEAMWORK

Teams are complex units with the capacity to innovate and perform at a high level (Wu et al., 2020). Although a number of factors are known to promote team success, researchers have also identified organizational- and individual-related barriers that can hinder their effectiveness. Several, such as communication and leadership, can have either a positive or negative effect on team performance depending upon the way in which they are managed (Figure 7.3).

Poor leadership is consistently reported as the most common cause of team dysfunction from an organizational perspective (Trent, 2019). Leaders who have not considered the requisite team size or individual competencies that are needed to work on a given project are likely to assemble unproductive teams. Also, failure to provide members with a clear explanation of the purpose and anticipated goals may leave the team unable to address the

FIGURE 7.3 Successful teamwork depends on effective communication and leadership. *fizkes, iStock / Getty Images Plus*

task for which it was assembled. Members in these situations often lose interest and end up leaving a team due to ineffective leadership (Nuhn, Heidenreich, & Wald, 2018).

A leader's personal leadership style can also be problematic and serve as a barrier to effective teamwork. Researchers have noted that an authoritarian leadership style has a negative effect on team performance and on members' engagement and creativity (Chiang et al., 2020; Lee et al., 2020). Similar findings have been reported in teams where laissez-faire leadership is practiced (Wellman et al., 2019). The perceived lack of direction and support is often detrimental to team cohesiveness, innovation, and productivity.

Unethical and inconsistent leadership have also been shown to serve as organizational barriers to team effectiveness. Members may gradually withdraw their commitment when leaders exhibit a lack of integrity and/or engage in lying, cheating, and unfair treatment (Mooijman et al., 2019; Sam, 2020). They also lose confidence in leaders who are unpredictable, ambiguous, and unable to manage conflict. Wong et al. (2019) suggested that these barriers are avoided when leaders model high ethical and moral standards and form respectful relationships with team members. As a result, their teams experience less conflict, improved work satisfaction, and increased productivity.

Individuals can also serve as barriers to a team's effectiveness. For example, a member's aversive personality (e.g., domineering, disgruntled, demanding) can disrupt a team's dynamics, communication, and working relationships (Carter et al., 2019). When these behaviors occur, there is a tendency for other members to stop participating, which can diminish the quantity and quality of team productivity.

───────────────── *Connecting Points* ─────────────────

During recent staff meetings, you have sensed an underlying tension that seems to exist between newly hired and senior teachers. For example, some of the tenured teachers unknowingly shake their head, roll their eyes, or smirk in disbelief when a new teacher suggests changes to a long-standing procedure.

- What effect(s) is this apparent division likely to have on team dynamics?
- How would you address this situation as the team leader?
- What measures would you take to improve team unity?

Generational differences can also affect team dynamics in terms of what individuals' value and perceive to be important (Burton et al., 2019; Weeks & Schaffert, 2019). For example, Generation Y (millennial) members are known to be interested in open communication and shared decision-making endeavors. They tend to be self-confident and do not expect to be recognized for their efforts. Generation Z individuals have expressed a preference for meaningful work, direct instruction, and continuous feedback. Although some multigenerational differences may exist, perceptive leaders understand that members share many positive qualities in common and are interested in maintaining team solidarity to achieve the organization's goals. They are able to address employee differences so that team unity is preserved.

Individuals who lack trust and commitment can also present a significant barrier to team effectiveness (Benishek & Lazzara, 2019; Naicker & Parumasur, 2018). Their distrust can exert a contagious and negative influence on team morale, creativity, and interpersonal relationships (Rezvani, Barrett, & Khosravi, 2019). As a result, communications may be disrupted and limit a team's access to critical information that may be needed to complete their work.

Individuals who withdraw early from a project can diminish the team's stability and progress (Benishek & Lazzara, 2019). Some members may leave because they have underestimated the time commitment that is required. For others, the rewards are not deemed sufficiently motivating to outweigh the necessary effort.

Motivational leaders must anticipate that barriers such as these will likely occur as teams form and conduct their work. They can often minimize the negative impact that such barriers can have on team performance by monitoring early changes in team dynamics and addressing any problems. Many potential barriers can also be prevented when motivational leaders provide meaningful guidance, strengthen team cohesion and camaraderie, empower their team members, and acknowledge individuals' efforts.

SUMMARY

- Teams and a team-based approach are commonly used in organizations today, and they have proven to be an effective and efficient strategy for addressing complex problems. Despite the advantages, a team approach also has its limitations.
- Several factors must be considered when assembling a team. What is the team's intended purpose? How many members should be invited? What diversity of knowledge, skills, and/or expertise should members possess? What combination of member personality traits will assure that the team can work together?
- Teams undergo a maturational process: forming, storming, norming, performing, and adjourning. The nature of member interactions, effectiveness, and performance differs during each brief stage. The process is repeated whenever a member leaves or is added to the team.
- Team leaders may hold a permanent title, be appointed temporarily, or emerge from the membership. They are responsible for providing initial guidance and ongoing support. Ineffective leadership is a common cause of team dysfunction.
- Team members have essential roles and responsibilities to fulfill if a team is to achieve its goals and purpose.
- Teams may encounter barriers, such as adverse member behavior, poor leadership, or lack of communication, that may interfere with their performance.

APPLICATION ACTIVITIES

1. Select and watch two of the following movies: *Cool Runnings, Invictus, Hoosiers, Miracle, Apollo 13, The Avengers, Coach Carter, Sister Act*. Respond to the following questions and record your answers on Application Sheet 7-1.

   a. How did the "leader" arrive at his/her leadership position?

   b. What personal qualities contributed to this individual's success as a leader?

c. What strategies did this leader use to foster cohesiveness and a teamwork mentality?

d. In what ways were the strategies used by the leaders in each movie similar and different?

2. Describe three team-building activities that you could use to help five new employees begin to assimilate and bond with their co-workers. Use Application Sheet 7-2 to record the information.

3. Recall a time that you had the pleasure of serving on a team or committee (e.g., high school, college, sports, professional, community). What aspects of team membership did you find rewarding? What aspects were particularly frustrating? If you had been the team or committee leader, what steps would you have taken to manage the frustrating experiences? Record your responses on Application Sheet 7-3.

REVIEW POINTS

1. What are two benefits of team participation for an individual?
2. How does psychological safety affect team members' willingness to take risks?
3. What are the advantages and disadvantages of limiting team size to five or six members?
4. What effect does social loafing have on team creativity and innovation?
5. At what stage in a team's development is it most productive? Why?
6. What measures can motivational leaders take to maintain participants' involvement in teamwork?
7. What obligations are individual team members expected to uphold?
8. In what ways does unethical leadership affect a team's performance?

KEY TERMS DEFINED

psychological safety—a feeling of protection from negative consequences that an individual experiences when they are part of a team or group

social loafing—an individual's tendency to exert less effort when working in a group

homogeneous—similar or alike

heterogeneous—dissimilar or unlike

norms—informal social rules or behavioral expectations established by a group

shared leadership—a leadership model whereby responsibilities and power are distributed among two or more individuals

REFERENCES

Aggarwal, I., & Woolley, A. W. (2019). Team creativity, cognition, and cognitive style diversity. *Management Science, 65*(4), 1586–1599.

Amir, O., Amir, D., Shahar, Y., Hart, Y., & Gal, K. (2018). The more the merrier? Increasing group size may be detrimental to decision-making performance in nominal groups. *PLoS One, 13*(2), e0192213. https://doi.org/10.1371/journal.pone.0192213.

Anderson, G., Keith, M., Albrecht, C., Spruill, A., & Pettit, C. (2019). Optimizing software team performance with cultural differences. *Proceedings of the 52nd Hawaii International Conference on System Sciences*, 3–13. http://hdl.handle.net/10125/59441.

Appelbaum, N. P., Lockeman, K. S., Orr, S., Huff, T. A., Hogan, C. J., Queen, B. A., & Dow, A. W. (2020). Perceived influence of power distance, psychological safety, and team cohesion on team effectiveness. *Journal of Interprofessional Care, 34*(1), 20–26.

Avis, P. (2019). Boosting productivity through health and wellbeing benefits. *Occupational Health & Wellbeing, 71*(10), 18–19.

Belbin, M. (1981). *Management teams: Why they succeed or fail.* London: Heinemann.

Bell, S. T., Brown, S. G., Colaneri, A., & Outland, N. (2018). Team composition and the ABCs of teamwork. *American Psychologist, 73*(4), 349–362.

Benishek, L. E., & Lazzara, E. H. (2019). Teams in a new era: Some considerations and implications. *Frontiers in Psychology, 10*, 1–15.

Bouwmans, M., Runhaar, P., Wesselink, R., & Mulder, M. (2019). Stimulating teachers' team performance through team-oriented HR practices: The roles of affective team commitment and information processing. *The International Journal of Human Resource Management, 30*(5), 856–878.

Breuer, C., Hüffmeier, J., Hibben, F., & Hertel, G. (2020). Trust in teams: A taxonomy of perceived trustworthiness factors and risk-taking behaviors in face-to-face and virtual teams. *Human Relations, 73*(1), 3–34.

Burton, C., Mayhall, C., Cross, J., & Patterson, P. (2019). Critical elements for multigenerational teams: A systematic review. *Team Performance Management, 25*(7/8), 369–401.

Carter, K. M., Mead, B. A., Stewart, G. L., Nielsen, J. D., & Solimeo, S. L. (2019). Reviewing work team design characteristics across industries: Combining meta-analysis and comprehensive synthesis. *Small Group Research, 50*(1), 138–188.

Chiang, J. T., Chen, X. P., Liu, H., Akutsu, S., & Wang, Z. (2020, February). We have emotions but can't show them! Authoritarian leadership, emotion suppression climate, and team performance. *Human Relations.* https://doi.org/10.1177/0018726720908649.

Clark, M. (2019). Edges and boundaries: Finding community and innovation as an early childhood educator. *Early Childhood Education Journal, 47*, 153–162.

Curseu, P. L., Ilies, R., Vîrgă, D., Maricutoiu, L., & Sava, F. A. (2019). Personality characteristics that are valued in teams: Not always "more is better"? *International Journal of Psychology, 54*(5), 638–649.

Czyz, S. H., Szmajke, A., Kruger, A., & Kubler, M. (2016). Participation in team sports can eliminate the effect of social loafing. *Perceptual and Motor Skills, 123*(3), 754–768.

Dinh, J. V., Traylor, A. M., Kilcullen, M. P., Perez, J. A., Schweissing, E. J., Venkatesh, A., & Salas, E. (2020). Cross-disciplinary care: A systematic review on teamwork processes in health care. *Small Group Research, 51*(1), 125–166.

Eckert, J. (2019). Collective leadership development: Emerging themes from urban, suburban, and rural high schools. *Educational Administration Quarterly, 55*(3), 477–509.

Emich, K. J., & Vincent, L. C. (2020). Shifting focus: The influence of affective diversity on team creativity. *Organizational Behavior and Human Decision Processes, 156*, 24–37.

Espedido, A., Searle, B. J., & Griffin, B. (2019). Peers, proactivity, and problem-solving: A multilevel study of team impacts on stress appraisals of problem-solving demands. *Work & Stress, 34*(3),1–10.

García, G., Gonzales-Miranda, D., Gallo, O., & Roman-Calderon, J. (2019). Employee involvement and job satisfaction: A tale of the millennial generation. *Employee Relations, 41*(3), 374–388.

Gonzalez-Mulé, E., Cockburn, B. S., McCormick, B. W., & Zhao, P. (2020). Team tenure and team performance: A meta-analysis and process model. *Personnel Psychology, 73*(1), 161–198.

Han, S. J., Lee, Y., & Beyerlein, M. (2019). Developing team creativity: The influence of psychological safety and relation-oriented shared leadership. *Performance Improvement Quarterly, 32*(2), 159–182.

Hill, N. S., Offermann, L. R., & Thomas, K. (2019). Mitigating the detrimental impact of maximum negative affect on team cohesion and performance through face-to-face communication. *Group & Organization Management, 44*(1), 211–238.

Kaiser, B., & Rasminsky, J. S. (2020). Valuing diversity: Developing a deeper understanding of all young children's behavior. *Teaching Young Children, 13*(2), 20–23.

Larson, L., & DeChurch, L. A. (2020). Leading teams in the digital age: Four perspectives on technology and what they mean for leading teams. *The Leadership Quarterly, 31*(1), 1–18.

La Salle, T. P., Wang, C., Wu, C., & Neves, J. R. (2020). Racial mismatch among minoritized students and white teachers: Implications and recommendations for moving forward. *Journal of Educational and Psychological Consultation, 30*(3), 314–343.

Lee, A., Legood, A., Hughes, D., Tian, A. W., Newman, A., & Knight, C. (2020). Leadership, creativity and innovation: A meta-analytic review. *European Journal of Work and Organizational Psychology, 29*(1), 1–35.

Maloney, M. M., Shah, P. P., Zellmer-Bruhn, M., & Jones, S. L. (2019). The lasting benefits of teams: Tie vitality after teams disband. *Organizational Science, 30*(2), 260–279.

Markowitz, A. J., Bassok, D., & Grissom, J. A. (2020). Teacher-child racial/ethnic match and parental engagement with Head Start. *American Educational Research Journal.* https://doi.org/10.3102/0002831219899356.

Maynard, M. T., Mathieu, J. E., Gilson, L. L., Sanchez, D. R., & Dean, M. D. (2019). Do I really know you and does it matter? Unpacking the relationship between familiarity and information elaboration in global virtual teams. *Group & Organization Management, 44*(1), 3–37.

Mitchell, R., Boyle, B., & Von Stieglitz, S. (2019). Professional commitment and team effectiveness: A moderated mediation investigation of cognitive diversity and task conflict. *Journal of Business Psychology, 34*, 471–483.

Mooijman, M., van Dijk, W. W., van Dijk, E., & Ellemers, N. (2019). Leader power, power stability, and interpersonal trust. *Organizational Behavior and Human Decision Processes, 152*, 1–10.

Mueller, J. S. (2012). Why individuals in larger teams perform worse. *Organizational Behavior and Human Decision Processes, 117*(1), 111–124.

Naicker, D., & Parumasur, S. B. (2018). The prevalence and magnitude of social loafing, and biographical influences, in a team-based organizational setting. *Journal of Economics and Behavioral Studies, 10*(3), 37–51.

Neto, R., Rodrigues, V. P., Campbell, K., Polega, M., & Ochsankehl, T. (2020). Teamwork and entrepreneurial behavior among K–12 teachers in the United States. *The Educational Forum, 84*(2), 179–193.

Nuhn, H. F., Heidenreich, S., & Wald, A. (2018). The role of task-related antecedents for the development of turnover intentions in temporary project teams. *The International Journal of Human Resource Management, 29*(15), 2284–2302.

Page, J., & Eadie, P. (2019). Coaching for continuous improvement in collaborative, interdisciplinary early childhood teams. *Australasian Journal of Early Childhood, 44*(3), 270–284.

Pérez-Vallejo, C., & Fernández-Muñoz, J. J. (2020). Quality of leadership and organizational climate in a sample of Spanish workers. The moderation and mediation effect of recognition and teamwork. *International Journal of Environmental Research and Public Health, 17*(1), 32.

Ramírez, R., López, L. M., & Ferron, J. (2019). Teacher characteristics that play a role in the language, literacy, and math development of dual language learners. *Early Childhood Education Journal, 47*(1), 85–96.

Rasheed, D. S., Brown, J. L., Doyle, S. L., & Jennings, P. A. (2020). The effect of teacher–child race/ethnicity matching and classroom diversity on children's socioemotional and academic skills. *Child Development, 91*(3), e597–e618. https://doi.org/10.1111/cdev.13275.

Redding, C. (2019). A teacher like me: A review of the effect of student-teacher racial/ethnic matching on teacher perceptions of students and student academic and behavioral outcomes. *Review of Educational Research, 89*(4), 499–535.

Rezvani, A., Barrett, R., & Khosravi, P. (2019). Investigating the relationships among team emotional intelligence, trust, conflict and team performance. *Team Performance Management, 25*(1/2), 120–137.

Rodríguez, I., Kozusznik, M. W., Peiró, J. M., & Tordera, N. (2019). Individual, co-active and collective coping and organizational stress: A longitudinal study. *European Management Journal, 37*(1), 86–98.

Rutishauser, L., & Sender, A. (2019). Effect of team-member exchange on turnover intention: A cross-cultural perspective on a selected aspect of employee engagement. *International Studies of Management & Organization, 49*(1), 43–62.

Sam, C. H. (2020, February). What are the practices of unethical leaders? Exploring how teachers experience the "dark side" of administrative leadership. *Educational Management Administration & Leadership.* https://doi.org/10.1177/1741143219898480.

Sanz-Martínez, L., Er, E., Martínez-Monés, A., Dimitriadis, Y., & Bote-Lorenzo, M. L. (2019). Creating collaborative groups in a MOOC: A homogeneous engagement grouping approach. *Behaviour & Information Technology, 38*(11), 1107–1121.

Steiner, I. (1972). *Group process and productivity.* New York: Academic Press.

Stipelman B. A., Rice, E. L., Vogel, A. L., & Hall, K. L. (2019). The role of team personality in team effectiveness and performance. In K. Hall, A. Vogel, & R. Croyle (Eds.), *Strategies for team science success* (pp. 189–196). Springer Publishing.

Tok, T. N. (2019). The relationship between the perceptions of personality traits and social loafing behaviors of candidate teachers. *Journal of Teacher Education and Educators, 8*(1), 55–77.

Tremblay, M., Gaudet, M., & Vandenberghe, C. (2019). The role of group-level perceived organizational support and collective affective commitment in the relationship between leaders' directive and supportive behaviors and group-level helping behaviors. *Personnel Review, 48*(2), 417–437.

Trent, R. J. (2019). Making sure the reality matches the hype: Understanding what hinders or promotes team performance. *Journal of Applied Business and Economics, 21*(8), 151–166.

Tuckman, B. W. (1965). Developmental sequence in small groups. *Psychological Bulletin, 63*(6), 384–399.

Tuckman, B. W., & Jensen, M. C. (1977). Stages of small-group development revisited. *Group & Organization Studies, 2*(4), 419–427.

van Veelen, R., & Ufkes, E. G. (2019). Teaming up or down? A multisource study on the role of team identification and learning in the team diversity-performance link. *Group and Organization Management, 44*(1), 38–71.

Wang, J., Cheng, G. H., Chen, T., & Leung, K. (2019). Team creativity/innovation in culturally diverse teams: A meta-analysis. *Journal of Organizational Behavior, 40*(6), 693–708.

Weeks, K. P., & Schaffert, C. (2019). Generational differences in definitions of meaningful work: A mixed methods study. *Journal of Business Ethics, 156,* 1045–1061.

Weiss, M., & Hoegl, M. (2016). Effects of relative team size on teams with innovative tasks: An understaffing theory perspective. *Organizational Psychology Review, 6*(4), 324–351.

Wellman, N., Newton, D. W., Wang, D., Wei, W., Waldman, D. A., & LePine, J. A. (2019). Meeting the need or falling in line? The effect of laissez-faire formal leaders on informal leadership. *Personnel Psychology, 72*(3), 337–359.

Wong, A., Wang, X., Wang, X., & Tjosvold, D. (2019). Ethical leaders manage conflict to develop trust. *Leadership & Organization Development Journal, 41*(1), 133–146.

Wu, Q., Cormican, K., & Chen, G. (2020). A meta-analysis of shared leadership: Antecedents, consequences, and moderators. *Journal of Leadership & Organizational Studies, 27*(1), 49–64.

Yam, P. P., Ng, G. T., Au, W. T., Tao, L., Lu, S., Leung, H., & Fung, J. M. (2018). The effect of subgroup homogeneity of efficacy on contribution in public good dilemmas. *PLoS ONE, 13*(7), e0201473.

Zaheer, S., Ginsburg, L., Wong, H. J., Thomson, K., Bain, L., & Wulffhart, Z. (2019). Turnover intention of hospital staff in Ontario, Canada: Exploring the role of frontline supervisors, teamwork, and mindful organizing. *Human Resources for Health 17*, 66. https://doi.org/10.1186/s12960-019-0404-2.

Zinsser, K. M., Main, C., Torres, L., & Connor, K. (2019). Patching the pathway and widening the pipeline: Models for developing a diverse early childhood workforce in Chicago. *Community Psychology, 63*(3–4), 459–471.

ONLINE RESOURCES

McCormick Center for Early Childhood Leadership (see, "Resources"): https://mccormickcenter.nl.edu/

MindTools.com (see, "Skill Areas"): https://www.mindtools.com/

University of California-Berkeley (see, "Guide to Managing Human Resources"): https://hr.berkeley.edu/

University of Colorado (see, "Team Effectiveness Questionnaire"): https://www.cu.edu/sites/default/files/Team_effectiveness_questionnaire.pdf

APPLICATION SHEET 7-1

I. The first movie I watched: _____.

    a. How did the "leader" arrive at his/her leadership position?

    b. What personal qualities made this individual a successful leader?

    c. What strategies did this leader use to foster cohesiveness and a teamwork mentality?

II. The second movie I watched: _____.

    a. How did the "leader" arrive at his/her leadership position?

    b. What personal qualities made this individual a successful leader?

    c. What strategies did this leader use to foster cohesiveness and a teamwork mentality?

III. In what ways were the strategies used by the leaders in each movie similar and different?

APPLICATION SHEET 7-2

Describe three team-building activities that you could use to help five new employees begin to assimilate and bond with their co-workers.

A.

B.

C.

APPLICATION SHEET 7-3

Team or committee (e.g., high school, college, sports, professional, community) on which I participated: _____.

a. What aspects did you find rewarding?

b. What aspects were particularly frustrating?

c. If you had been the team or committee leader, what steps would you have taken to manage the frustrating experience(s)?

Putting It All Together: Meaningful Motivation

OBJECTIVES

After reading this chapter, you will be able to do the following:

- Identify and describe three factors that contribute to employee demotivation.
- Explain why monetary rewards typically fail to produce sustained motivation.
- Describe how job enlargement, job enrichment, and job rotation can motivate employee engagement and professional growth.
- Design an in-service workshop based on adult learning principles.
- Discuss how factors, such as culture and age, influence an individual's perception of gratitude.
- Explain why it is important to continuously evaluate motivational reward systems.

KEY TERMS

- demotivate
- andragogy
- mentoring
- coaching
- gratitude

■ ■ ■

Motivation is the art of getting people to do what you want them to do because they want to do it.

—Dwight D. Eisenhower, Thirty-Fourth United States President

INTRODUCTION

Consider how you felt the first time you wore a new dress or drove a new car, ate at a new restaurant, embarked on a trip to a city that you had always dreamed of visiting, or purchased something new for your apartment or home. Very likely those feelings included a combination of joy, eagerness, excitement, enthusiasm, pleasure, and/or anticipation. The question is, do you still experience such feelings with the same intensity a year later?

In most instances, individuals respond with a resounding no. But why did these initial feelings diminish? What has changed and lessened the exhilaration and anticipation that once existed? What role could motivation play in these feelings?

Several motivational theories were discussed in chapter 3. In this chapter, you will learn how to apply that information in creative and effective ways to increase employee engagement, performance, morale, and motivation.

Connecting Points

Recall your initial emotions when you began a new job or higher education degree.

- What made you feel enthusiastic or excited about the opportunity?
- What factors reduced your enthusiasm after a period of time?
- How did you feel when you received a reward, such as a favorable grade, praise, pay increase, or promotion?
- How long did the "good" feelings last before your enthusiasm began to fade?

WHY EMPLOYEES LOSE THEIR MOTIVATION

Leaders across the business spectrum cite workforce retention as one of their most challenging responsibilities (Hom, Allen, & Griffeth, 2019). Annual turnover rates are reported to be greater than thirty percent in fields such as early childhood programs and as high as one-hundred fifty percent in the fast food industry (Rosenbaum, 2019; Whitebook et al., 2018).

Why do employees who were once passionate about working for a business lose their interest so quickly? Reasons vary and are often specific to an organization or business type. However, one of the most common explanations given for leaving a job is a loss of motivation (Clark & Saxberg, 2019; Lee et al., 2019a; Vui-Yee & Paggy, 2020).

These results prompt another question: What causes employees to feel less fulfilled or motivated after a short period of time? Their reasons are often attributed to ineffective leadership practices, which **demotivate** employees' interest and engagement in their work (Cote, 2019; Hom, Allen, & Griffeth, 2019; Wilkens, 2020) (Textbox 8.1).

Motivational leaders realize that their actions and inactions influence employees' engagement and commitment to an organization (Figure 8.1). For example, leaders should understand that employees want frequent performance feedback. However, if only criticism or negative information is provided, they are more likely to withdraw, devote less effort to their work, or eventually leave (Brower & Dvorak, 2019). Similarly, a director who often ignores teachers' suggestions creates an environment in which individuals are likely to feel discouraged and unappreciated.

Motivational leaders build trust and meaningful working relationships with their employees by taking time to learn more about them as individuals, not just as a qualified team member (Textbox 8.2). They ask questions, listen, and observe in order to identify a person's unique qualities, preferences, talents, and what they find motivating. Motivational leaders then use such information to create a workplace environment that employees find enjoyable and supportive, meets their needs, and makes them want to stay.

LEADERSHIP PRACTICES LINKED TO EMPLOYEE DEMOTIVATION

Employees are more likely to leave their job when leaders:

- fail to acknowledge or show appreciation for their efforts;
- overburden them with work and provide no additional compensation;
- fail to keep them informed or to provide constructive feedback;
- micromanage their work and prevent or discourage autonomy;
- ignore their ideas and/or requests;
- engage in behaviors that cause them to lose trust or respect in leadership;
- do not encourage or support employees' career development;
- overlook opportunities to challenge and keep employees interested in their work; or
- are ineffective in preventing or resolving conflict among co-workers.

FIGURE 8.1 A leader's behavior exerts a strong influence on employees' work ethic and commitment. *fizkes, iStock / Getty Images Plus*

"GETTING TO KNOW YOU" ACTIVITIES

The following are but a few examples of the many ways that leaders can begin to learn more about their employees.

One-on-One

"Eat and meet"—One day of each week (or month) invite one or two employees to join you for lunch or to take a short walk together. Ask about their day. (What was surprising? Funny? Frustrating or challenging? Suggestions?) Gradually shift the conversation to things that are more personal (e.g., their hobbies, favorite foods, travels, pets, family). Share some of the same information about yourself to establish a personal connection.

"Ask one question"—Hang a large piece of paper (or whiteboard) in the break room on which you pose a question for teachers to answer, such as, "What is your favorite color (dessert)?"; "What secret talent do you have that no one knows about?"; "What was the last movie you watched?"; "If you could have any pet, what would it be?"; "What do you like to do on your day off?" Post a different question each week. You will learn a lot about your staff, and they will also learn more about one another.

Motivation preference surveys—Search online for free, downloadable surveys. The results will enable you to identify and deliver meaningful acknowledgment for a job well done.

"Would you rather"—This can be a quick, fun way to learn a lot about an employee and his/her personal preferences. For example, "Would you rather get up early or stay up late?"; "Would you rather go on a hike or to a movie?"; "Would you rather live where it is warm or where it snows?"; "Would you rather eat healthy or exercise every day?" Construct your own questionnaire or locate any of the "would you rather" questions posted online.

As a Group

Ask the same question—Post a question on your staff meeting agenda that everyone will be expected to answer. For example, "If you could be on any television show, which one would it be?"; "What is your favorite way to unwind after work?"; "What is most likely to make you laugh?"; "What is one trend you hope never comes back?" Begin your meeting by having everyone respond to the question. Their answers will reveal interesting things about one another and begin the meeting on a light-hearted note.

Please pass the . . . —Fill a small bowl with M&Ms, fish-shaped crackers, teddy bear graham snacks, blueberries, or another small edible item. Pass the bowl and have everybody remove the desired number of pieces with a spoon. Next, each person must tell one interesting thing about themselves for each piece they have taken.

Show and tell (adult style)—Ask teachers to bring an item that represents or tells something about themself to share at the next staff meeting.

Flying high—Arrange staff in a circle. Have each person write three facts about themself or things they dream of doing in their lifetime on a blank piece of paper. Next, fold the sheet into a paper airplane and throw it across the room when given a signal. Each person should pick up an airplane (not your own), read aloud what is written, and see if the group can guess the author.

The ability to provide meaningful motivation also requires leaders to remain vigilant. Things that an employee once found inherently motivating are likely to change as they age, progress in their careers, and develop new interests (Furner & McCulla, 2019; Heinrichs et al., 2020). For example, a novice teacher may welcome a pay raise, regardless of the amount. A senior teacher may prefer opportunities to attend professional development events or to assume more leadership responsibilities.

Cultural values may also influence the type of reward that is motivating to an employee (Gagandeep & Sharma, 2019; Gesthuizen, Kovarek, & Rapp, 2019). For example, an individual from a collectivist background may be embarrassed if acknowledged or presented an award in front of her colleagues. As a result, she may subsequently refrain from the behavior that earned her the recognition. An employee who has grown up in a marginalized community may place a high value on job security and be motivated by a promotion or salary increase. In contrast, an employee of Japanese or Middle Eastern heritage may be less driven to attain power or social status and more intent on achieving a satisfactory work-life balance (Zhao & Pan, 2017). A leader who does not consider an individual's unique needs, values, and goals will likely fail to provide rewards that continue to motivate and inspire employee engagement. Questionnaires are available online to use for determining an employee's motivational preferences.

Successful early childhood leaders recognize that reward systems must be timely, meaningful to the individual, and specific to an achievement in order to motivate continued and improved performance. They also understand that a combination of monetary and nonmonetary motivators will address individuals' intrinsic and extrinsic needs. Leaders are likely to be rewarded for their motivational efforts by employees who are happy, productive, inspired, and committed to a program for the long-run. Occasionally, leaders may encounter an employee who chooses to resist their motivational efforts. In these cases, it is important that they continue to show the individual support and respect without prejudice.

MONETARY REWARDS

Organizations often use financial incentives, such as a pay raise, bonus, or fringe benefit, to acknowledge employees' contributions and accomplishments. The additional compensation is generally welcomed and appreciated, especially among younger and lower-salaried employees. It also serves as an important form of social recognition that can boost a person's self-esteem.

However, not all employees are motivated by financial incentives, so caution must be exercised in assuming that everyone will consider this token rewarding. For example, a senior teacher who is close to retirement and stays on because she enjoys working with the children may not be impressed with a forty-dollar monthly raise.

Employees' productivity and job satisfaction have been shown to increase for a short time following the receipt of an extrinsic reward, such as a salary increase or bonus. However, the motivating effect also tends to be transient unless it continues to be reinforced (Bareket-Bojmel, Hochman, & Ariely, 2017; Ponta, Delfino, & Cainarca, 2020). Antoni et al. (2017) noted one exception. They found that rewards in the form of benefits, such as health insurance, significantly increased employees' long-term commitment to an organization.

Researchers have also noted that most extrinsic rewards reduce or "crowd out" the things that an individual once found intrinsically motivating about their job. This is more likely to occur when employees consider the reward too small or insufficient relative to the task they are being asked to perform (Burson & Harvey, 2019; Coccia, 2019). As a result, they may feel unappreciated and lose passion for work they formerly enjoyed. For example, a talented teacher may give up a recent promotion to an assistant directorship after deciding that the added workload and stress was simply not worth the small salary increase that was offered. Such negative responses are particularly challenging for early childhood programs given their limited financial resources.

Monetary rewards are often tied to an employee's performance evaluation. An advantage of incentives awarded in this manner is their immediate and positive effect on employee morale and job satisfaction (Froese et al., 2019). For example, an individual may feel re-energized following a favorable review and express interest in learning new skills, devoting more effort to their work, and/or volunteering for additional responsibilities.

The disadvantages associated with performance-based rewards, or merit pay, are several. Employees have a tendency to resume their earlier work habits once the initial enthusiasm of a merit incentive wears off. They may question the accuracy of appraisals and, thus, the fairness of compensation awarded on this basis, if they are not pleased with the results. However, Wenzel, Krause, and Vogel (2019) found that these perceptions could be mitigated to some degree by including employees in the appraisal and goal-setting processes.

Performance-based rewards have also been criticized for increasing employees' stress and decreasing their creativity and spontaneity. Parker et al. (2019) reported that employees experienced a significant increase in pro-social behaviors and stress in their efforts to achieve the expected performance goals. Dahl and Pierce (2020) examined the potential mental health effects associated with rewards tied to performance appraisals. Employees who worked in these companies experienced increased rates of anxiety and depression. This was particularly common among employees who were evaluated as "poor performers." The authors also concluded that many employees who are subjected to performance-based rewards are more likely to either leave their job or end up seeking medical treatment for a mental health disorder.

BEYOND MONETARY REWARDS

Improved compensation remains a serious and pressing issue in the early childhood education field. Until this matter is fully resolved, leaders must rely on nonmonetary reward opportunities within a program to motivate, inspire, and empower a dedicated early childhood workforce. These rewards will not eliminate retention challenges, but they do yield an impactful and long-lasting favorable effect because of their intrinsic value (Buric & Moe, 2020; Vui-Yee & Paggy, 2020). Only a few of the many creative nonmonetary ways that early childhood leaders can motivate and inspire employees are presented here.

Job Design

The job design concept refers to a systematic process of distributing tasks and responsibilities among an organization's employees. Motivational leaders are in an ideal position to understand the duties that are essential to an organization's efficient and successful operation. They are able to design positions based upon factors such as these:

- employee qualifications
- job responsibilities
- task significance or importance
- degree of autonomy

In addition, motivational leaders can envision how positions complement one another and are aligned with organizational goals and resources. Once the plan is complete, the information can be formulated into comprehensive job descriptions and used for recruitment, evaluation, and training purposes (Textbox 8.3).

TEXTBOX 8.3

KEY ELEMENTS OF A WRITTEN POSITION DESCRIPTION

A well-written position description is an essential recruitment and evaluative tool, and should include the following:

- job title
- description of the position and responsibilities—brief (one or two paragraphs), clear, and specific; a statement about the primary duties (use action verbs), work environment (e.g., noisy, outdoors), population to be served, expected work hours, etc.
- required and preferred qualifications—skills, knowledge, education, experience, and any physical or other special requirements
- person to whom the employee reports
- frequency of performance evaluations
- salary range

The allocation of job responsibilities can have a significant positive or negative effect on employees' behavior (Figure 8.2). Individuals are more likely to experience job satisfaction, motivation, and inspiration when job expectations are matched to their skills, interests, and talents. Researchers have also found that employees are more engaged and productive and less likely to be absent when the work itself becomes intrinsically meaningful (Diamantidis & Chatzoglou, 2019; Peiro et al., 2020). Conversely, employees who lack requisite competencies, autonomy, or clear direction regarding their expected responsibilities are more likely to become frustrated and demotivated (Hester, Romano, & Rollins, 2020; Parker, Van den Broeck, & Holman, 2017).

FIGURE 8.2 Job responsibilities can be motivating and inspiring when they meet an employee's intrinsic needs. *globalmoments, iStock / Getty Images Plus*

Job design is an ongoing process that allows motivational leaders to make adjustments based upon their observations and employee input. Specific elements of a job can be modified to improve employee performance and organizational efficiency once the basic design framework is in place. For example, it may become apparent that more than one teacher may need to be assigned to playground maintenance or that the cook may require additional training to improve his adherence to sanitation practices.

Leaders can also use job design strategies to restructure existing jobs in order to boost employee morale, motivation, and organizational commitment. The three approaches most commonly used include job enlargement, job enrichment, and job rotation. Each modifies the employee's current responsibilities in a slightly different way.

Before initiating any job redesign initiative, motivational leaders should give careful thought to the potential limitations. Some employees may be uncomfortable with change. Involving them in the planning process provides an opportunity for individuals to express their concerns and to opt out if they prefer. Leaders must also consider the time and cost involved in providing additional training and/or mentoring that may be needed to facilitate an employee's transition into a new role. Plans must also be in place for evaluating the employee's performance and possible effect(s) that the job changes may have on other staff and the program itself.

Job Enlargement

Job enlargement is sometimes referred to as horizontal job loading (Cote, 2019). This redesign strategy involves adding new responsibilities of a similar nature to an employee's job. For example, a director may shuffle and reassign several duties currently assigned to other teachers. Or a head teacher who has worked in the same toddler classroom for the last five years may be asked to help set up a new toddler classroom, mentor several assistant teachers, or manage children's enrollment paperwork for her classroom. In most cases, no additional training is needed because the employee already possesses the requisite skills and knowledge to perform the new responsibilities.

The goal of job enlargement is to reduce an employee's potential for work-related boredom by increasing task variety. Employees often find newly assigned responsibilities refreshing and motivating because they create a feeling of autonomy, ownership, and accountability. Job enlargement also expands employees' skill attainment and promotes professional growth. Job enlargement plans should always be discussed with the employee before changes are made. It is important that they understand the purpose of these changes and do not perceive them simply as uncompensated responsibilities that are being added to their existing workload. If the employee expresses concern about performing an unfamiliar task, advanced arrangements should be made to provide training or mentoring. Leaders should also follow up with the employee to determine if the additional workload is manageable and continues to be of interest.

Job Enrichment

Job enrichment involves the redesign of an employee's job to include meaningful responsibilities that are more complex, challenging, and significant in importance. One goal is to improve organizational efficiency. Another is to increase an employee's intrinsic motivation and job satisfaction by delegating tasks and providing opportunities that foster personal achievement, recognition, increased responsibility, individual growth, and advancement (Textbox 8.4).

Many job enrichment programs are based on the principles of Frederick Herzberg's (1966) hygiene-motivator theory (see chapter 3). Herzberg found that when employees described the things that made them feel good about their jobs, they tended to identify factors directly associated with the content of the job: achievement, recognition, the work itself, responsibility, and advancement. He concluded that the only way to make meaningful changes in work design was to include more of the following motivational factors:

- *Accountability—employees are held accountable for their own work performance.* Leaders must communicate clear expectations for employees, provide frequent performance feedback, and consistently hold everyone accountable, including administrators.
- *Achievement—employees feel that they are accomplishing something worthwhile.* Leaders must be transparent and share information with employees so they understand the "big picture," including the program's goals and successes. They must also show their appreciation by acknowledging employees' efforts and accomplishments, even when the outcome is unsuccessful.

HOW TO DELEGATE EFFECTIVELY

Understand that it is likely to take an employee longer to complete a new task the first time. Successful delegation requires patience and can be achieved in these ways:

- Identifying and precisely defining the task to be delegated.
- Selecting an individual who possesses the necessary skills, knowledge, and experience to complete the task or is willing to learn.
- Describing the task, intended deadlines, expected outcomes, and accountability; providing the information in written form reduces the potential for misunderstanding. Avoid giving "how to" instructions to encourage the employee's creativity in determining how the task might best be performed.
- Providing resources, including training, that may be needed.
- Monitoring, without micromanaging, the individual's progress from time to time and providing constructive feedback.
- Evaluating the final results and rewarding the individual's efforts.

- *Control over resources—employees have some control over their resources and costs.* Leaders can involve teachers in decision-making processes and in budget planning so they understand program expenses and available resources. For example, teachers may be given a budget to use for purchasing classroom supplies.
- *Feedback—employees receive direct and timely information about their performance from the job itself.* Leaders can be instrumental in helping employees to see the results of their work through children's progress and learning, parent feedback, regulatory inspections or accreditation visits, and the achievement of classroom and program goals. Employees consider feedback especially important when they undertake new responsibilities (Umukoro & Egwakhe, 2019).
- *Personal growth and development—employees have the opportunity to learn new skills.* Motivational leaders encourage employees to continuously enhance their skills and competencies by providing more responsibility, such as mentoring opportunities, special project assignments, committee membership, or professional development event participation.
- *Work pace—employees are able to set their own work pace, and have the flexibility to schedule breaks.* Leaders should look for opportunities to provide job flexibility, such as offering a four ten-hour-day workweek staffing plan, flexible break schedules, or an occasional early departure to support employees' work/life balance.
- *Client relationships—employees develop a relationship with clients and know if they are satisfied with the services provided.* Building relationships with families is critical to children's developmental progress and a program's success. Multiple opportunities should be available for families to interact with teachers and become involved with the program through classroom participation, social events, advisory committees, conferences, open houses, etc.

Although job enrichment can be an effective nonmonetary motivational strategy, leaders must be sure that the individual desires more responsibility and possesses the necessary skills to be successful. The newly assigned duties must also be interesting and meaningful to the person, or they will fail to have any motivating effect. There is also the possibility that an employee will regret the additional oversight or monitoring that may be necessary during the transition period. For these reasons, motivational leaders must work closely with employees before making any changes to their current job responsibilities.

Job Rotation

Job rotation involves moving employees temporarily from one job to another within a program. This redesign approach creates job flexibility, reduces boredom, and helps employees gain an appreciation for different roles and activities. Job rotation also enables individuals to acquire a broader range of knowledge and experiences and, in turn, improve team effectiveness. Because employees are familiar with each other's position, they are able to step in if there is an unexpected absence or emergency.

The concept of job rotation may be more difficult to implement in early childhood programs because teacher-child consistency is important to maintain. However, job rotation can be made manageable in the following ways:

- Exchanging roles for short periods of time. Teachers can be scheduled to trade places for one or two hours during key times of the day so they get a true feeling for a different role. For example, one teacher might assist the cook in preparing the lunch meal or to work with the director on a special project.
- Exchanging jobs for one day each month. For example, one teacher may trade places with a teacher in a different classroom or age group. The following month, another teacher from each area swaps roles. This can be an effective strategy to help teachers gain perspective and to "walk a mile" in someone else's shoes.
- Exchanging visits with a nearby early childhood program. This allows employees to network with other early childhood professionals and to observe different facilities, educational philosophies, and program frameworks. Teachers' experiences can be shared and discussed during team meetings.

Although job rotation can be a positive motivator, it is also important to consider the potential disadvantages. Individuals may not be immediately efficient or effective until they have had time to acclimate to a new environment and set of responsibilities. Employees who are comfortable with their current position may find job rotation stressful and eventually decide to leave the program. This type of reaction may be more common among older and long-term employees who are content and not eager for change (Ann & Blum, 2020; Cote, 2019).

Job Crafting

The concept of job crafting is a less common form of job redesign. It refers to an employee's proactive efforts to change some aspect(s) of his or her job so that the work becomes more intrinsically meaningful. Such changes may involve an alteration in tasks, relationships, or personal beliefs about the value or importance of one's work (Figure 8.3).

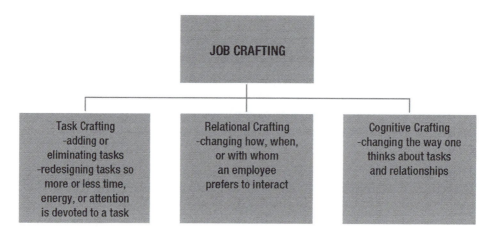

FIGURE 8.3 Job Crafting Elements

The distinguishing feature that separates job crafting from other redesign forms is that the employee initiates the desired changes. For example, a teacher may find new ways to establish stronger relationships with the children's families when the center reopens during the coronavirus pandemic. Or the same teacher may seek additional training in an effort to overcome her resistance to integrating more technology into the children's curriculum. Job crafting has been shown to significantly improve an employee's work-related interest, engagement, and satisfaction (Frederick & VanderWeele, 2020; Kuijpers, Kooij, & van Woerkom, 2020; Zhang & Li, 2020).

Employees should give careful thought to specific things they want to modify before implementing any changes. Their motive(s) will determine how co-workers view the changes and whether they are likely to be supportive or alienated (Tims & Parker, 2020). For example, an assistant teacher's offer to take on several additional tasks to lighten the head teacher's workload is likely to be well-received. In contrast, a teacher whose motives are perceived as self-serving or interfering with their co-workers' ability to perform a job can anticipate a negative reaction.

Employees who are interested in adding or deleting duties must first discuss such intentions with their director. Self-limited modifications, such as the manner in which a teacher decides to conduct a lesson or reframe her ideas about working with children who have challenging behaviors, do not require permission. However, employees may want to discuss their plans with colleagues if they have concerns or want suggestions. The effectiveness of any alterations should also be evaluated after a period of time so that necessary adjustments can be made.

Did You Know? ·

More than sixty percent of millennial employees who were surveyed said they wanted formal evaluation feedback at least once every month or two.

· ·

PROFESSIONAL DEVELOPMENT

Motivational leaders understand the importance of supporting employees' and their own participation in continuous professional development activities. They recognize that learning is a lifelong process. They invest in opportunities to help staff and themselves acquire new skills and knowledge, improve their effectiveness, network with other educators, explore new interests, and advance their careers.

Researchers have noted that teachers' participation in professional development experiences results in increased self-efficacy, reduced stress, and improved compassion and understanding (Harding et al., 2019; Hatton-Bowers et al., 2020). They have also found that it significantly improves engagement and retention rates (Kohli, 2019; Mansfield & Gu, 2019).

Some benefits may not be immediately apparent or may even produce unintended results. For example, Hanno and Gonzalez (2020) reported an unexpected reduction in preschool children's absenteeism following teachers' participation in training designed to improve the quality of teacher-child interactions. The effect on absenteeism was not a planned objective.

Teachers' satisfaction with professional development training, however, is not always positive. Compulsory one-time workshops are frequently viewed as lacking in relevant content, new ideas that advance teachers' skills or careers, respect for what they already know, or opportunities for participation and follow-up (Avidov-Ungar, 2020; Schachter, Gerde, & Hatton-Bowers, 2019; Svendsen, 2020). As a result, teachers often consider their attendance as a "waste of time" and simply fulfilling mandated professional development hours to meet licensing and/or accreditation requirements.

Researchers continue to address these criticisms and to suggest strategies for improving the quality and design of professional development activities. Many of their recommendations are based on Malcolm Knowles's (1970) theory of adult learning. Knowles described adults' learning needs and styles as unique from those of children, and referred to the differences as **andragogy** (Textbox 8.5).

Did You Know? ·

Employees who participated in a recent LinkedIn survey said they would not have left a company if it had invested in educational activities for employees.

· ·

Powell and Bodur (2019) conducted an empirical study to determine if online professional development learning modules reflected adult learning principles and achieved the intended outcomes. Teachers considered design features, such as content relevancy and usefulness, authentic tasks and experiences, opportunities to interact and collaborate with other educators, and reflection activities as being essential to their learning. Interestingly, the qualities that teachers perceived to be most important to a training's effectiveness mirrored those proposed by Knowles decades ago!

Professional development activities are offered in many forms, including conferences, courses (virtual, in person), workshops (online, face-to-face), professional learning communities, onsite speakers, observations, and printed materials. This variety provides individuals

KNOWLES'S SIX PRINCIPLES OF ADULT LEARNING

Knowles's six guiding principles are designed to improve the effectiveness of adult learning experiences.

- *Adults are self-motivated and self-directed learners.* They know what they need and want to learn and take the initiative to find appropriate resources; adults learn best when they are involved in identifying learning activities of interest.
- *Adults have accumulated years of life experience.* Learning activities should build upon and advance existing skills and knowledge, not repeat what individuals may already know.
- *Adults are goal-oriented.* They want learning to be meaningful and applicable.
- *Adults are motivated by learning what is relevant.* They want to know why something is important to learn and how it will benefit them personally and/or professionally.
- *Adults are practical.* They want theory translated into everyday practice; they want to be engaged and involved in hands-on experiences so they understand how to apply the information.
- *Adult learners want respect.* They are motivated by learning what acknowledges their competence, improves their performance, earns recognition, and satisfies intrinsic needs.

with flexibility in identifying opportunities that will meet their differences in learning needs, styles, and experience. Involving teachers in the selection of professional development learning activities has been shown to increase their interest, receptiveness, and engagement (Osman & Warner, 2020; Veldman et al., 2020). The likelihood that teachers implement what they have learned also is greater when leadership supports and reinforces their efforts.

Connecting Points

Your teachers need to complete additional in-service training hours before the next license renewal visit. You make arrangements for a speaker to come to the school and present a two-hour workshop on identifying signs of child abuse. During the session, you observe several teachers attending to their cell phones and whispering to one another. The next day, you ask the teachers what they thought about the session, and they replied, "We already knew this stuff."

- What lesson did you learn from this experience?
- What steps might you take now to build on the teachers' current knowledge and skills?
- What measures can you take in the future to avoid a similar occurrence?

Mentoring and Coaching

Mentoring and **coaching** can be described as alternative forms of professional development that are particularly beneficial for novice teachers. These arrangements have been shown to improve teacher engagement, effectiveness, retention, and well-being (Kutsyuruba & Godden, 2019; Whalen, Majocha, & Van Nuland, 2019). Morettini, Luet, and Vernon-Dotson (2020) observed new teachers who were faced with challenging teaching assignments. They noted that teachers experienced lower stress rates and developed increased resilience and self-efficacy when formal and informal mentoring was provided for a period of time.

Although the terms *mentoring* and *coaching* are often used interchangeably, they describe roles and responsibilities that differ. Mentors are usually colleagues who have considerable experience and work closely with a less experienced teacher. They play an important role in helping a novice or recently hired teacher transition to a new program and/or position. Mentors provide their mentee(s) with information, guidance, feedback, role-modeling, and personal and professional support. Their relationship is one built on trust and often continues as the teacher advances in his/her career.

The role of a coach differs somewhat from that of a mentor. Coaches are usually brought into a program to share specific expertise with novice or veteran teachers in order to improve and advance their skills. Their arrangement with a recipient teacher tends to be more formal and focused on instruction than that of a mentor-teacher relationship. For example, a person with behavioral training may be brought in to work with a teacher who has several children with autism in her classroom. Or a speech therapist may spend several days helping a teacher to modify learning activities for a child who is deaf. Coaching interventions are most often successful when:

- mutual goals are established;
- coaches model the desired instructional strategy;
- teachers implement and practice the strategy and reflect on their performance; and
- coaches provide constructive feedback, reinforcement, and encouragement.

There is considerable empirical evidence linking high-quality mentoring and coaching with teacher improvement and positive outcomes for children (Elek & Page, 2019; Siraj, Kingston, & Neilsen-Hewett, 2019). For example, Egert, Dederer, and Fukkink (2020) noted that teachers' instructional skills and interactions with children were more effective and positive following their experience with quality coaching and mentoring initiatives. The authors also determined that providing opportunities for teachers to self-reflect on the training activity was fundamental to a successful outcome.

DIRECTOR'S SHOWCASE

Study after study reports the positive effects that motivation has on employee engagement, job satisfaction, and retention. What advice would you offer to new program directors given your many years of experience?

I would agree that finding ways to motivate my staff is one of my most important and challenging jobs as a director. However, I have not always been successful but continue to learn from my mistakes. I made this plaque that says, "You are a star!" When a teacher did something outstanding, like getting a toddler to use the potty or an autistic preschooler to say a word, I would hang the plaque on their classroom door. One day, I did this for a teacher who had spent time with a parent who was quite upset. I also recognized her during our staff meeting. I could tell that she was embarrassed by the attention. Now I make it a point to talk with our new teachers when they are hired to find out what they find motivating.

—Darlene, program director

RANDOM ACTS OF GRATITUDE

The term **gratitude** describes a pleasurable feeling that people experience when they encounter something pleasing or meaningful (Ghosh, 2018). This emotion may be expressed in the form of praise, a favor, or a gift to show one's appreciation. Something as simple as a verbal "thank you for meeting with the cook to discuss Mia's special dietary needs" conveys a powerful message of caring. It informs the teacher that her efforts are valued and make an important contribution to the program.

Scientists have used imaging studies to determine how the brain responds to expressions of gratitude (Fox et al., 2015; Yu et al., 2018). They discovered that the acts of giving and receiving gratitude activate specific areas of the brain. This activity, in turn, triggers the release of brain chemicals (neurotransmitters), which produce sensations of happiness and pleasure and have a positive effect on a person's psychological well-being.

Gratitude is also known to foster prosocial behavior by establishing an emotional bond between the recipient and provider (Eisenberger, Shanock, & Wen, 2020; Pillay et al., 2020) (Figure 8.4). This connection is perceived as a reward for appropriate behavior and reinforces the likelihood that the same or similar conduct will be repeated. Employees who are treated with respect and gratitude also tend to treat their peers in a similar manner. One only needs to look at athletic teams to understand how essential gratitude is to team trust, cohesion, and successful performance.

Motivational leaders who practice gratitude create a workplace culture in which employees enjoy working, are engaged and productive, and likely to remain with a program (Cain et al., 2019; Cortini et al., 2019; Lee et al., 2019b). However, it is important that leaders do not limit their expressions of appreciation to only positive outcomes. Successes, large and small, as well as efforts that may not have had a favorable result should be celebrated.

Expressed gratitude will only have a positive and motivating effect for the individual when it is:

- *sincere*—words and body language should convey an honest and genuine message.
- *relevant*—meaningful praise should be descriptive and specific to the behavior for which one is grateful. "It was thoughtful of you to have the papers ready for Tanya's mother when she arrived this morning" versus "Thanks for helping out this morning."
- *time-sensitive*—praise delivered in a timely manner increases its significance. Praise that is withheld until the next staff meeting or semi-annual performance review loses its value.

FIGURE 8.4 An acknowledging of employees' efforts can be highly motivating. *SDI Productions*

- *personalized*—recognition presented in person or with a written thank-you note is viewed as being more authentic and sincere. A leader's personal effort also communicates a deeper sense of caring and respect than praise offered in an email or newsletter announcement.

Scientists have studied other factors to determine if they have any influence on individuals' need for, and response to, gratitude. Chopik and his colleagues (2019) noted a positive relationship between age and gratitude. Older adults and women tended to express gratitude at the highest rates. The study authors suggested that this behavior may reflect a desire to initiate increased social interaction. However, they also noted that age made no difference in terms of gratitude's effect on a person's emotional well-being. These findings reinforce the significant role that gratitude plays in satisfying basic human needs for belonging, respect, and self-actualization.

Researchers have also examined the way in which culture influences a person's perception of gratitude and its effect on emotional well-being. Corona et al. (2020) noted distinct differences among East Asians, Latinos, and European Americans in the way that gratitude was expressed and experienced. For example, Latinos regarded the appropriateness, frequency, and intensity of expressing gratitude of greater importance than did East Asians. However, European Americans considered the receipt and expression of gratitude more appropriate than both groups. These findings suggest that leaders use caution in assuming that all employees desire and experience gratitude in the same way.

Successful motivational leaders have many inexpensive options at their disposal for acknowledging employees' efforts and accomplishments (Textbox 8.6). They understand that practicing random acts of gratitude on a regular basis creates an environment in which employees feel empowered, enjoy working, and are inspired to perform to the best of their ability.

EXAMPLES OF RANDOM ACTS OF GRATITUDE

There are many simple, effective ways that can be used to express one's gratitude.

- Say "thank you" in person or in a written note; this action establishes a powerful emotional connection between the giver and recipient.
- Create a "gratitude board" (e.g., blackboard, bulletin board, whiteboard); encourage staff to post notes about something for which they are grateful—that day, week, or always.
- Celebrate employment anniversaries. Create a paper "ticket" that says, "We are proud to have had you on board for _____ years," and post it on the person's classroom door.
- Begin staff meetings by asking each person to share something they are grateful for.
- Surprise staff with "a treat just because." Provide items such as cookies, cupcakes, yogurt and various toppings, or a fruit or vegetable plate and leave it in the break room or share it during a staff meeting.
- Encourage employees to give "cheers from your peers." They are often the first to know about one another's interests and achievements, such as completing a marathon, adopting a dog or cat, trying to eat healthier foods, buying a new car, taking a trip, reading a good book, etc.
- Plan a staff "sleepover." Provide movies and games, snacks, and breakfast in the morning.
- Distribute staff appreciation bags; fill them with inexpensive items (e.g., candies, gum, "footies" or gloves, purse-size hand cream, small picture frame, "scratch off" ticket, etc.). Or host a staff appreciation picnic at the end of the day.
- Designate a VIP parking spot for a selected "employee of the week or month."
- Give out impromptu "time off" coupons that allow an employee to leave thirty minutes early or arrive thirty minutes later than usual.
- Provide an opportunity for a teacher to work in the front office for a day or to conduct the next staff meeting. This may be a chance for them to realize a new talent.
- Maintain a suggestion box and encourage employees to share their ideas and concerns. Be sure to act on their contributions or they will stop offering them.

EVALUATING REWARD AND RECOGNITION EFFECTIVENESS

Motivational leaders understand that employee reward and recognition programs must be evaluated periodically to ensure that they are achieving the desired motivational outcomes. One of the simplest and most direct ways to obtain feedback is to have employees complete an anonymous survey. A limited number of questions will elicit the critical information that is needed:

- Were the rewards and recognition forms meaningful?
- Did you find them motivating?
- Did you consider them to be fair and equitable?
- What would improve current recognition efforts?

The effectiveness of a program's motivational reward system can also be measured in terms of its impact on employee performance, job satisfaction, collegiality, and retention. Employees who feel valued and appreciated tend to enjoy their work, offer to help with extra tasks, look for ways to grow personally and professionally, and are less likely to be absent or to leave the program (Hom, Allen, & Griffeth, 2019; Jeon & Wells, 2018). Conducting an exit interview with employees who do leave can be helpful for determining if the reward system failed to meet their needs.

Evaluative data can also be obtained from family surveys and children's progress reports. Both sources yield information regarding teachers' performance and satisfaction or dissatisfaction with a program's leadership. By soliciting feedback from multiple sources, leaders can be relatively confident that their current reward and recognition efforts are either effective or in need of modification to improve employee satisfaction.

SUMMARY

- Leaders play a critical role in creating a workplace culture that motivates and inspires their employees. They understand what motivates each employee and work to build trust and meaningful relationships. They know that failure to address employees' motivational needs can lead to poor morale and attrition.
- Monetary incentives are usually appreciated but do not provide long-lasting intrinsic fulfillment.
- Job redesign (e.g., enlargement, enrichment, rotation, crafting) provides effective non-monetary options for renewing employee interest, engagement, motivation, and organizational commitment.
- Employees respect leaders who support their professional development. Continued learning opportunities satisfy an individual's self-actualization needs. However, they must be designed to meet adults' unique learning needs and style to be effective.
- Motivational leaders who express frequent and sincere gratitude create a positive workplace culture that fosters employee resilience, engagement, and commitment.
- Reward systems must be evaluated often to determine if they remain effective in supporting and motivating employee performance.

APPLICATION ACTIVITIES

1. Compile a list of ten work-related things that you find motivating. Next to each item, indicate if the motivational value is primarily intrinsic or extrinsic. Comment on the result. Use Application Sheet 8-1 for this activity.

2. Create a position description using Application Sheet 8-2 for the following job advertisement: Experienced teacher wanted to head a nature-based classroom for eighteen children ages three and four. Must be passionate about science and have an early childhood degree. If interested, call the Everything Nature Center to speak with the director.

3. Make changes to your current position description using the following job redesign concepts: job enlargement, job enrichment, job rotation, and job crafting. Which option would you find most inspiring and motivating, and why? Record your responses on Application Sheet 8-3.

4. List three things that you found gratifying today. Repeat this exercise every day for the next two weeks. Briefly discuss the effect this exercise has had on your daily outlook. Record your responses on Application Sheet 8-4.

5. Expand the list of Random Acts of Gratitude provided in Textbox 8.6. Describe a minimum of five additional ways to motivate and acknowledge employees' contributions using Application Sheet 8-5.

REVIEW POINTS

1. What leadership practices are likely to reduce the potential for employee demotivation?
2. Why do monetary rewards tend to have a limited, short-term effect on employee motivation?
3. What steps should leaders take to assure that employees will consider job redesign a positive motivational change?
4. What steps can a presenter take to design an in-service workshop that is appealing and advances participants' learning?
5. What makes an expression of gratitude meaningful and motivational for the recipient?
6. How is a verbal compliment interpreted by the brain?
7. Why is it important for motivational leaders to periodically evaluate their reward system?

KEY TERMS DEFINED

demotivate—a loss of interest or enthusiasm

andragogy—theory and principles of adults' learning style

mentoring—a supportive relationship formed between individuals for the purpose of sharing knowledge, skills, and experience

coaching—the process of guiding another individual's learning in a specific area for improved performance

gratitude—feeling thankful; an expression of appreciation

REFERENCES

Ann, S., & Blum, S. C. (2020). Motivating senior employees in the hospitality industry. *International Journal of Contemporary Hospitality Management, 32*(1), 324–346.

Antoni, C. H., Baeten, X., Perkins, S. J., Shaw, J. D., & Vartiainen, M. (2017). Reward management: Linking employee motivation and organizational performance. *Journal of Personnel Psychology*, *16*(2), 57–60.

Avidov-Ungar, O. (2020, May). The professional learning expectations of teachers in different professional development periods. *Professional Development in Education*. https://doi.org/10.1080 /19415257.2020.1763435.

Bareket-Bojmel, L., Hochman, G., & Ariely, D. (2017). It's (not) all about the Jacksons: Testing different types of short-term bonuses in the field. *Journal of Management*, *43*(2), 534–554.

Berg, J. M., Dutton, J. E., & Wrzesniewski, A. (2013). Job crafting and meaningful work. In B. J. Dik, Z. S. Byrne, & M. F. Steger (Eds.), *Purpose and meaning in the workplace* (pp. 81–104). Washington, DC: American Psychological Association.

Brower, C., & Dvorak, N. (2019). *Why employees are fed up with feedback*. Gallup. Retrieved from https://www.gallup.com/workplace/267251/why-employees-fed-feedback.aspx.

Buric, I., & Moe, A. (2020). What makes teachers enthusiastic: The interplay of positive affect, self-efficacy and job satisfaction. *Teaching and Teacher Education*, *89*, 103008. https://doi.org/10.1016/j .tate.2019.103008.

Burson, J., & Harvey, N. (2019). Mo money, Mo problems: When and why financial incentives backfire. *Journal of Management Information and Decision Sciences*, *22*(3), 191–206.

Cain, I. H., Cairo, A., Duffy, M., Meli, L., Rye, M. S., & Worthington, E. L. (2019). Measuring gratitude at work. *The Journal of Positive Psychology*, *14*(4), 440–451.

Chopik, W. J., Newton, N. J., Ryan, L. H., Kashdan, T. B., & Jarden, A. J. (2019). Gratitude across the life span: Age differences and links to subjective well-being. *The Journal of Positive Psychology*, *14*(3), 292–302.

Clark, R. E., & Saxberg, B. (2019). 4 reasons good employees lose their motivation. *Harvard Business Review*. Retrieved from https://hbr.org/2019/03/4-reasons-good-employees-lose-their-motivation.

Coccia, M. (2019). Intrinsic and extrinsic incentives to support motivation and performance of public organizations. *Journal of Economics Bibliography*, *6*(1), 20–29.

Corona, K., Senft, N., Campos, B., Chen, C., Shiota, M., & Chentsova-Dutton, Y. (2020). Ethnic variation in gratitude and well-being. *Emotion*, *20*(3), 518–524.

Cortini, M., Converso, D., Galanti, T., Di Fiore, T., Di Domenico, A., & Fantinelli, S. (2019). Gratitude at work works! A mix-method study on different dimensions of gratitude, job satisfaction, and job performance. *Sustainability*, *11*(14), 3902. DOI:10.3390/su11143902.

Cote, R. (2019). Motivating multigenerational employees: Is there a difference? *Journal of Leadership, Accountability and Ethics*, *16*(2), 15–29.

Dahl, M. S., & Pierce, L. (2020). Pay-for-performance and employee mental health: Large sample evidence using employee prescription drug usage. *Academy of Management Discoveries Journal*, *6*(1), 12–38.

Diamantidis, A. D., & Chatzoglou, P. (2019). Factors affecting employee performance: An empirical approach. *International Journal of Productivity and Performance Management*, *68*(1), 171–193.

Egert, F., Dederer, V., & Fukkink, R. G. (2020). The impact of in-service professional development on the quality of teacher-child interactions in early education and care: A meta-analysis. *Educational Research Review*, *28*, 100309. https://doi.org/10.1016/j.edurev.2019.100309.

Eisenberger, R., Shanock, L. R., & Wen, X. (2020). Perceived organizational support: Why caring about employees counts. *Annual Review of Organizational Psychology and Organizational Behavior*, *7*, 101–124.

Elek, C., & Page, J. (2019). Critical features of effective coaching for early childhood educators: A review of empirical research literature. *Professional Development in Education, 45*(4), 567–585.

Fox, G. R., Kaplan, J., Damasio, H., & Damasio, A. (2015). Neural correlates of gratitude. *Frontiers in Psychology, 6,* 1481. DOI: 10.3389/fpsyg.2015.01491.

Frederick, D. E., & VanderWeele, T. J. (2020). Longitudinal meta-analysis of job crafting shows positive association with work engagement. *Cogent Psychology, 7*(1), 1746733. https://doi.org/10.1080/233 11908.2020.1746733.

Froese, F. J., Peltokorpi, V., Varma, A., & Hitotsuyanagi-Hansel, A. (2019). Merit-based rewards, job satisfaction and voluntary turnover: Moderating effects of employee demographic characteristics. *British Journal of Management, 30*(3), 610–623.

Furner, C., & McCulla, N. (2019). An exploration of the influence of school context, ethos and culture on teacher career-stage professional learning. *Professional Development in Education, 45*(3), 505–519.

Gagandeep, K., & Sharma, R. R. (2019). Linkages between culture (national, organizational and professional) and total reward expectation of employees: A conceptual framework. *IUP Journal of Organizational Behavior, 18*(4), 25–49.

Gesthuizen, M., Kovarek, D., & Rapp, C. (2019). Extrinsic and intrinsic work values: Findings on equivalence in different cultural contexts. *The Annals of the American Academy of Political and Social Science, 682*(1), 60–83.

Ghosh, S. K. (2018). Happy hormones at work: Applying the learnings from neuroscience to improve and sustain workplace happiness. *NHRD Network Journal, 11*(4), 83–92.

Hanno, E. C., & Gonzalez, K. E. (2020). The effects of teacher professional development on children's attendance in preschool. *Journal of Research on Educational Effectiveness, 13*(1), 3–28.

Harding, J. F., Connors, M. C., Krauss, A. F., Aikens, N., Malone, L., & Tarullo, L. (2019). Head Start teachers' professional development, well-being, attitudes, and practices: Understanding changes over time and predictive associations. *Community Psychology, 63*(3–4), 324–337.

Hatton-Bowers, H., Smith, M. H., Huynh, T., Bash, K., Durden, T., Anthony, C. . . . Lodl, K. (2020). "I will be less judgmental, more kind, more aware, and resilient!": Early childhood professionals' learnings from an online mindfulness module. *Early Childhood Education Journal, 48*(3), 379–391.

Heinrichs, K., Angerer, P., Li, J., Loerbroks, A., Weigl, M., & Müller, A. (2020). Changes in the association between job decision latitude and work engagement at different levels of work experience: A 10-year longitudinal study. *Work & Stress, 34*(2), 111–126.

Herzberg, F. (1966). *Work and the nature of man.* Cleveland, OH: World Publishing Co.

Hester, O., Romano, S., & Rollins, L. (2020). "Overworked and underappreciated": Special education teachers describe stress and attrition. *Teacher Development, 24*(2), 1–18.

Hom, P. W., Allen, D. G., & Griffeth, R. W. (2019). *Employee retention and turnover: Why employees stay or leave.* New York: Routledge.

Jeon, L., & Wells, M. (2018). An organizational-level analysis of early childhood teachers' job attitudes: Workplace satisfaction affects Early Head Start and Head Start teacher turnover. *Child & Youth Care Forum, 47*(4), 563–581.

Knowles, M. S. (1970). *The modern practice of adult education. Andragogy versus pedagogy.* New York: Association Press.

Kohli, R. (2019). Lessons for teacher education: The role of critical professional development in teacher of color retention. *Journal of Teacher Education, 70*(1), 39–50.

Kuijpers, E., Kooij, D. T., & van Woerkom, M. (2020). Align your job with yourself: The relationship between a job crafting intervention and work engagement, and the role of workload. *Journal of Occupational Health Psychology, 25*(1), 1–16.

Kutsyuruba, B., & Godden, L. (2019). The role of mentoring and coaching as a means of supporting the well-being of educators and students. *International Journal of Mentoring and Coaching in Education, 8*(4), 229–234.

Lee, A., Kim, H., Faulkner, M., Gerstenblatt, P., & Travis, D. J. (2019a). Work engagement among child-care providers: An application of the job demands—resources model. *Child & Youth Care Forum, 49*(1), 77–91.

Lee, H. W., Bradburn, J., Johnson, R. E., Lin, S. H., & Chang, C. H. (2019b). The benefits of receiving gratitude for helpers: A daily investigation of proactive and reactive helping at work. *Journal of Applied Psychology, 104*(2), 197–213.

Mansfield, C., & Gu, Q. (2019). "I'm finally getting that help that I needed": Early career teacher induction and professional learning. *Australian Educational Researcher, 46*, 639–659.

Morettini, B., Luet, K., & Vernon-Dotson, L. (2020). Building beginning teacher resilience: Exploring the relationship between mentoring and contextual acceptance. *The Educational Forum, 84*(1), 48–62.

Osman, D. J., & Warner, J. R. (2020). Measuring teacher motivation: The missing link between professional development and practice. *Teaching and Teacher Education, 92*, 103064. https://doi.org/10.1016/j.tate.2020.103064.

Parker, S. K., Van den Broeck, A., & Holman, D. (2017). Work design influences: A synthesis of multilevel factors that affect the design of jobs. *Academy of Management Annals, 11*(1), 267–308.

Parker, S. L., Bell, K., Gagné, M., Carey, K., & Hilpert, T. (2019). Collateral damage associated with performance-based pay: The role of stress appraisals. *European Journal of Work and Organizational Psychology, 28*(5), 691–707.

Peiro, J., Bayona, J., Caballer, A., & Fabio, A. (2020). Importance of work characteristics affects job performance: The mediating role of individual dispositions on the work design-performance relationships. *Personality and Individual Differences, 157*, 109808. https://doi.org/10.1016/j.paid.2019.109808.

Pillay, N., Park, G., Kim, Y. K., & Lee, S. (2020). Thanks for your ideas: Gratitude and team creativity. *Organizational Behavior and Human Decision Processes, 156*, 69–81.

Ponta, L., Delfino, F., & Cainarca, G. C. (2020). The role of monetary incentives: Bonus and/or stimulus. *Administrative Sciences, 10*(1), 1–18.

Powell, C. G., & Bodur, Y. (2019). Teachers' perceptions of an online professional development experience: Implications for a design and implementation framework. *Teaching and Teacher Education, 77*, 19–30.

Rosenbaum, E. (2019). *Panera is losing nearly 100% of its workers every year as fast-food turnover crisis worsens.* Retrieved from https://www.cnbc.com/2019/08/29/fast-food-restaurants-in-america-are-losing-100percent-of-workers-every-year.html.

Schachter, R. E., Gerde, H. K., & Hatton-Bowers, H. (2019). Guidelines for selecting professional development for early childhood teachers. *Early Childhood Education Journal, 47*(2), 395–408.

Siraj, I., Kingston, D., & Neilsen-Hewett, C. (2019). The role of professional development in improving quality and supporting child outcomes in early education and care. *Asia-Pacific Journal of Research in Early Childhood Education, 13*(2), 49–68.

Svendsen, B. (2020). Inquiries into teacher professional development—What matters? *Education, 140*(3), 111–130.

Tims, M., & Parker, S. K. (2020). How coworkers attribute, react to, and shape job crafting. *Organization Psychology Review, 10*(1), 29–54.

Umukoro, J. E., & Egwakhe, A. J. (2019). Job-characteristics dimensions and employee continuance commitment. *Global Journal of Management and Business Research: Administration and Management, 19*(10), 21–31.

Veldman, M. A., Van Kuijk, M. F., Doolaard, S., & Bosker, R. J. (2020). Implementation of cooperative learning: Differences in teachers' attitudes and beliefs. *Teachers and Teaching, 26*(1), 103–117.

Vui-Yee, K., & Paggy, K. (2020). The effect of work fulfilment on job characteristics and employee retention: Gen Y employees. *Global Business Review, 21*(2), 313–327.

Wenzel, A., Krause, T. A., & Vogel, D. (2019). Making performance pay work: The impact of transparency, participation, and fairness on controlling perception and intrinsic motivation. *Review of Public Personnel Administration, 39*(2), 232–255.

Whalen, C., Majocha, E., & Van Nuland, S. (2019). Novice teacher challenges and promoting novice teacher retention in Canada. *European Journal of Teacher Education, 42*(5), 591–607.

Whitebook, M., McLean, C., Austin, L. J., & Edwards, B. (2018). *Early childhood workforce index—2018.* Berkeley, CA: Center for the Study of Child Care Employment, University of California, Berkeley. Retrieved from http://cscce.berkeley.edu/topic/early-childhood-work-force-index/2018/.

Wilkens, M. (2020). Employee churn in after-school care: Manager influences on retention and turnover. *Journal of Youth Development, 15*(1), 94–121.

Yu, H., Gao, X., Zhou, Y., & Zhou, X. (2018). Decomposing gratitude: Representation and integration of cognitive antecedents of gratitude in the brain. *Journal of Neuroscience, 38*(21), 4886–4898.

Zhang, T., & Li, B. (2020). Job crafting and turnover intention: The mediating role of work engagement and job satisfaction. *Social Behavior and Personality, 48*(2), 1–9.

Zhao, B., & Pan, Y. (2017). Cross-cultural employee motivation in international companies. *Journal of Human Resource and Sustainability Studies, 5*(4), 215–222.

ONLINE RESOURCES

OMES Recognition Toolkit: https://omes.ok.gov/sites/g/files/gmc316/f/RecognitionTookKit.pdf

The Society for Human Resource Management (SHRM): https://www.shrm.org/

University of California Irvine (recognition preference questionnaire): http://training.uci.edu/staff/engagement-recognition/recognition/EmployeeRecognitionQuestionnaire.pdf

U.S. Small Business Administration (SBA): https://www.sba.gov/

Your Partner in HR (employee recognition survey): http://yourpartnerinhr.com/wp-content/uploads/Employee-Recognition-Survey.pdf

APPLICATION SHEET 8-1

Ten work-related items that I personally find motivating:
(Note next to each item whether the value is extrinsic or intrinsic.)

Comment on your results.

APPLICATION SHEET 8-2

Prepare a position description from the following newspaper advertisement: Experienced teacher wanted to head a nature-based classroom for eighteen children ages three and four. Must be passionate about science and have an early childhood degree. If interested, call the Everything Nature Center to speak with the director.

APPLICATION SHEET 8-3

Rewrite your current position description using the job enlargement approach:

Repeat this exercise using job enrichment:

Repeat this exercise using job rotation:

Repeat this exercise using job crafting:

APPLICATION SHEET 8-4

Three things that I am grateful for today:

1.

2.

3.

Continue to record your responses every day for the next two weeks. Briefly describe any effect(s) this exercise has had on your daily outlook.

APPLICATION SHEET 8-5

Five additional examples of Random Acts of Gratitude:

1.

2.

3.

4.

5.

Future Challenges

OBJECTIVES

After reading this chapter, you will be able to do the following:

- Describe the leader's role in advancing early childhood education as a field of professional practice.
- Discuss two ways that leaders can support program quality improvements.
- Identify two advantages that professional status would offer for the recruitment and retention of early childhood educators.
- Discuss two strategies that motivational leaders can use to reduce the potential for -isms in the workplace.
- Explain the concept of director credentialing and why it is beneficial.
- Justify the importance of family-school-community partnerships in early childhood education.

KEY TERMS

- -isms
- implicit bias
- explicit bias
- credentialing

■ ■ ■

Education is the most powerful weapon which you can use to change the world.
—Nelson Mandela, Nobel Prize winner, South Africa's first black president

INTRODUCTION

The early childhood field has entered a period that is unique in its long history. The clientele served, services provided, and authorities with whom it interacts create a combination that often leads to challenges and discussion. Newer and current challenges in a different form are some of the most thought-provoking it will now have to address. Among them are implicit and explicit biases, discipline disparities, equitable access, funding, assessment pressures, retention, public expectations, leadership development, and professionalism achievement.

Early childhood leaders will have to acknowledge, understand, and react to the potential turmoil and dissent such issues and others may provoke. These challenges should be viewed as opportunities for change and improvement. They also serve as guides for discussion and control of future actions and direction.

Several emerging developments are described and discussed in this final chapter. The purpose is to raise leaders' awareness, understanding, and ability to serve as catalysts for effective change. It is also intended to convey the importance of leadership's role in recruiting, mentoring, and motivating a new generation of early childhood leaders as reflective and action processes take place.

ACHIEVING PROFESSIONAL RECOGNITION

NAEYC's vision for defining and advancing early childhood education as a field of professional practice is presented in the document *Unifying Framework for the Early Childhood Education Profession* (see chapter 1). The initiative is described as "a national collaboration to define the early childhood profession by establishing a unifying framework for career pathways, knowledge, and competencies, qualifications, standards, and compensation." The complete text is available on the organization's website (http://powertotheprofession.org/).

The proposed restructuring involves a significant departure from the existing arrangement of varied—and often minimal—qualification requirements and accountability standards established by individual states. The current approach would be replaced with a cohesive, three-tiered credentialing system that explicitly defines who childhood educators are, what they know, and what they do. Each state would follow and enforce the identical standards, thus unifying all early childhood educators as professional members.

Changes of this magnitude will undoubtedly raise questions, apprehension, resistance, and criticism among personnel who currently work in and operate early childhood programs. NAEYC anticipated this possibility and countered by inviting and engaging public involvement throughout the developmental process. Furthermore, NAEYC has offered reassurance that new requirements and regulations would not be implemented until adequate public investment is guaranteed. Once this occurs, reasonable deadlines will support a gradual transition to the new system.

Although challenges are likely to be encountered along the way, it is important that leaders continue to move the initiative forward and build on the public's increasing understanding of early childhood education's inherent value (Figure 9.1):

> These investments are well worth the cost. They are investments in our nation's essential infrastructure, as important as other public goods such as highways and clean drinking water. They are investments in people who are the most valuable resource our country has, and who represent the cornerstone of quality in early childhood education. With the voices of educators at the forefront of the movement, we must take advantage of this moment, for the good of our country's children, families, educators, businesses, and economy. (NAEYC, 2020)

FIGURE 9.1 Achieving professional status has important implications for early childhood teacher recognition, respect, and compensation. *FatCamera, E+*

The recent pandemic drew greater attention to the essential role that early childhood education plays in our society and raised concerns about the need to improve program quality, equity, and access for all children. It also served to highlight inherent struggles in the field, including a lack of respect and fair wages, that dedicated, hard-working educators experience. Allvin and Hogan (2020) noted, "If our economy is to recover, it will require a reimagined approach to financing and structuring the systems that support high-quality child care."

The achievement of professional status will require strong and sustained leadership. Early childhood leaders will need to be proactive in answering teachers' questions about the proposed changes, advocating and gaining the support of stakeholders and policymakers, and controlling the direction of future developments. They must also collaborate closely with institutions of higher learning to develop new professional training programs that prepare educators to meet competency standards. In other words, attaining the bold changes that NAEYC proposes will require a coordinated team effort.

IMPROVING PROGRAM QUALITY

Results from countless empirical studies support the conclusions that participation in quality early childhood programs leads to increased cognitive development, lower criminal activity rates, greater lifetime earning potential, and reduced need for special education services (Carr et al., 2019; Domond et al., 2020; Philpott et al., 2019). However, experts have long recognized that high standards of learning and environmental conditions are not evident in all programs across the nation. As a result, calls for improving the consistent quality of early childhood education programs continue to dominate national discussions.

A number of early evaluative tools remain in use to address inequities in program quality, such as Quality Rating and Improvement Systems (QRIS), NAEYC Accreditation Standards, Early Childhood Environment Rating Scales (ECERS–R), Classroom Assessment Scoring System (CLASS), National Health and Safety Performance Standards, state-specific Early Learning Standards, and others. Increased funding initiatives, such as Race to the Top, Federal Preschool Development Grants, Head Start, and state-supported pre-K, have been established to reinforce early childhood program efforts in achieving improvement goals. However, progress in delivering consistently high-quality early childhood programs has been uneven despite these efforts.

Many rationales have been offered to explain the field's slow progress. One often cited reason centers on the inconsistent interpretation and administration of quality measurement systems (Perlman et al., 2020; Sabol, Ross, & Frost, 2020). Another points to programs' failed use of assessment results to implement any noteworthy quality improvements, such as hiring teachers with advanced early childhood education credentials (Boyd-Swan & Herbst, 2020). In other cases, existing programs are simply unwilling or unable to modify current practices.

These findings are of significant importance for the early childhood leadership community. Leaders have a fundamental and ethical obligation to engage in continuous program evaluation and to use the results for improvement (NAEYC, 2018). Equally important is their role in advocating for, and building, a unified assessment and accountability system to replace the current fragmented approach. These changes would yield meaningful information that program leaders could use to better serve diverse child, family, and workforce populations. They would also produce reliable data needed to inform early childhood education policy, funding, and legislative developments.

The achievement of high-quality standards across all early childhood programs is important for optimization of young children's development, attraction and retention of outstanding teachers, and garnering of public respect and recognition. Supporting and maintaining these efforts will require increased financial investments. Additional research is also needed to identify obstacles that may impede program improvements and to develop effective means to overcome them. Equally important will be the need for strong, visionary leadership to articulate the value of engaging in a unified system of program improvement.

ATTRACTING AND RETAINING HIGH-QUALITY TEACHERS

Program leaders will continue to struggle with recruitment and retention issues until they are able to pay highly qualified early childhood teachers an acceptable living wage. Currently, more than half of the field's teachers depend on federal assistance programs (such as Supplemental Nutrition Assistance Program [SNAP], Medicaid, Temporary Assistance for Needy Families [TANF], and Children's Health Insurance Program [CHIP]) to supplement their income and simply survive (McLean, Whitebook, & Roh, 2019). Data analysis also shows that low wages continue to perpetuate gender and racial disparities in the field. Half of all early childhood teachers are women of color and fewer than three percent are male (Austin et al., 2019; Mader, 2019).

Declining enrollments in teacher preparation programs will further exacerbate efforts to attract and hire highly qualified teachers. Higher education schools in almost every state report a thirty- to fifty-percent drop in applicants (Partelow, 2019). Stagnant wages and increased responsibilities are often cited as deterring individuals from entering the teaching profession (Sutcher, Darling-Hammond, & Carver-Thomas, 2016; Wiggan, Smith, & Watson-Vandiver, 2020). Current shortages are likely to become even greater as more teachers retire or leave the field to pursue a different career.

NAEYC's call to professionalize the field may be the much-needed stimulus that helps to alleviate the teacher shortage. The proposed framework would establish a highly recognized career path along which teachers can advance and earn a salary commensurate with their education and responsibilities. It also includes plans for financial support to help teachers pursue an advanced degree.

Accepting and approving these bold changes will require additional resources and strong, sustained advocacy. Even then, it will take time before the benefits associated with professional status can be fully realized. In the interim, it is incumbent upon leaders to create inspirational and motivational workplace environments that are conducive to the retention of highly qualified teachers.

ADDRESSING "–ISMS"

Racism, classism, sexism, ageism, ableism, and other "-**isms**" have attracted increased attention in recent years. They have served as catalysts for extensive dialogue among educators and the implementation of pedagogical and instructional changes. For example, inclusive and anti-bias practices and curricula that teach children acceptance, respect, and social justice are significantly more predominant in early childhood classrooms today. Programs also have made policy changes and provided more sensitivity training.

These are certainly noteworthy efforts. However, they fail to address the **implicit** and **explicit biases**, or "-isms," that can influence the recruitment and retention of teachers, especially those of color. Currently, only twenty percent of public school teachers identify their race/ethnicity as non-white (NCES, 2020). In contrast, teachers of a minority background account for fifty percent of the early childhood workforce (McLean, Whitebook, & Roh, 2019). Low wages and few entry qualifications may explain, in part, this stark discrepancy (Austin et al., 2019).

Sexism, another persistent "-ism," is illustrated by the underrepresentation of male early childhood teachers. Currently, eleven percent of public school teachers at the secondary level are male; only three percent of early childhood teachers are male (Mader, 2019; NCES, 2020). Traditional and cultural biases have influenced male teaching career choices in this and many other countries. For example, researchers have noted that male teachers are often viewed with skepticism and distrust, as being incompetent or overqualified, or having questionable motives (Bristol & Goings, 2018; Cruickshank, 2019; Reich-Shapiro, Cole, & Plaisir, 2020). The fact that these concerns persist is evidence that male teachers still face considerable bias.

Building an early childhood workforce that mirrors the population's diversity is important. Researchers have noted that children are more motivated, engaged in learning and positive social interactions, and less likely to be absent when teacher diversity more closely parallels their own race and/or ethnicity (Rasheed et al., 2020). Children also exhibit fewer disruptive and/or challenging behaviors that may result in expulsion when they share characteristics in common with their teachers (Wymer, Williford, & Lhospital, 2020).

It is imperative, given these findings, that leaders examine their recruitment and hiring practices to ensure that they do not discriminate against qualified individuals (Abawi & Eizadirad, 2020; Kim & Cooc, 2020; Scott & Alexander, 2019). Program policies must also be reviewed to safeguard the dignity and equality of all employees and protect against potential discrimination and/or harassment.

Early childhood leaders will continue to face "-ism" challenges in the workplace. Practices that foster a culture of acceptance, understanding, respect, and open dialogue about topics that may be uncomfortable to discuss must be implemented. Success in achieving positive outcomes also requires leaders to examine their own personal biases and to work closely with employees as they conduct their own examinations. Acknowledging that biases exist and influence a person's decisions and actions is essential to creating a collaborative environment where teachers want to work and children are more likely to emulate tolerance and respect.

Did You Know? . . . .

Many males are discouraged from becoming early childhood teachers due to stereotypical attitudes and lack of personal role models.

. . . .

DIRECTOR CREDENTIALING

Links between teacher preparation and quality learning outcomes for young children have received substantial attention in recent research studies (Eckhardt & Egert, 2020; Hooper, 2018; Manning, Wong, & Fleming, 2019). Results consistently show the relationship is positive and statistically significant. Much less attention has been focused on director qualifications and their potential bearing on program quality. This is unfortunate given that there are an estimated 66,700 directors who oversee early childhood programs and centers, and many more who operate independent home-based programs (U.S. Bureau of Labor Statistics, 2020). Also, the demand for directors is expected to increase by double-digit percentages in the near future.

Daily operation oversight and the shaping of complex workplace and learning cultures are pivotal activities carried out by program directors. Their decisions and actions directly and indirectly influence overall program quality. States typically rely on their respective child care licensing authorities to establish the minimal training and experience qualifications that directors are expected to meet. In some cases, these amount to only limited observation, volunteer, or in-classroom hours.

National accrediting organizations view director preparation as essential to program quality and, thus, have established higher standards. For example, NAEYC requires directors of accredited programs to have a baccalaureate degree and additional coursework in business and program administration (NAEYC, 2018). Many states include similar requirements in their QRIS (Quality Rating and Improvement System) standards. Programs that receive federal funding, such as Head Start and military child care centers, also require their directors to have an advanced degree and specialized early childhood education coursework.

Many early childhood program directors are former teachers who have risen up through the ranks (Figure 9.2). Some have degrees, but they may not possess the requisite skills to be successful leaders. Increased concerns about school readiness and program quality issues have led numerous states to require all directors of licensed early childhood programs to be credentialed.

Specialized director degree, credential, and certificate programs are frequently offered in online and in-person formats by many higher education institutions. Individuals who complete a director credential or certificate program gain a better understanding of the responsibilities and demands inherent in a leadership position. They also develop critical skills that enable them to work effectively with employees, provide high-quality learning experiences for children, establish short- and long-term goals, foster meaningful relationships with families, address financial matters, and work closely with community partners.

FIGURE 9.2 A program director credential is an important step for the improvement of early childhood education quality. *SDI Productions*

Achieving universal director **credentialing** is a worthy and attainable goal. However, caution is required so that the rich racial, ethnic, cultural, and linguistic diversity that defines the early childhood workforce is preserved. Financial, personnel, and programmatic concerns should not impede working adults from pursuing their interests in becoming a program director. Leaders will be called upon to help secure additional resources and continue their advocacy to assure that affordable programs, financial assistance, and ample supports are available to all those who are interested in advancing in the field.

FAMILY-SCHOOL-COMMUNITY PARTNERSHIPS

Research evidence continues to support positive outcomes associated with equitable family-school-community partnerships (Smith et al., 2020; Wong, Thomas, & Boben, 2020). Teachers gain a better understanding of children and their families and, in turn, are able to provide learning experiences that are more respectful and meaningful. Children show improved academic achievements and reductions in health and behavior problems. Parents build confidence and enhanced parenting skills and, thus, also benefit from these relationships (Burke et al., 2020; Jeon et al., 2020).

Perhaps one of the most overlooked aspects, however, may be the impact that such partnerships have on local, state, and national governments. The child care industry contributes an estimated 99 billion dollars to these economies (Committee for Economic Development, 2019). This figure includes wages paid to personnel, salaries of self-employed owners, dollars spent on supplies and services, and goods and services purchased by employees. Gains are also realized in terms of reduced spending on special intervention services, lower crime rates, improved graduation rates, and increased per capita income (Cannon et al., 2018; Garcia, Heckman, & Ziff, 2019). For example, it is estimated that government agencies experience substantial savings for every dollar they invest in early childhood education programs (Heckman, 2018; Meloy, Gardner, & Darling-Hammond, 2019).

Recent public health and economic crises have drawn national attention to the critical role that early childhood programs play in maintaining workforce participation. Mandated school closures left many families without child care. An estimated thirteen percent of working mothers quit their jobs because child care was not available (Long, 2020). Many early childhood programs were forced to close permanently due to lost revenue. Program closures eliminated approximately 4.5 million available child care spaces in this country (Jessen-Howard & Workman, 2020). These collective developments have clearly exposed the fragility of an underfunded child care industry and its supporting role in the nation's economy.

Crises often serve as motivators for change. The recent pandemic may prove to be the catalyst that highlights the critical service that early childhood educators provide in our society. Public awareness regarding program closures, child care shortages, and teachers leaving the field may bring about long overdue changes. Efforts to address these challenges will require meaningful family-school-community partnerships, strong leadership advocacy, and evidence-based decisions. They will also necessitate the support of policymakers who are willing to legislate additional funding and other resources so that all children have access to high-quality early childhood education programs.

Did You Know? ·

An estimated $4.2 billion in tax revenue is lost each year because parents must leave paid employment to care for their children.

· ·

CLOSING THOUGHTS

The challenges described and discussed in this chapter and elsewhere in the book are among the most daunting the early childhood field has encountered. Leaders will be called upon to use their expertise, leadership skills, tenacity, and resilience to navigate difficult situations and to achieve meaningful change when prudent and necessary.

Early childhood practitioners and leaders have historically faced significant problems and have responded by developing and implementing workable solutions. Those achievements often were accomplished over a relatively long time period—decades in some instances. The field now faces numerous new situations constrained by multiple factors. Time, resource availability, social and educational structures, economics, public engagement, and nationwide health concerns have combined to form an unusually large, complicated, and problematic matrix. Plans for "what could and should be" will require urgent and substantial leadership.

New research endeavors are also needed to inform data-driven decisions. Calls for policy change and increased public funding for early childhood education programs will be dependent upon an updated and accurate portrayal of today's diverse child population. Early childhood workforce restructuring, program delivery effectiveness, increased use of digital instruction, equity-building strategies, and cost-benefit returns on educational investments are among the many topics that will necessitate additional in-depth research.

Changes in the early childhood field also will have implications for higher education. Institutions must be responsive to decreasing enrollments as well as emerging developments in the field. Early childhood teacher and leadership preparation programs and continuing education offerings will require revision to align with new competency standards. Program delivery and instructional practices must incorporate innovative approaches to ensure that adults' unique learning needs and styles are met. For example, how can time and delivery systems meet the needs of those who are both working and pursuing an education at the same time? What role(s) might online instruction only for required classes, self-paced classes with more than a semester time limit, and alternative time scheduling play in the curriculum? Attention to such opportunities will also necessitate financial assistance to support the preparation of new teacher and leadership cohorts.

These and other issues should not be considered as unsolvable obstacles. Although progress may be slow at times, and new initiatives may not pass as quickly as they should, each experience ultimately can contribute to a better outcome. Early childhood leaders who believe in—and practice—a motivational and empowering leadership style will serve as an inspiration to others throughout daily trials and tribulations. They will help to achieve greater recognition and stronger commitments toward high-quality early childhood programs. They will be able to foster teachers' personal and professional growth and energize those who ultimately make a difference in young children's lives.

Perhaps Kermit the Frog and Fozzie Bear may have given us the best advocacy advice:

Movin' right along in search of good times and good news
With good friends you can't lose
This could become a habit
Opportunity knocks once let's reach out and grab it!

Hop on board and prepare for an adventurous road trip ahead . . . one to be anticipated, shared, and celebrated as early childhood education sets out to redefine itself!

SUMMARY

- The early childhood field currently faces a number of noteworthy challenges that require decisive, inspirational, and motivational leadership.
- NAEYC has proposed a systemic restructuring of early childhood education for the purpose of achieving professional recognition for the field. A gradual phase-in process would establish consistent preparation and compensation standards for teachers.
- Concerted efforts are needed to ensure that early childhood programs are of a high quality and that all children have an equal access to optimal learning experiences.
- Early childhood program leaders face significant challenges in maintaining a qualified workforce. Stressful working conditions and poor compensation cause many teachers to leave their jobs and pursue a different career. Until adequate funding is available to pay appropriate wages, leaders must rely on their creativity and motivational skills to attract and retain qualified employees.
- Early childhood leaders have a professional and ethical responsibility to create workplace environments in which all employees are treated in an accepting and respectful manner.
- Many states require early childhood program directors to be credentialed.
- Children, families, teachers, and communities all benefit from effective partnerships.

APPLICATION ACTIVITIES

1. Survey a minimum of five early childhood programs in your community to identify the major issues leaders/directors are facing. Include a cross-section of different program types (e.g., publicly funded centers; privately owned programs; home-based, nature-, art-, or religious-oriented programs). What challenges do they share in common? What issues are unique to an individual program? Use Application Sheet 9-1.

2. Job titles may elicit gender-linked stereotypes. Identify the gender you are most likely to attribute to each of the occupations listed on the Application Sheet 9-2. Compare your responses to data posted by the U.S. Bureau of Labor Statistics (https://www.bls.gov/cps/cpsaat11.htm). Discuss your results in terms of implicit gender biases.

3. Select and watch any two of the *New York Times'* short videos on implicit bias: https://www.nytimes.com/video/who-me-biased. Write a one-page reaction paper on Application Sheet 9-3 summarizing the primary focus of each video and your feelings about the message.

4. Download and read the NAEYC document *Unifying Framework for the Early Childhood Education Profession* (http://powertotheprofession.org/). Prepare a six-slide promotional slideshow to present to a local early childhood affiliate group. The first five slides should summarize the main initiative features. The sixth slide should include four to five discussion questions, including one that elicits participants' feelings about the proposed workforce restructuring. Use Application Sheet 9-4 to begin.

REVIEW POINTS

1. What aspects of NAEYC's proposed workforce restructuring are most likely to meet resistance from early childhood educators? Why? What steps can be taken to address their concerns?
2. Why isn't a high standard of quality evident across all early childhood programs at this time?
3. What measures can be taken to improve the recruitment and retainment of highly qualified early childhood teachers?
4. What factors have created an early childhood workforce that is more diverse than is typical at other grade levels?
5. Why is it imperative that all early childhood program directors be credentialed?
6. In what ways do communities benefit from having high-quality early childhood programs in their neighborhoods?

KEY TERMS DEFINED

-isms—derogatory or discriminatory beliefs

implicit bias—prejudiced feelings, judgments, or actions that a person may not be aware of; feelings that may contradict conscious beliefs

explicit bias—intentional discriminatory attitudes and/or practices

credentialing—an acknowledgment that a person has met established qualifications

REFERENCES

Abawi, Z., & Eizadirad, A. (2020). Bias-free or biased hiring? Racialized teachers' perspectives on educational hiring practices in Ontario. *Canadian Journal of Educational Administration and Policy, 193*, 18–31.

Allvin, R. E., & Hogan, L. (2020, May 6). *There's no going back: Child care after COVID-19*. NAEYC. Retrieved from https://www.naeyc.org/resources/blog/theres-no-going-back-child-care-after-covid-19.

Austin, L. J., Edwards, B., Chávez, R., & Whitebook, M. (2019, December 19). *Racial wage gaps in early education employment*. Retrieved from https://cscce.berkeley.edu/racial-wage-gaps-in-early-education-employment/.

Boyd-Swan, C., & Herbst, C. M. (2020). Influence of quality credentialing programs on teacher characteristics in center-based early care and education settings. *Early Childhood Research Quarterly, 51*(2nd Quarter), 352–365.

Bristol, T. J., & Goings, R. B. (2018). Exploring the boundary-heightening experiences of Black male teachers: Lessons for teacher education programs. *Journal of Teacher Education, 70*(1), 51–64.

Burke, M. M., Rios, K., Garcia, M., & Magaña, S. (2020). Examining differences in empowerment, special education knowledge, and family–school partnerships among Latino and White families of children with autism spectrum disorder. *International Journal of Developmental Disabilities, 66*(1), 75–81.

Cannon, J. S., Kilburn, M. R., Karoly, L. A., Mattox, T., Muchow, A. N., & Buenaventura, M. (2018). Investing early: Taking stock of outcomes and economic returns from early childhood programs. *Rand Health Quarterly, 7*(4), 6.

Carr, R. C., Mokrova, I. L., Vernon-Feagans, L., & Burchinal, M. R. (2019). Cumulative classroom quality during pre-kindergarten and kindergarten and children's language, literacy, and mathematics skills. *Early Childhood Research Quarterly, 47*(2nd Quarter), 218–228.

Committee for Economic Development (CED). (2019). *Child care in state economies: 2019 Update.* Retrieved from https://www.ced.org/assets/reports/childcareimpact/181104%20CCSE%20 Report%20Jan30.pdf.

Cruickshank, V. (2019). Male primary teachers' fear and uncertainty surrounding physical contact. *Education 3–13, 47*(2), 247–257.

Domond, P., Orri, M., Algan, Y., Findlay, L., Kohen, D., Vitaro, F., Tremblay, R. E., & Côté, S. M. (2020). Child care attendance and educational and economic outcomes in adulthood. *Pediatrics, 146*(1), e20193880.

Eckhardt, A. G., & Egert, F. (2020). Predictors for the quality of family child care: A meta-analysis. *Children and Youth Services Review, 116*, 105205.

Garcia, J. L., Heckman, J. J., & Ziff, A. L. (2019). Early childhood education and crime. *Infant Mental Health Journal, 40*(1), 141–151.

Heckman, J. J. (2018). *Why early investment matters.* Retrieved from https://heckmanequation.org/ resource/why-early-investment-matters/.

Hooper, A. (2018). The influence of early childhood teacher certification on kindergarten and first-grade students' academic outcomes. *Early Child Development and Care, 188*(10), 1419–1430.

Jeon, S., Kwon, K., Guss, S., & Horm, D. (2020). Profiles of family engagement in home- and center-based Early Head Start programs: Associations with child outcomes and parenting skills. *Early Childhood Research Quarterly, 53*, 108–123.

Jessen-Howard, S., & Workman, S. (2020, April 24). *Coronavirus pandemic could lead to permanent loss of nearly 4.5 million child care slots.* Center for American Progress. Retrieved from https://www .americanprogress.org/issues/early-childhood/news/2020/04/24/483817/coronavirus-pandemic -lead-permanent-loss-nearly-4-5-million-child-care-slots/.

Kim, G. M., & Cooc, N. (2020). Recruiting and retaining Asian American and Pacific Islander teachers. *The Urban Review.* https://doi.org/10.1007/s11256-020-00571-1.

Long, H. (2020, July 3). The big factor holding back the U.S. economic recovery: Child care. *Washington Post.* Retrieved from https://www.washingtonpost.com/business/2020/07/03/big -factor-holding-back-us-economic-recovery-child-care/.

Mader, J. (2019, November 28). What is it like to be a male teacher in early ed? *The Hechinger Report.* Retrieved from https://hechingerreport.org/what-is-it-like-to-be-a-male-teacher-in-early-ed/.

Manning, M., Wong, G. T., & Fleming, C. M. (2019). Is teacher qualification associated with the quality of the early childhood education and care environment? A meta-analytic review. *Review of Educational Research, 89*(3), 370–415.

McLean, C., Whitebook, M., & Roh, E. (2019). *From unlivable wages to just pay for early educators.* Berkeley, CA: Center for the Study of Child Care Employment, University of California, Berkeley.

Retrieved from https://cscce.berkeley.edu/files/2019/05/From-Unlivable-Wages-to-Just-Pay-for-Early-Educators.pdf.

Meloy, B., Gardner, M., & Darling-Hammond, L. (2019). *Untangling the evidence on preschool effectiveness: Insights for policymakers.* Learning Policy Institute. Retrieved from https://learningpolicyinstitute.org/sites/default/files/product-files/Untangling_Evidence_Preschool_Effectiveness_REPORT.pdf.

National Association for the Education of Young Children (NAEYC). (2020). *Unifying framework for the early childhood education profession: Executive summary.* Retrieved from http://powertotheprofession.org/wp-content/uploads/2020/03/Power-to-Profession-Framework-exec-summary-03082020.pdf.

NAEYC. (2018). *Early learning program accreditation standards and assessment items.* Retrieved from https://www.naeyc.org/accreditation/early-learning/standards.

National Center for Education Statistics (NCES). (2020). *Characteristics of public school teachers.* Retrieved from https://nces.ed.gov/programs/coe/indicator_clr.asp.

Partelow, L. (2019, December 3). *What to make of declining enrollment in teacher preparation programs.* Center for American Progress. Retrieved from https://www.americanprogress.org/issues/education-k-12/reports/2019/12/03/477311/make-declining-enrollment-teacher-preparation-programs/.

Perlman, M., Howe, N., Gulyas, C., & Falenchuk, O. (2020). Association between directors' characteristics, supervision practices and quality of early childhood education and care classrooms. *Early Education and Development, 31*(4), 507–523.

Philpott, D. F., Young, G., Maich, K., Penney, S. C., & Butler, E. (2019). *The preemptive nature of quality early child education on special educational needs in children.* Research Report. Memorial University of Newfoundland, St. John's, Newfoundland and Labrador. Retrieved from https://research.library.mun.ca/13571/1/The%20Preemptive%20Nature%20of%20ECE%2C%20Feb%2012.pdf.

Rasheed, D. S., Brown, J. L., Doyle, S. L., & Jennings, P. A. (2020). The effect of teacher-child race/ethnicity matching and classroom diversity on children's socioemotional and academic skills. *Child Development, 91*(3), e597–e618. https://doi.org/10.1111/cdev.13275.

Reich-Shapiro, M., Cole, K., & Plaisir, J. Y. (2020). "I *am* the teacher": How male educators conceptualize their impact on the early childhood classroom. *Journal of Early Childhood Teacher Education.* DOI: 10.1080/10901027.2020.1754310.

Sabol, T. J., Ross, E. C., & Frost, A. (2020). Are all Head Start classrooms created equal? Variation in classroom quality within Head Start centers and implications for accountability systems. *American Educational Research Journal, 57*(2), 504–534.

Scott, L. A., & Alexander, Q. (2019). Strategies for recruiting and retaining Black male special education teachers. *Remedial and Special Education, 40*(4), 236–247.

Smith, T. E., Sheridan, S. M., Kim, E. M., Park, S., & Beretvas, S. N. (2020). Effects of family-school partnership interventions on academic and social-emotional functioning: A meta-analysis exploring what works for whom. *Educational Psychology Review, 32,* 511–544.

Sutcher, L., Darling-Hammond, L., & Carver-Thomas, D. (2016). *A coming crisis in teaching? Teacher supply, demand, and shortages in the U.S.* Learning Policy Institute. Retrieved from https://learningpolicyinstitute.org/sites/default/files/product-files/A_Coming_Crisis_in_Teaching_REPORT.pdf.

U.S. Bureau of Labor Statistics. (2020). *Preschool and child care center directors.* Retrieved from https://www.bls.gov/OOH/management/preschool-and-childcare-center-directors.htm.

Wiggan, G., Smith, D., & Watson-Vandiver, M. J. (2020). The national teacher shortage, urban education and the cognitive sociology of labor. *Urban Review*. https://doi.org/10.1007/s11256-020 -00565-z.

Wong, K., Thomas, C., & Boben, M. (2020). Providence talks: A citywide partnership to address early childhood language development. *Studies in Educational Evaluation, 64*, 100818. Retrieved from https://www.sciencedirect.com/science/article/pii/S0191491X18304024.

Wymer, S. C., Williford, A. P., & Lhospital, A. S. (2020). Exclusionary discipline practices in early childhood. *Young Children, 75*(3), 36–44.

ONLINE RESOURCES

Alliance for Early Success: https://earlysuccess.org

America for Early Ed: http://www.americaforearlyed.org

Childhood Education International: https://ceinternational1892.org

Foundation for Child Development: https://www.fcd-us.org

NAEYC (Power to the Profession): https://www.naeyc.org/our-work/initiatives/profession

PEACH (Partnerships in Education, Articulation, and Collaboration in Higher Education): https:// www.peach4ece.org

W. K. Kellogg Foundation: https://www.wkkf.org

APPLICATION SHEET 9-1

Interview results: Identify the program type and major issues facing each director.

1.

2.

3.

4.

5.

What challenges do the directors share in common?

What issues are unique to an individual program?

APPLICATION SHEET 9-2

Note the gender you are most likely to associate with each of the following occupations:

doctor

principal

chef

forest ranger

teacher

dental hygienist

computer technician

nurse

pilot

hairdresser

coach

pharmacist

architect

paramedic

clergy

librarian

Discuss your results in terms of implicit gender biases.

APPLICATION SHEET 9-3

The videos I watched:

My reaction summarizing the primary focus of the videos and my feelings about the message:

APPLICATION SHEET 9-4

Overview of NAEYC's initiative, Unifying Framework for the Early Childhood Education Profession:

Slide #1

Slide #2

Slide #3

Slide #4

Slide #5

Slide #6

Employment and Labor Laws

Employers must be familiar and compliant with federal laws that address work regulations and employee rights. It is also important that they check with local and state laws, which may establish higher standards than those set by federal legislation. Programs receiving federal funding may have additional requirements to meet.

Federal laws that apply to any employer:

- **Consumer Credit Protection Act (CCPA)**—employers must comply with wage garnishment requirements. The amount that can be garnished per week is limited. Employers are prevented from firing an employee with this mandate.
- **Employee Retirement Income Security Act (ERISA)**—requires employers to provide employees with information regarding private pension and health plan, including features and contributions.
- **Equal Pay Act (EPA)**—requires employers to pay equal compensation to men and women who perform the same or similar work. A 2009 amendment (Lilly Ledbetter Fair Pay Act) allows employees who experience pay discrimination to file a federal antidiscrimination claim.
- **Fair and Accurate Credit Transactions Act (FACT)**—requires employers to dispose of employee credit information in a manner that is secure and prevents unsanctioned access.
- **Fair Labor Standards Act (FLSA)**—establishes minimum wage, overtime eligibility, and child labor standards for part- and full-time employees, as well as employer recordkeeping requirements.
- **Federal Income Tax Withholding**—requires employers to withhold and pay to the federal government (IRS) a predetermined percentage of an employee's wages.
- **Federal Insurance Contributions Act (FICA)**—requires employers to withhold and pay to the federal government (IRS) a predetermined percentage of an employee's wages for Social Security and Medicare.

- **Health Insurance Portability and Accountability Act (HIPAA)**—prevents employers from requesting an employee's information from health care providers.
- **Immigration Reform and Control Act (IRCA)**—prevents employers from hiring employees who are not authorized to work in the United States. Workers must have a current Form I-9 on file.
- **Jury System Improvement Act (JSIA)**—prevents employers from firing or punishing employees who are summoned to jury duty in federal court. Most states have similar laws protecting employees who are called to jury duty.
- **National Labor Relations Act (NLRA)**—prevents employers from punishing employees for forming or joining a union.
- **Occupational Safety and Health Act (OSHA)**—requires employers to provide workplace conditions that meet federal health and safety standards. Programs with more than eleven employees must maintain records showing compliance with regulations.
- **Uniform Guidelines on Employee Selection Procedures**—prohibits employers from discriminating against applicants or employees on the basis of race, color, religion, sex, national origin, disability, or age. The law applies to all hiring, promotion, demotion, referral, licensing, and membership decisions. It also addresses the proper use of tests and other selection procedures.
- **Uniformed Services Employment and Reemployment Rights Act (USERRA)**—prohibits employers from discriminating against individuals who have served in military service, including the reserves, and grants the right to reemployment. Employers are also expected to make reasonable efforts to accommodate veterans' disabilities.

Employers with fifteen or more employees:
- **Americans with Disabilities Act (ADA)**—prevents discrimination, in terms of employment, against individuals who have a qualified disability; provides access to state and local government services, public accommodations, transportation, and telecommunications.
- **Title VII, Civil Rights Act of 1964**—prohibits employers from discrimination against an individual because of his or her race, color, religion, sex (including sexual harassment), or national origin.

Employers with twenty or more employees:
- **Affirmative Action Law (AAL)**—prohibits businesses with fifteen or more employees from discriminating against individuals based on race, color, sex or sexual orientation, religion, national or ethnic origin, or physical capability in hiring, compensating, promoting, training, and dismissing employees. Employers are encouraged to actively recruit and train minorities, women, individuals with disabilities, and military veterans. Additionally, the law allows state and federal governments to give preference to women- and minority-owned businesses when awarding contracts.
- **Age Discrimination in Employment Act (ADEA)**—forbids employers from discriminating against employees or applicants who are age forty or older.

- **Consolidated Omnibus Budget Reconciliation Act (COBRA)**—requires employer-sponsored group health insurance plans to offer continued coverage (for up to eighteen months) to eligible employees and their dependents in the event of voluntary or involuntary job loss or reduction in hours worked or transitioning between jobs, death, divorce, and other life events (for up to thirty-six months). Qualified individuals may be required to pay the premium.

Employers with fifty or more employees:
- **Affordable Care Act (ACA)**—requires programs/companies employing fifty or more full-time employees (or the equivalent) in the previous tax year to offer affordable health insurance options to their employees. The law also requires companies to maintain strict records of all transactions.
- **Family and Medical Leave Act (FMLA)**—requires employers to provide up to twelve weeks of unpaid, job-protected leave following the birth, adoption, or foster placement of an employee's child or serious family illness in a given twelve-month period. Health insurance coverage is to continue with the same conditions as if the employee were working.

ADDITIONAL LEGISLATION:
- **Setting Every Community Up for Retirement Enhancement Act of 2019 (SECURE)**—provides tax incentives that encourage small businesses to offer affordable retirement plans (e.g., 401(k), IRAs, college savings funds) to full- and part-time employees. The law also increases the mandatory age at which funds must be withdrawn and allows individuals to continue contributing indefinitely to their plans.

ADDITIONAL INFORMATIONAL RESOURCES:
- Shiftboard (potential upcoming changes to labor laws, such as paid break time, sick leave): https://www.shiftboard.com/blog/2020-labor-laws/
- USA.gov (description of current labor laws): https://www.usa.gov/labor-laws
- U.S. Department of Labor (state labor offices and contact information): https://www.dol.gov/agencies/whd/state/contacts
- U.S. Department of Labor (summary of all major labor laws): https://www.dol.gov/general/aboutdol/majorlaws
- U.S. Equal Employment Opportunity Commission (small business requirements): https://www.eeoc.gov/employers/smallbusiness/requirements.cfm

Glossary

accommodating—a conflict management style in which one party gives up their demands in order to satisfy the wishes of others

andragogy—theory and principles of adults' learning style

asynchronous communication—information exchanges that do not occur in person or simultaneously (e.g., memo, voice mail, text message, blog, email)

attributes—personal qualities or characteristics (e.g., sincere, helpful, patient, reliable)

attrition—the loss of employees due to intentional choice, death, or retirement

authentic—sincere; genuine

autocratic leadership—leaders who maintain full control of all decisions and limit employee input

avoiding—a management style in which a leader ignores or chooses not to become involved in conflict

burnout—a physical or emotional response to prolonged stress; a lack of interest and commitment

charismatic leadership—leaders who use their charm, communication skills, and convincing personalities to attract and influence followers

coaching—the process of guiding another individual's learning in a specific area for improved performance

collaborating—a conflict management style in which an agreement or solution is reached that satisfies the desires of everyone involved

collectivist—a political or cultural philosophy that emphasizes group welfare over individual or personal gain. Collectivist cultures are represented in many Asian and Latino countries

commensurate—appropriate or suitable according to specific criteria

communication competence—knowledge of effective and appropriate communication (e.g., language, grammar, rules, styles, barriers) to achieve meaning that is mutually understood

compensatory—to make up for a loss or deficiency

competencies—a combination of knowledge, skills, and abilities

competing—a conflict management style in which one individual controls and makes the decisions

compromising—a conflict management style in which both parties relinquish some of their demands to achieve a mutually acceptable resolution

conflict—a difference of opinion or perceived incompatibility of interests, goals, or needs

constructive feedback—information that is specific, nonjudgmental, and meaningful regarding an employee's performance and opportunities for improvement

consultative leadership—leaders who listen to employees' suggestions before making decisions

credentialing—an acknowledgment that a person has met established qualifications

decode—the mental process used to translate what is heard into thoughts or ideas

demographic—a statistical description of various human population characteristics, such as the number of employed fathers or the number of children per family

demotivate—a loss of interest or enthusiasm

downward communication—information that flows from leadership to subordinates

emotional intelligence—the ability to recognize and understand emotions (personal and those of others) and to use the information to guide one's decisions

encode—the process used to translate thoughts or ideas into words or expressions that another individual will understand

environment—the sum of an individual's surroundings; includes physical and psychological factors

explicit bias—intentional discriminatory attitudes and/or practices

extrinsic motivators—tangible rewards (e.g., salary increase, designated parking space, birthday gift, movie tickets) that an individual finds personally gratifying

grapevine communication—informal hallway or "watercooler" conversations, rumors, or gossip that take place among employees or supervisors and employees

gratitude—feeling thankful; an expression of appreciation

heterogeneous—dissimilar or unlike

homogeneous—similar or alike

horizontal communication—information that flows laterally among individuals on a similar hierarchy level

hygienes—a term Herzberg used to describe workplace conditions that contribute to employee satisfaction or displeasure

implicit bias—prejudiced feelings, judgments, or actions that a person may not be aware of; feelings that may contradict conscious beliefs

incivility—disrespectful or offensive treatment directed toward another individual

individualist—cultures that encourage and value individual effort and achievement. Individualism is predominant in many European and American countries

intrinsic motivators—rewards or recognition (e.g., job promotion, title change, praise, being named employee of the month) that provide a feeling of personal satisfaction, pride, or pleasure

-isms—derogatory or discriminatory beliefs

laissez-faire leadership—leaders who grant employees full decision-making control and provide little or no guidance

mentoring—a supportive relationship formed between individuals for the purpose of sharing knowledge, skills, and experience

motivation—a perceived need that shapes the purpose and direction of a person's behavior

norms—informal social rules or behavioral expectations established by a group

one-way communication—information that is only transmitted from sender to recipient

participative leadership—leaders who encourage, involve, and respect employee participation in decision-making activities

perception checking—a strategy used to determine another person's understanding of information that has been communicated

physiological needs—basic functions (e.g., food, water, shelter) that are required for survival

psychological safety—a feeling of protection from negative consequences that an individual experiences when they are part of a team or group

regression—to retreat or move backward

self-actualization—the personal need for satisfaction that an individual derives from using their skills and talents to accomplish a task

self-efficacy—a person's belief in her or his ability to succeed in accomplishing a desired task or goal

servant leadership—a style characterized by a leader's devotion to meeting employees' needs and developing their abilities to achieve organizational goals

shared leadership—a leadership model whereby responsibilities and power are distributed among two or more individuals

social loafing—an individual's tendency to exert less effort when working in a group

stress—a sense of frustration, tension, or anxiety that may develop when an event or response differs from what a person expected

subjective—relating to a personal belief, bias, or interpretation that is not based on fact

synchronous communication—a face-to-face or real-time exchange of information between sender and recipient(s)

traits—characteristics unique to an individual

transactional—a give-and-take exchange of information between a sender and recipient

transactional leadership—a style characterized by the outcomes or accomplishments resulting from a leader's efforts; task or product orientation

transformational leadership—a style that reflects a leader's concern with building employee relationships to achieve desired outcomes; process orientation

two-way communication—a back-and-forth exchange of information between sender and recipient

upward communication—information that flows up the administrative hierarchy, from subordinates to administration

Index

Note: Page numbers in *italics* refer to tables and figures.

About the Author

Lynn R. Marotz received a PhD in Educational Policy and Leadership from the University of Kansas, an MEd in Adult Education from the University of Illinois, and a BS in Nursing from the University of Wisconsin. She is professor emerita in the Department of Applied Behavioral Science, University of Kansas, and served as the associate director of the Edna A. Hill Child Development Center for thirty years. Her primary teaching and research interests focused on leadership and administration, children's health-safety-nutrition, and parenting. She has worked closely with early childhood teachers and program directors throughout her career and has a deep respect for their dedication to promoting children's development.

Lynn is the author of numerous early childhood textbooks and invited chapters. She has also produced many digital courseware products and webinars, and served as a consultant for films and trade magazine articles. In addition, she has presented extensively at international, national, and state conferences, and remains active in national, state, and local initiatives that advocate on behalf of the early childhood education field.